Security Monitoring with Cisco Security MARS

Gary Halleen

Greg Kellogg

Cisco Press

Cisco Press
800 East 96th Street
Indianapolis, IN 46240 USA

Security Monitoring with Cisco Security MARS

Gary Halleen

Greg Kellogg

Copyright© 2007 Cisco Systems, Inc.

Published by:
Cisco Press
800 East 96th Street
Indianapolis, IN 46240 USA

First Printing June 2007

Library of Congress Cataloging-in-Publication Data

Halleen, Gary.

  Security monitoring with Cisco security MARS/Gary Halleen, Greg Kellogg.

     p. cm.

  ISBN 978-1-58705-270-5 (pbk.)

  1. Computer networks—Security measures. 2. Computer security—Evaluation. I. Kellogg, Greg. II. Title.

  TK5105.59.H345 2007

  005.8—dc22

                                   2007021272

ISBN-10: 1-58705-270-9

ISBN-13: 978-1-58705-270-5

Warning and Disclaimer

This book is designed to provide information about day-to-day operations, configuration, and customization capabilities of the Cisco Security MARS appliances. Every effort has been made to make this book as complete and as accurate as possible, but no warranty or fitness is implied.

The information is provided on an "as is" basis. The authors, Cisco Press, and Cisco Systems, Inc. shall have neither liability nor responsibility to any person or entity with respect to any loss or damages arising from the information contained in this book or from the use of the discs or programs that may accompany it.

The opinions expressed in this book belong to the author and are not necessarily those of Cisco Systems, Inc.

Trademark Acknowledgments

All terms mentioned in this book that are known to be trademarks or service marks have been appropriately capitalized. Cisco Press or Cisco Systems, Inc. cannot attest to the accuracy of this information. Use of a term in this book should not be regarded as affecting the validity of any trademark or service mark.

Feedback Information

At Cisco Press, our goal is to create in-depth technical books of the highest quality and value. Each book is crafted with care and precision, undergoing rigorous development that involves the unique expertise of members from the professional technical community.

Readers' feedback is a natural continuation of this process. If you have any comments regarding how we could improve the quality of this book, or otherwise alter it to better suit your needs, you can contact us through e-mail at feedback@ciscopress.com. Please make sure to include the book title and ISBN in your message.

We greatly appreciate your assistance.

Corporate and Government Sales

Cisco Press offers excellent discounts on this book when ordered in quantity for bulk purchases or special sales.

For more information please contact: U.S. Corporate and Government Sales
1-800-382-3419
corpsales@pearsontechgroup.com

For sales outside the U.S. please contact: International Sales
international@pearsoned.com

Publisher	Paul Boger
Associate Publisher	David Dusthimer
Cisco Representative	Anthony Wolfenden
Cisco Press Program Manager	Jeff Brady
Executive Editor	Brett Bartow
Managing Editor	Patrick Kanouse
Senior Development Editor	Christopher Cleveland
Project Editor	Tonya Simpson
Copy Editor	John Edwards
Technical Editors	Greg Abelar, Francesca Martucci
Team Coordinator	Vanessa Evans
Book Designer	Louisa Adair
Composition	Mark Shirar
Indexer	Ken Johnson

Americas Headquarters	Asia Pacific Headquarters	Europe Headquarters
Cisco Systems, Inc.	Cisco Systems, Inc.	Cisco Systems International BV
170 West Tasman Drive	168 Robinson Road	Haarlerbergpark
San Jose, CA 95134-1706	#28-01 Capital Tower	Haarlerbergweg 13-19
USA	Singapore 068912	1101 CH Amsterdam
www.cisco.com	www.cisco.com	The Netherlands
Tel: 408 526-4000	Tel: +65 6317 7777	www-europe.cisco.com
800 553-NETS (6387)	Fax: +65 6317 7799	Tel: +31 0 800 020 0791
Fax: 408 527-0883		Fax: +31 0 20 357 1100

Cisco has more than 200 offices worldwide. Addresses, phone numbers, and fax numbers are listed on the Cisco Website at **www.cisco.com/go/offices.**

About the Authors

Gary Halleen is a security consulting systems engineer with Cisco. He has in-depth knowledge of security systems, remote access, and routing/switching technology. Gary is a CISSP and ISSAP and has been a technical editor for Cisco Press. Before working at Cisco, he wrote web-based software, owned an Internet service provider, worked in Information Technology at a college, and taught computer science courses. His diligence was responsible for the first successful computer crimes conviction in the state of Oregon. Gary is a regular speaker at security events, and he presents at Cisco Networkers conferences. He lives in Salem, Oregon, with his wife and children.

Greg Kellogg is the vice president of security solutions for Calence, LLC, which is based out of Tempe, Arizona. He is responsible for managing the company's overall security strategy, as well as developing new security solutions and service offerings, establishing strategic partnerships, managing strategic client engagements, and supporting business development efforts. Greg has more than 15 years of networking industry experience, including serving as a senior security business consultant for the Cisco Systems Enterprise Channel organization. While at Cisco, Greg helped organizations understand regulatory compliance, policy creation, and risk analysis to guide their security implementations. He was recognized for his commitment to service with the Cisco Technology Leader of the Year award. Additionally, Greg worked for Protego Networks, Inc. (where MARS was originally developed). While there, he was responsible for developing channel partner programs and helping solution providers increase their security revenue. Greg currently resides in Spring Branch, Texas, with his wife and four children.

About the Technical Reviewers

Greg Abelar has been an employee of Cisco since December 1996. He was an original member of the Cisco Technical Assistance Security team, helping to hire and train many of the engineers. He has held various positions in both the Security Architecture and Security Technical Marketing Engineering teams at Cisco. Greg is the primary founder and project manager of the Cisco written CCIE Security exam. Greg is the author of the Cisco Press title *Securing Your Business with Cisco ASA and PIX Firewalls* and coauthor of *Security Threat Mitigation and Response: Understanding Cisco Security MARS*. In addition, he has been a technical editor for various Cisco Press security books.

Francesca Martucci is the lead technical marketing engineer for CS-MARS, and she played an instrumental role in the support of the product after the acquisition. Francesca has a very strong background across all the different security technologies. She has been working at Cisco for more than seven years within the Security Technology Group, covering different roles as test engineer first and TME later.

Dedications

Gary Halleen: I would like to dedicate this book to my beautiful wife, Pam, and my children (Amber, Harry, Ashley, Kristin, Jordan, and Bailey). They are all fantastic, and they motivate me to always be the best I can be.

I would also like to dedicate this book to my dad, Arne, for always being there.

Greg Kellogg: This book is dedicated to my incredible and beloved wife, Lynette, for her dedication, vision, and strength. I owe every bit of my success to her.

And

To my children, Max, Briggs, Gage, and Indianna. You kids truly light up my life.

And

To my mom and dad, Kelly and Gloria, for always forcing me to understand why…

Acknowledgments

Gary Halleen:

I would like to thank Greg Kellogg for writing this book with me. We began talking about this book a few years ago, sitting on a bench in San Francisco. It feels good to see it completed.

I would also like to thank Phil Chiu for his support in getting the process started, the entire MARS team at Cisco, for making me part of their team, and Steve Wells, for being a good friend and coworker.

Greg Kellogg:

First, I would like to thank my coauthor, Gary Halleen. This book never would have been completed if it wasn't for his diligence, intelligence, and drive.

I would also like to thank my Protego "Brothers & Sisters"—"If you build it, they will come." This also includes Paul and Phil; thanks for putting up with me.

Finally, thank you Cisco and Calence, LLC, two of the finest employers I have ever had.

This Book Is Safari Enabled

The Safari® Enabled icon on the cover of your favorite technology book means the book is available through Safari Bookshelf. When you buy this book, you get free access to the online edition for 45 days.

Safari Bookshelf is an electronic reference library that lets you easily search thousands of technical books, find code samples, download chapters, and access technical information whenever and wherever you need it.

To gain 45-day Safari Enabled access to this book:

- Go to http://www.ciscopress.com/safarienabled
- Complete the brief registration form
- Enter the coupon code M1RK-D8LQ-GVQF-UMQ9-R4X8

If you have difficulty registering on Safari Bookshelf or accessing the online edition, please e-mail customer-service@safaribooksonline.com.

Contents at a Glance

Contents

Icons Used in This Book

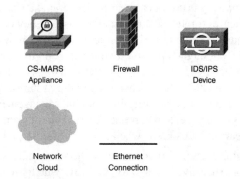

CS-MARS
Appliance

Firewall

IDS/IPS
Device

Network
Cloud

Ethernet
Connection

Command Syntax Conventions

The conventions used to present command syntax in this book are the same conventions used in the IOS Command Reference. The Command Reference describes these conventions as follows:

- **Boldface** indicates commands and keywords that are entered literally as shown. In actual configuration examples and output (not general command syntax), boldface indicates commands that are manually input by the user (such as a show command).

- *Italics* indicate arguments for which you supply actual values.

- Vertical bars (|) separate alternative, mutually exclusive elements.

- Square brackets [ ] indicate optional elements.

- Braces { } indicate a required choice.

- Braces within brackets [{ }] indicate a required choice within an optional element.

Foreword

If a tree falls in the forest but nobody is around to hear it, does it make a sound? Philosophers and physicists have volleyed that brainteaser for years. But consider it as a metaphor for your computer systems. If an event is logged on your network, but nobody monitors your logs, how can you determine whether an attack occurred? By missing out on the opportunity to catch bad guys early through solid event analysis, you've extended and deepened your exposure to the attacker's foul plot. You'll never know what's going on until the bad guys start making blatant changes on your systems, wreaking all kinds of damage. In many modern enterprise networks, Security Information Management tools, or SIMs for short, are crucial in helping to manage, analyze, and correlate a mountain of event data. Increasingly, SIM solutions act as our eyes and ears to let us know when trees start falling in our networks.

Have you ever seen the television show *24*? If you haven't, the story centers around a high-tech Counter Terrorism Unit (CTU) working exhaustive hours to foil bad guys who try to deal death and destruction to innocent victims. Jack Bauer, played by Kiefer Sutherland, is the world's ultimate good-guy field agent, heading up each action-packed episode. While Jack's skills are important, he relies heavily on the technical wizardry and information analysis abilities of his coworkers back at the office. In almost every nail-biting episode, these data analysts pull the proverbial needle out of the information haystack just in the nick of time to help Jack save civilization. With all the data flowing into CTU, these analysts must rely on the ultimate SIM infrastructure to work their magic.

So what does *24* have to do with this book? Besides the passing resemblance of this book's authors to Jack Bauer, *24* highlights the importance of information management in thwarting bad guys: integrating and correlating data from a myriad of system types. I'm sorry to say that this book won't turn you into Jack Bauer, nor will it let you create a mythical SIM solution that matches the functionality of the all-seeing analysts of the *24* TV show. But if you read this book and live by its principles, you can design and deploy a SIM solution that maximizes your abilities to understand and monitor your systems using the Cisco MARS product.

Unfortunately, many SIM deployments are not well planned and result in either abject failure or an infrastructure that barely scratches the surface of potential MARS functionality. That's why deploying and using MARS without reading this book is like throwing money away. Greg Kellogg and Gary Halleen have distilled an immense amount of extremely valuable knowledge in these pages. By relying on the wisdom of Kellogg and Halleen embedded in this book, you will vastly improve your MARS deployment, helping your own metaphorical field agents detect, dodge, and even stop falling trees.

—Ed Skoudis

December 2006

Vice President of Security Strategy

Predictive Systems

Introduction

Security Event Management (SEM) systems, Security Information Management (SIM) systems, and Security Threat Mitigation (STM) systems are all solutions with a primary goal of making it easier to determine when bad things are happening on your network. Ideally, the tools we use to correlate events between various network and security devices or software will detect malicious behavior before damage is done, rather than letting us know when we've already been compromised.

This book is intended to describe how a third-generation tool, the Cisco Security Monitoring, Analysis, and Response System (CS-MARS), performs as an STM solution.

Goals and Methods

The goal of this book is to provide the information you need to successfully use the CS-MARS appliances in a real network, on a day-to-day basis. No SIM or STM solution, out of the box, is a perfect fit for every network. As you read through the chapters, we hope you find tidbits that help you make the most of your investment. We also hope you learn enough to avoid some of the common mistakes and misconfigurations.

CS-MARS is a powerful tool that can dramatically increase your knowledge of activity, whether malicious or not, on your network. There are many case studies and other examples throughout the book that show you how this STM functions in a real-world network. Hopefully, some of these examples will bear a resemblance to your own network.

By the time your finish this book, you should have a good understanding of the overall operations and maintenance tasks involved with a CS-MARS deployment. Some of the things you will learn include:

- How to properly design and size a CS-MARS deployment
- Protection of the information contained with CS-MARS
- Incident investigation techniques
- Customization features to allow support of applications and devices that aren't natively supported
- Creation of custom reports and queries

This Book's Audience

The primary audience for this book comprises information security analysts, security officers, and anyone who is tasked with monitoring or maintaining devices and software, such as:

- Firewalls
- Intrusion prevention systems (IPS) or intrusion detection systems (IDS)
- Antivirus systems
- Host intrusion protection systems
- Virtual Private Network (VPN) devices

- Authentication systems
- Web servers
- Vulnerability assessment systems

This book assumes that you have a basic understanding of networking technologies and security technologies. It also assumes that you are able to perform basic CS-MARS installation tasks and have a basic proficiency with Linux or other UNIX operating systems.

How This Book Is Organized

This book is organized into three parts, each with a number of chapters. Part I introduces CS-MARS and Security Threat Mitigation systems. It describes features and strategies for using CS-MARS as your STM solution. In addition, Part I covers regulatory issues and discusses design and sizing scenarios. Part II focuses on day-to-day operations and forensics. Part III discusses more advanced topics, such as integration with other management solutions or technologies, as well as customization features. The appendixes provide a sample script for parsing MARS data from a third-party application, in addition to useful links and a command reference.

The chapters in this book cover the following topics:

- Part I: Introduction to CS-MARS and Security Threat Mitigation

  Chapter 1: Introducing CS-MARS—This chapter discusses differences between different log aggregation and correlation systems. It also covers an introduction to the various MARS components, the user interface, and the types of devices that typically log to MARS.

  Chapter 2: Regulatory Challenges in Depth—This chapter examines many of the regulatory and industry requirements businesses face today, and how MARS assists in meeting these requirements.

  Chapter 3: CS-MARS Deployment Scenarios—This chapter examines the various ways local controllers, standalone controllers, and global controllers can be deployed to best meet your needs. Additionally, it covers techniques for properly sizing your deployment.

- Part II: CS-MARS Operations and Forensics

  Chapter 4: Securing CS-MARS—This chapter focuses on why you need to secure CS-MARS and other security management or monitoring products, and how to protect MARS from attack.

  Chapter 5: Rules, Reports, and Queries—This chapter covers how to understand and use the reporting and query interfaces.

  Chapter 6: Incident Investigation and Forensics—This chapter focuses on what to do when CS-MARS detects an attack.

  Chapter 7: Archiving and Disaster Recovery—This chapter focuses on data retention, archiving, and recovering from a disaster.

- Part III: CS-MARS Advanced Topics

  Chapter 8: Integration with Cisco Security Manager—Cisco Security Manager is a management product for Cisco security products. This chapter demonstrates integration between the two products and describes how to use the strengths of each.

  Chapter 9: **Troubleshooting CS-MARS**—This chapter discusses what to do when things don't work like they should. What do you do before calling TAC?

  Chapter 10: **Network Admission Control**—This chapter discusses the Cisco Network Admission Control set of products that allow or deny network access based on a host's capability to meet a certain posture level, and describes how NAC integrates into CS-MARS.

  Chapter 11: **CS-MARS Custom Parser**—This chapter dives into configuring CS-MARS to use security logs from officially unsupported devices and software.

  Chapter 12: **Global Controller Operations**—This chapter focuses on what is involved in using a global controller to manage and monitor a group of MARS local controllers.

- Part IV: Appendixes

  Appendix A: Querying the Archive—This appendix discusses how the MARS archiving feature allows integration with command-line and other applications, to provide a lightweight query capability. A sample Python script is provided.

  Appendix B: CS-MARS Command Reference—This appendix provides a reference to the various commands available from the MARS command-line interface.

  Appendix C: Useful Websites—This appendix provides a list of websites the authors have found useful in working with CS-MARS.

## PART I

Introduction to CS-MARS and Security Threat Mitigation

## CHAPTER 1

Introducing CS-MARS

A Security Information/Event Manager (SIEM, or commonly called a SIM) is a relatively simple tool. In its most basic sense, these devices collect Simple Network Management Protocol (SNMP) and syslog data from security devices and software, and insert it into a database. These devices then provide you with an easy user interface with which to access that information.

By itself, this is nothing special, but what is done after the data is received is important.

The Cisco Security Monitoring, Analysis, and Response System (CS-MARS) product was built to enhance this somewhat common tool by sessionizing the data and providing it with intelligence and knowledge of the network topology. *Sessionization* refers to the initial summarization of events from multiple devices, providing the knowledge to intelligently identify data streams, sources, and destinations of interesting traffic.

Additionally, CS-MARS gives you false-positive detection and provides instructions for mitigating attacks based on that topology. The CS-MARS appliance can help organizations meet compliance standards and assist in adhering to governmental regulations.

CS-MARS provides a 50,000-foot view of what is occurring on your network. You can think of CS-MARS as an Airborne Warning and Control System (AWACS) for networks.

This chapter explains the basics of the CS-MARS appliance. By the end of this chapter, you should understand what MARS is, what the typical requirements are, and the types of data it collects. You should also understand the basic operation of the MARS appliance.

This book is not an exhaustive guide on how to install, configure, and otherwise operate the MARS appliance. The goal of this book is to provide guidance for designing your MARS deployment and understanding the day-to-day operations of security forensics, the MARS way. It also provides useful information for expanding the default capabilities of MARS through its custom parsing capabilities.

NOTE   If this is your first exposure to the MARS appliance, you can review the comprehensive MARS guides at http://www.cisco.com/go/mars.

NOTE   Cisco acquired Protego Networks, Inc., which initially developed the MARS appliance technology, in February 2005.

Introduction to Security Information Management

The following sections discuss the role of a SIM in today's networks, the challenges you face, and the minimum set of features you should look for in a SIM appliance.

The Role of a SIM in Today's Network

In recent years, the SIM has become a more important system than was previously envisioned. First-generation SIM products were essentially event correlation systems, taking event logs from multiple security products and providing basic correlation, graphing, and reporting functionality. Not enough information existed to allow an administrator to trust his eyes and ears (and sometimes scripts) to determine what was occurring on his networks, let alone provide the ability to respond in real time, with mitigation recommendations.

NOTE   The primary role of a SIM is to create order where chaos exists.

The situation is different with today's networks. In the past, it was usually not critical to review security logs in a timely fashion. Today it is critical. Modern threats are coming more rapidly, and the attacks are more dangerous and fast-acting. Additionally, legal obligations require companies to perform regular reviews of logs and to take immediate action when malicious activity is discovered. For example, many states have enacted legislation requiring mandatory disclosure when sensitive personal or financial information has been compromised. Stiff penalties can be imposed when organizations fail to comply.

In recent years, incidents of misappropriation of corporate dollars, falsification of trading reports, and theft of private financial and identification information have created a need for new laws and rules from the federal and state governments in an effort to hold organizations accountable for poor security practices.

Today, chief security officers and other executives, including the CEO, are held accountable for their actions by the government and private organizations, even when the organization itself does not hold itself accountable. The Payment Card Industry Data Security Standard is a perfect example, where the combined forces of the major credit card companies have organized to require and enforce a rigid set of standards for protecting their customers' financial information. Chapter 2, "Regulatory Challenges in Depth," provides an overview of recent regulatory issues.

Without regulatory controls, organizations will never hold themselves to the same level of accountability that the public—and shareholders—demand. It is an interesting fact that

"an organization will typically spend less on security personnel and countermeasures than they do on their coffee budget." (Richard Clarke, Former Special Advisor to the President for Cyberspace Security)

In addition to regulatory and other compliance reasons, a well-designed and -implemented SIM provides an invaluable tool to the security and network teams. It can pinpoint where a hacker, virus, or worm has compromised a server. It can also identify where policy violations have occurred, such as when an employee has attempted to access data that she doesn't have rights to, or when peer-to-peer (P2P) applications (such as Kazaa, Morpheus, and so on) are in use.

Most organizations that handle sensitive computer information do not have more than one person dedicated to security, or to monitoring log information. The SIM's role in a production network today is to help fill the gap between inadequate personnel, inadequate budgets, and ever-increasing security requirements.

CS-MARS can prioritize security incidents and events, and can help demonstrate compliance with the regulations and laws. This is far more efficient than in the days past, when understanding what occurred on your network meant combing through extensive logs that existed on multiple servers and network devices throughout the organization.

Common Features for SIM Products

SIM products are differentiated from other event collection applications and devices by their capability to analyze a variety of different reporting devices (firewalls, intrusion protection devices, applications, and so on) and make sense of them in a usable fashion. Each SIM product must include the following minimum set of features:

- **Event collection and correlation**—As a minimum requirement, you should expect a SIM to collect and correlate security event logs from your firewalls, intrusion detection systems/intrusion prevention systems (IDSs/IPSs), routers, switches, and servers. The capability of the SIM to receive syslog or SNMP events should be mandatory. A nice additional feature would be for a SIM to allow you to collect NetFlow data from NetFlow-capable devices such as switches and routers. The SIM should also be able to custom-parse data from devices that are not natively supported by the SIM.

- **Reporting**—Reporting is the primary reason why organizations purchase a SIM. The interface needs to be intuitive and responsive to the commands issued. The capability to pull important, relevant information out of the SIM in a rapid fashion is critical.

- **Alerting**—If you're collecting information and reporting on the data, you must be able to receive alerts in real time, especially when anomalies are detected. At the minimum, a system needs to be capable of sending e-mails to SIM administrators.

Additional capabilities that you should consider for a SIM include sending syslog messages and SNMP traps and paging you out of band if the network has been compromised.

Desirable Features for SIM Products

The common SIM features are what you can expect any SIM product to be capable of. Modern SIM products provide new capabilities that expand on what a traditional SIM can provide. These new features allow a SIM to do more than simple correlation, reporting, and alerting. SIM products that provide the following cutting-edge capabilities are often referred to as Security Threat Mitigation (STM) devices:

- **Sessionization**—The capability of an STM to sessionize data is a key differentiator when comparing it to other SIM products. Sessionization, simply stated, is the capability of the STM to collect related events from multiple hosts and security or network devices, identify that the events are related to the same traffic flow, and give you a summary of what has occurred. This provides the security analyst with a 30,000-foot view. This high-level view allows a rapid understanding of what has occurred. Sessionization is similar to a detective taking statements from witnesses to a crime and comparing it to other evidence. A single piece of evidence, or event, usually is not enough to accurately describe what has happened, but multiple related pieces of evidence, or events, can be.

- **Topology awareness**—An STM that can understand the network topology is in a class of its own. This rare feature enables the STM to understand the significance of the relative position of security devices. This feature enables the STM to evaluate security and network events so that the STM can determine whether an attack was successful.

- **Mitigation**—With mitigation capability, the STM can react rapidly to anomalous and malicious traffic on the network, and by understanding the network layout (or topology), provide the security administrator with an accurate recommendation for protecting the network from that traffic. On small- or medium-sized networks, this capability can greatly reduce staffing needs.

As you can see, new SIM features increase the value of the SIM, making it valuable in mitigating security threats, rather than simply reporting on event data.

A traditional SIM might page someone in the middle of the night when a web server is attacked. An STM, however, might look at the same set of events and determine that, although an attack against the web server was attempted, your network's IPS stopped the attack before it could reach the web server and cause damage. Rather than paging someone in the middle of the night, the STM can provide a summary that someone can read in the morning.

Challenges in Security Monitoring

Organizations have a lot of challenges when it comes to security monitoring. One of the biggest challenges is in the sheer volume of logs. Nearly every piece of equipment that is used on a network can also produce logs. Additionally, every host produces logs, and nearly every application on every host produces logs. Some of these logs typically stay local to the host, but others are intended to be sent to a monitoring system. Traditionally, however, each type of log has its own monitoring system, and those systems don't communicate with each other.

In addition to the volume of logs you have to deal with, drastic differences also exist in the way various hosts, devices, and applications log. No real standard exists for log messages. Different vendors have their own log formats, and often a single vendor uses different log formats for different products.

Some logs are easy to read, whereas others use cryptic codes instead of words and phrases.

When a regulation says that a company must comply with certain laws or standards by monitoring security and application logs, it can be like trying to make a square peg fit into a round hole. When you need to respond rapidly to a threat, such as when a new worm appears in your network or a database server has been compromised, all the pegs and holes need to be round. You cannot rely on multiple individual log-monitoring systems. Instead, you need a single system that can understand all your logs.

In the past, the general thought was that simply collecting logs was enough. The task of having to actually read and respond to them has created challenges most organizations did not anticipate.

The sections that follow provide brief descriptions of the various types of log messages you might want or need to monitor. Although this is not an exhaustive list, it should help you understand the various log types.

Types of Events Messages

The sections that follow provide some overview information on the various types of events messages. See the documentation for your security or network devices or applications for a complete description of each of the log types your devices use. Cisco.com also provides excellent information.

NetFlow

NetFlow was created by Cisco to address several needs by service providers and larger enterprise customers. NetFlow allows administrators to monitor a network in real time by creating flows, or sessions, based on the packets that flow through the interfaces. NetFlow can be used for the following purposes:

- Application profiling and monitoring
- User profiling and monitoring
- Network interface monitoring, for capacity planning
- Accounting and billing
- Security monitoring

NetFlow can be enabled on many Cisco switches and routers. When used with CS-MARS, NetFlow helps provide accurate views of which hosts, networks, and applications are generating the most network traffic. It's one of the key logging types for early detection of worms.

Syslog

Syslog is perhaps the most widely used of all the logging protocols. It is a general-purpose message protocol, and it can send virtually any type of message from a device to a syslog server. Most, but not all, syslog messages are simple text, and they are easy to read without special software.

Examples of systems that commonly use syslog include the following:

- Firewalls
- Routers
- UNIX servers

Most network devices can communicate at this level. Syslog provides a facility for communication between network devices, servers, and hosts. One property that makes syslog so useful is its simplicity. Syslog uses User Datagram Protocol (UDP) port 514. UDP is connectionless, and syslog provides rapid transmission of messages, but it does not guarantee delivery to the target server. The host or device that sends a syslog message assumes that it reaches the destination, but the protocol does not guarantee the delivery. For this reason, some systems use TCP instead of UDP for syslog messages. TCP guarantees message delivery, but it is not as fast. It also has the side effect of failing if the hard drive of the monitoring system gets full. When this happens, network traffic through the host or device can fail as well. The decision to use UDP or TCP for syslog messages is one that you need to make. Be aware, though, that many monitoring systems do not support TCP delivery.

SNMP (Simple Network Management Protocol)

SNMP is considered the standard for network management communication. Like syslog, SNMP uses UDP for communications, providing rapid messages but no guarantee of message delivery. SNMP communicates using UDP port 162 for *traps*, which are SNMP log messages. SNMP also allows management communications from a console to a managed device, but this is not related to receiving log messages.

SNMP traps are cryptic and usually impossible to read without special software, called the Management Information Base (MIB). The MIB is a collection of information, organized in a hierarchical manner, that provides a common format for the manager to communicate with devices. Within the MIB are objects that represent specific characteristics for a specific device. All top-level MIBs belong to different standards organizations, while the objects can apply to different vendors or organizations.

Examples of systems that typically use SNMP include the following:

- Switches
- Routers
- Host protection software

Security Device Event Exchange (SDEE)

SDEE is a somewhat open standard used by many IPS/IDS vendors, including Cisco, ISS, Sourcefire, and TruSecure. "Somewhat open" means that you can use it, but it is ultimately owned by the International Computer Security Association (ICSA). SDEE uses Extensible Markup Language (XML) to organize the format of IDS alerts (or events) and specifies the protocol as HTTP. SDEE was designed to be both flexible and extensible. SDEE, when used on Cisco IDS/IPS sensors, is backward compatible with Remote Data Exchange Protocol (RDEP) (a similar, but older communication protocol for Cisco IDS devices).

The original idea for SDEE was to standardize the event and alerting format among vendors so that many different vendor IPS/IDS solutions could be supported within a customer's network.

The SDEE framework is built on top of XML and uses HTTP as a transport with Secure Socket Layer/Transport Layer Security (SSL/TLS) standards for encryption and secure authentication with passwords and certificates. This is the same standard used on many shopping, banking, and other sites that require secure communication.

Besides allowing a standard, secure event-logging protocol, SDEE also guarantees delivery of log messages. SDEE uses TCP for the transport protocol. It is also a pull method, meaning that the monitoring station pulls event logs from the device, just as your web browser pulls information from a web server. Syslog and SNMP, on the other hand, are push methods, meaning that they blindly fire event logs onto the network, without knowing whether they reach their destination.

Currently, SDEE is widely used by Cisco for all network IDS and IPS logs. Other vendors have committed to using it. Contact your IDS/IPS vendor to see whether it has implemented SDEE in its devices.

Understanding CS-MARS

So far, this chapter has discussed the features you need in a SIM or STM system and which protocols you might need to use. The following sections look at how CS-MARS can provide the capabilities you need.

These sections discuss the MARS appliance and interface. You will understand the different components of the MARS appliance and see how it operates at a high level. Later chapters in this book discuss the appliance and interface in greater detail.

Security Threat Mitigation System

CS-MARS was initially created to help solve the issues that organizations have with event log collection. In the past, the data collected from security and network devices, such as routers, switches, firewalls, IDSs, and servers, was collected into separate event systems. Each vendor, and often each product, used its own console for collecting events and reporting. Correlation did not exist, especially across multiple vendors, and administrators had to manually monitor these different devices. You probably have better things to do than to crawl through gigabytes of data trying to find that one bad event. The purpose of MARS is to automate the collection of event data, place it into a large database, and then crawl through it on your behalf and locate the sessions that identify exactly what a user (or bad guy) did, when he did it, and where he is.

Topology and Visualization

MARS understands where the hosts are located because it understands your network topology. It gains the topology information when it performs a "discovery" on your network devices. During discovery, MARS connects to a device or reads from a configuration file, learns its Layer 2 and 3 configuration, and populates that information into its database. Periodically, a rediscovery process runs to keep the topology information up to date. MARS offers flexibility in how you configure the rediscovery.

Discovery also happens on demand, as you are investigating security incidents. For example, CS-MARS can detect when a host on your network is infected with a worm. When you select the worm incident and begin investigating, MARS tracks down the infected host by reading the Address Resolution Protocol (ARP) and content addressable memory (CAM) tables on your network devices so that you are presented with the switch port to which the infected host is connected. You can see this information as well as diagrams that show where the infected host sits in relation to other hosts and devices.

The visualization feature can also permit you to view the diagrams while stepping through the worm infection process. It can even recommend actions to stop an attack. Because CS-MARS can determine to which switch port the worm-infected host is connected, it can also recommend commands to temporarily disable network access through that port.

This same process occurs with each investigation of incidents and greatly increases the accuracy and usability of the STM.

Robust Reporting and Rules Engine

CS-MARS provides a powerful query-based engine that allows you to easily create additional rules and reports. By default, CS-MARS has an extensive set of rules and reports, each of which is open and editable. The query engine allows you to quickly display, in a variety of formats, the information in which you are interested. Commonly used queries can also be saved as reports or rules to allow automation of the queries.

Chapter 5, "Rules, Reports, and Queries," provides more detailed information on the reporting engine and interface.

Alerts and Mitigation

MARS allows you to customize alerts based on incident type. For example, reconnaissance activity followed by an unsuccessful buffer overflow attack might be an incident in which you want to receive an e-mail, but more suspect behavior, such as reconnaissance activity followed by a *successful* buffer overflow incident, might require MARS to page a security administrator.

MARS has several ways to notify you of incidents:

- E-mail
- Syslog
- SNMP
- Paging
- Short Message Service (SMS)
- E-mail with XML file attached

Description of Terminology

CS-MARS uses terminology that might differ slightly from what you are used to. To understand MARS and the process of investigation or tuning, you should clearly understand what each of these terms means, as defined in the sections that follow.

Events

Each single log event, regardless of how it arrives on CS-MARS, is an *event*. An event can be from any supported method, including SNMP, syslog, RDEP, SDEE, Check Point's

LEA, or a message received through Server Message Block (SMB) from a Windows server or host. When viewing a single event, you are not looking at correlated data.

Sessions

CS-MARS correlates events, and watches for multiple events that are all related to the same network traffic, coming from one or multiple event sources. This correlation of event data results in the creation of a *session*.

A session is created when events are identified by timestamp or hold-down timer, source IP address, source port, destination IP address, destination port, and protocol, and MARS determines that they are related.

If you consider an HTML attack against a web server, such as a directory traversal attack, multiple network and security devices should create a log. You could see a session created with the following set of log events:

- Your firewall permits TCP port 80 traffic to the web server from the attacker and sends a log to MARS through syslog.

- Your IDS or IPS identifies a directory traversal attack and sends a log to MARS through SDEE.

- Your routers identify TCP port 80 traffic from the attacker to the web server and send a syslog to MARS.

- Your web server, which might be vulnerable to the directory traversal attack, logs the web request from the attacker and uses an HTML response code to show whether the request (attack) was successful. A response code of 200 would indicate a successful attack, while a response code of almost anything else, including 403, shows that the web server did not display the requested information and the attack failed.

Each of these log events is related to the same network traffic and would be correlated into a session.

Rules

Rules are descriptions of behavior. They are created using queries, which can be simple or complex. For example, a rule could be so simple that it says "show me when this keyword appears in any event," or it could be complex and say "show me all instances of when someone scans one of my networks, and then sometime later attempts to brute-force log in using Secure Shell (SSH) or Telnet, and is successful."

MARS uses rules extensively to identify activities you need to know about. Rules are also used in reports. Figure 1-1 shows one of the built-in rules.

Figure 1-1   *Access Web Customer Data Rule*

Offset	Open (	Source IP	Destination IP	Service Name	Event	Device	Reported User	Keyword	Severity	Count	)	Close	Operation
	Rule Name:		System Rule: Misc. Attacks: Access Web Customer Data									Status:	Active
	Action:		None									Time Range:	0h:30m
	Description:		This correlation rule detects malicious attempts to access customer data stored by web applications, preceded by reconnaissance attempts to that host, if any. Customer data typically contains sensitive information such as purchasing history, credit card numbers etc.										
1	(	ANY	SAME, $TARGET01, ANY	ANY	Probe/HostInfo/All, Probe/ServerInfo/Web, Penetrate/ViewFiles/DirTraversal/Web, Penetrate/ViewFiles/Sensitive	ANY	None	ANY	ANY	1			FOLLOWED-BY
2		ANY	SAME, $TARGET01, ANY	ANY	Penetrate/ViewFiles/WebOrderInfo	ANY	None	ANY	ANY	1	)		OR
3		ANY	SAME, $TARGET01, ANY	ANY	Penetrate/ViewFiles/WebOrderInfo	ANY	None	ANY	ANY	1			

MARS observes a probe or penetration activity, using reconnaissance techniques or directory traversal attacks.

This behavior is followed by the same host attempting to access files referred to as WebOrderInfo, which is a set of files that e-commerce websites typically use for customer data.

Or, if the attempted access of the customer data occurs without previous activities, the rule is still matched.

Incidents

An *incident* is triggered when network activity matches the description of a behavior seen in a rule. An incident describes the entire story of what happened in an attack. A single incident can contain anywhere from a single event to millions of events. This is the highest level of correlation possible.

Figure 1-2 shows an incident summary. This summary provides you with a high-level overview of the incident, prior to a closer investigation. The following list describes the columns in Figure 1-2:

- The first column shows the unique incident ID, which is created for each incident.

- The second column shows a short list of the types of events seen in this incident.

- The third column shows the rule that was triggered to create an incident.

- The fourth column shows which automated action was taken. This column is usually empty, but if a rule is configured to page or e-mail someone, or send a trap, that action appears.

- The fifth column shows the date and time the rule was triggered.

- The sixth column shows a couple of icons that give you a "session vector" view (see Figure 1-3) and the path and direction (see Figure 1-4).

- The final column shows whether this incident has been assigned for further investigation by linking it to a case number.

Figure 1-2 *Sample Incident Summary*

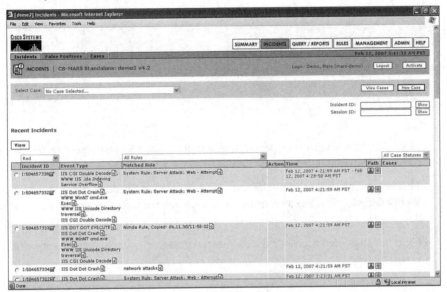

Figure 1-3 *Session Vector (Physical View) Diagram*

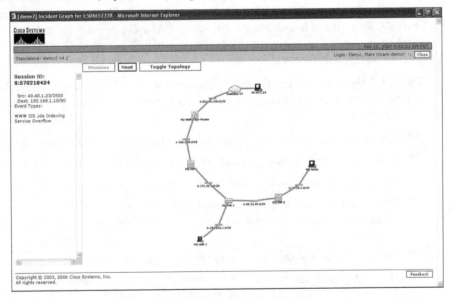

Figure 1-4   *Path and Direction (Logical View) Diagram*

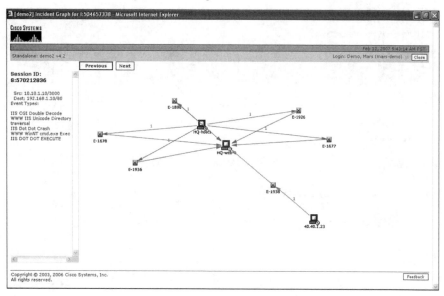

False Positives

CS-MARS considers a *false positive* an attack that was unsuccessful against the target, either because the host was not vulnerable to the attack or because other products prevented the attack from succeeding. This is somewhat of a misnomer, because the real definition of a false positive is when a product incorrectly identifies an attack, when in reality it was not an attack.

For example, if legitimate communication between a network printer and a host is incorrectly detected by your network-based IDS as an attack, this is, by definition, a false positive. However, this does not fit the definition used by CS-MARS. On the other hand, if a hacker launches an attack against your web server, and your network-based IDS accurately detects the attack but your web server is protected against the attack with updated software, CS-MARS considers this a system-determined false positive. By definition, it is not really a false positive; instead, it is a positively detected attack that was unsuccessful.

You need to understand the differences between the true definition of a false positive and the definition used by CS-MARS.

Figure 1-5 shows the following three types of false positives that are used in CS-MARS:

- Unconfirmed false positive type
- User-confirmed false positive type
- System-determined false positive type

Figure 1-5 *False Positive Page*

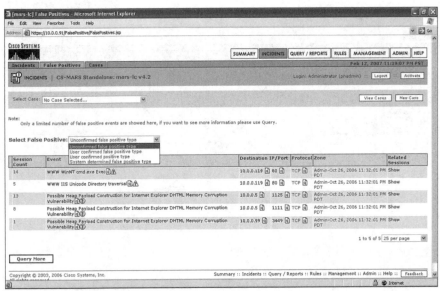

CS-MARS uses an integrated vulnerability assessment (VA) system that can be enabled on all or part of your network. The VA system more accurately determines whether attacks are real and can make the false positives described in this section more accurate. The system is designed to determine the following items:

- Operating system
- Version and patch level
- Servers that are running

Unconfirmed False Positives

An *unconfirmed false positive* is created when CS-MARS believes, but is not certain, that a host is not vulnerable to an attack. For example, the first unconfirmed false positive in Figure 1-5 is related to event "WWW WinNT cmd.exe Exec," which is a known vulnerability in older versions of Microsoft's IIS web server. Part of the investigation CS-MARS performs, when enabled, is a vulnerability assessment of the hosts under attack. This allows CS-MARS to determine things such as host operating system, patch level, services that are running, and versions of the services. If the vulnerability assessment shows that the targeted system is not vulnerable to the attack type, CS-MARS labels it as an unconfirmed false positive.

Periodically, you must check the unconfirmed false positives and confirm the results of the vulnerability assessment. Click the question mark to see why CS-MARS believes this is a false positive. Figure 1-6 shows the resulting window.

Figure 1-6   *Unconfirmed False Positive*

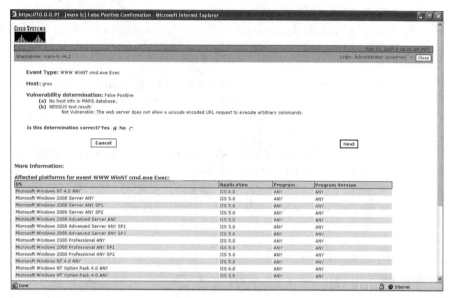

User-Confirmed False Positives

After you look at an unconfirmed false positive and agree with the determination CS-MARS has made, you confirm the false positive.

A *user-confirmed false positive* is simply your agreement that CS-MARS is correct in saying that a host is not vulnerable to a type of attack.

System-Determined False Positives

A *system-determined false positive* occurs when a device reports that it has stopped an attack. This occurs when some reporting devices indicate an attack while at least one other indicates the attack failed, or when the targeted host sends a log that the attack failed.

Consider the following example:

- An attacker (or worm) attempts a directory traversal attack against your Microsoft IIS web server. A directory traversal attack occurs when the attacker tricks the web server into accessing files outside the designated directories for the web server. Most commonly, this is an attempt to run Windows system files, such as the command prompt (cmd.exe).

- Several devices might report on this attack. Your firewall and routers will report on the traffic flow. Your IDS might identify the attack but might not be configured to respond to it.

- Your web server might have host protection software installed, such as Cisco Security Agent, or it might be patched so that it's not vulnerable to the attack. In this case, when the web request attack is sent to the web server, the server responds with an HTML response code, such as 404.

- You might also have an IPS that is configured to drop this type of attack. In this case, the attack never reaches the destination web server.

In this example, CS-MARS understands the topology of your network and knows when a device in the path of an attack prevents the attack from succeeding.

Figure 1-7 shows a system that was determined to be false positive.

Figure 1-7 *System Determined to Be False Positive*

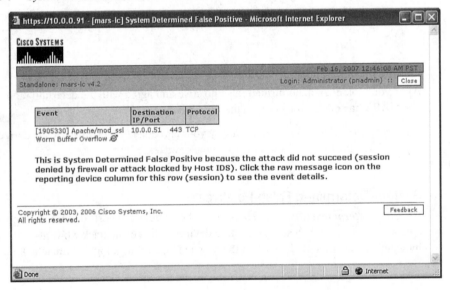

Mitigation

CS-MARS has multiple ways to assist you in mitigating threats and attacks. Because MARS understands topology and it understands where the specific threat exists, MARS can pinpoint the best method to mitigate an attack.

While you are investigating a security incident, you can click an icon to bring up a recommended mitigation. For example, if you appear to have an infected or compromised host on your network, MARS can tell which switch port it is connected to, and it can shut off that port for you. It can also recommend changes to your firewall or router access lists to shut down communication paths that are allowing an attack or infection.

CS-MARS User Interface

The CS-MARS user interface is easy to use and provides helpful information at a glance. The user interface is web based. Your web browser is all you need to access CS-MARS. You can view the security health of your network, run reports, search for events, and more.

Dashboard

The Dashboard is the main page within the user interface and is useful for seeing the overall security health of your network. As illustrated in Figures 1-8 and 1-9, the Dashboard is broken into subsections, each one offering its own view of the data as described in the list that follows. Statistics, graphs, drawings, and alerts are each represented. The purpose of looking at each of these in a different view is to validate the resultant data.

Figure 1-8   *CS-MARS Dashboard: Part 1*

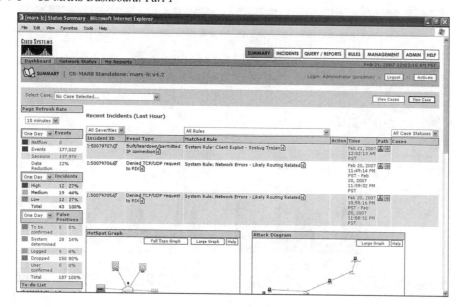

- **Events**—NetFlow, events, and sessions are calculated here. Sessionization can significantly reduce the overall amount of data. The percentage shown is an indication of how much data is being reduced in your environment.

- **Incidents**—This shows the number of incidents recorded in the last time period (one day, two days, one week, one month, one year) by level: red (severe), yellow (medium severity), and green (informational or low severity).

- **All False Positives**—This shows the total number of false positives in the last time period. Remember that just because MARS marks an event as a system-determined false positive, the event could still be a real incident, just ineffective against a target host.

- **Recent Incidents Table**—This table shows the last five incidents in the past hour that match the current filter. You can filter by severity, rule, rule group, and status of the case to which a rule might be assigned.

- **HotSpot Graph**—This graphic shows network devices and "hot" traffic. Using event counters, this window shows the hotspots of activity on the given network.

- **Attack Diagram**—This diagram shows the activity of communication and events between hosts without the muddle of network gear. The name *attack diagram* is really a misnomer; it would be better to refer to it as a *session vector diagram*. This pane/bow/window does not discriminate between an attack and typical network traffic. The color coding is as follows: brown is a source host (might be an attacker), red is a destination host (might be a target), and purple is a host that was recently communicated to and then began communicating to another host (might be an infected host).

Figure 1-9 *CS-MARS Dashboard: Part 2*

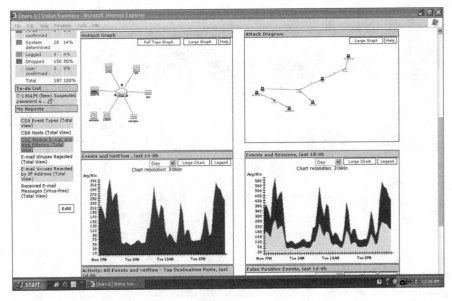

- **Events and NetFlow**—This chart compares events against NetFlow to aid in identifying a disparity. If NetFlow drops suddenly but events remain high, a misconfiguration or anomaly in the network could be present.

- **Events and Sessions**—This chart provides a visual indication of how much sessionization is occurring on the MARS appliance.

- **Activity: All Events and NetFlow–Top Destination Ports**—This graph is perhaps the most useful in identifying threats to your network. All worms and viruses have destination port patterns. For example, port 445, a commonly used port on any network that supports Microsoft Windows hosts, will have a generally stable number of events at any point during the day, typically ranking around mid-pack, as Figure 1-9 illustrates. When the Sasser worm hit the network and exploited the Windows services listening on port 445, it caused port 445 traffic to spike, creating an anomaly. This chart helps you pinpoint anomalies on your network and can also allow you to drill down on a specific port and identify the source and destination hosts involved in those sessions.

- **False Positive Events**—This chart tracks the false positives against real or undetermined false positives. If this chart goes out of norm, or false positives spike above what is normal, then you must investigate the anomaly.

Network Status

The Network Status page, described in the list that follows and shown in Figures 1-10 and 1-11, provides several graphs in addition to those shown on the Dashboard page.

Figure 1-10 *CS-MARS Network Status Page: Part 1*

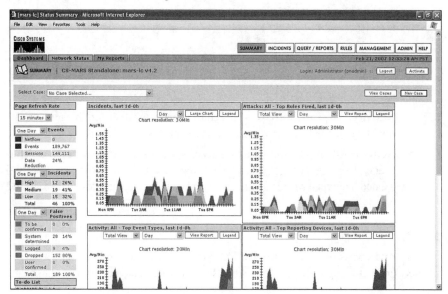

- **Incidents**—This chart is a graphical representation of high (red), medium (yellow), and low (green) incidents that have occurred over a specific time frame. The default is one day.

- **Attacks: All–Top Rules Fired**—This chart gives a representation of the rules fired. Clicking the Legend button on this graph (and any other graph) gives you specific details about rules that are being violated and are creating incidents.

- **Activity: All–Top Event Types**—This chart shows top events triggered on the network. Sudden changes can be anomalous, so you should review this chart often.

- **Activity: All–Top Reporting Devices**—This chart can assist in determining when a device has stopped reporting, which is reporting the most (busiest device), and so on.

Figure 1-11 *CS-MARS Network Status Page: Part 2*

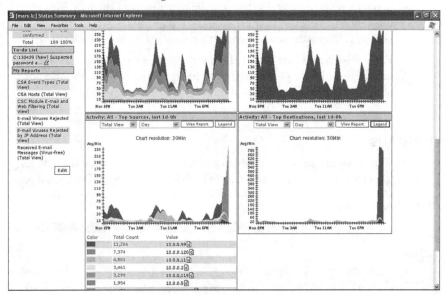

- **Activity: All–Top Sources**—This chart shows top talkers on the network. If you click the "Legend" button, IP addresses are listed as well.

- **Activity: All–Top Destinations**—This chart displays the top places to which packets/events are going. This graph can be useful in the case of a worm such a Nachi (known as a Good Samaritan worm). Nachi attempted to download the latest patches from Microsoft.

My Reports

The My Reports page, as illustrated in Figure 1-12, allows you to create a customized Network Status page. This is useful when specific events and incidents need to be monitored.

Figure 1-12 *My Reports Page*

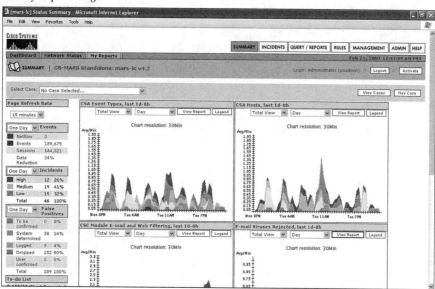

Summary

Regardless of the size of your organization, leveraging your existing investments is an important business initiative. Many organizations have invested millions of dollars in network hardware, security and monitoring applications such as antivirus applications and host-based IPSs, and more. The last thing an organization wants to do is to spend additional money on probes, servers, and databases to satisfy compliance requirements when the information it needs is already being collected.

It's ironic that the laws and regulations that have been implemented to protect the consumer end up costing businesses vast amounts of money in audit services, insurance, and hardware. You must leverage the existing investments your company has made.

CS-MARS solves some of these issues. It cannot make you compliant, but it can help you get there. It cannot stop all attackers, but it can tell you about when they attack and provide you with the information you need to mitigate and isolate the damage.

Today's networking environment is a battlefield. Enemies want your data, and they want access to your information and hosts. Sometimes these enemies might be your competitors. Other times, an enemy might be an overseas criminal looking to steal your data for profit. In the battlefield, monitoring sensors are placed in the ground and the air. You do the same thing by deploying IDSs, IPSs, firewalls, and other devices and software that can provide MARS with information.

CS-MARS gives your organization what it needs to use the existing devices as listening posts on your network, leveraging the investment made and giving you the visibility you need to meet organizational requirements.

## CHAPTER 2

Regulatory Challenges in Depth

Over the past several years, organizations have been faced with many new government and financial regulations. The general theme of the regulations is to force companies to take an active stance toward the security and privacy of their data. These regulations impose a set of challenges that require you to create security policies, implement various standards, and also prove that you are following the regulatory guidelines.

Some of the requirements, or guidelines, of these regulations include the following things:

- Development and enforcement of written security policies
- Encryption using Virtual Private Networks (VPN)
- Placement of firewalls
- Monitoring of attempted logins on systems that contain sensitive data
- Restricting access to sensitive data
- Placement of intrusion detection systems (IDS) or intrusion prevention systems (IPS)

Although each of these requirements is relatively simple to implement by itself, often the most difficult issue is how to monitor the network after protections are put in place. Various products come with their own monitoring tools or have tools available. However, with individual monitoring tools, you find that it's difficult, or even impossible, to adequately correlate events produced by the various tools. Additionally, this increases the staffing and knowledge required to adequately monitor the security events produced by the devices. For this reason, organizations have turned to Security Information Manager (SIM) and Security Threat Mitigation (STM) products such as the Cisco Security Monitoring, Analysis, and Response System (CS-MARS).

This chapter addresses many of the regulations and explains the key requirements you're likely to be faced with. The regulations covered are as follows:

- The Health Insurance Portability and Accountability Act of 1996 (HIPAA)
- The Gramm-Leach-Bliley Act of 1999 (GLB Act)
- The Sarbanes-Oxley Act of 2002 (SOX)
- The Payment Card Industry (PCI) data security standards of 2004

Reading this chapter is certainly not going to make you an expert on any of the regulations. The chapter can, however, give you a good overview of each of them.

Health Insurance Portability and Accountability Act of 1996 (HIPAA)

Most people in information technology think of HIPAA as a privacy or security regulation. However, that's only a portion of HIPAA. In 1996, when HIPAA was enacted, its purpose wasn't related to security. In fact, the primary focus of the legislation was to provide a set of standards for electronic transactions used within the medical field for billing and payment of services. Portability of data was the focus. Over time, it gained provisions for both privacy and security.

The three major areas within HIPAA are as follows:

- **Standards for Electronic Transactions**—Also referred to as Transactions, Code Sets, and Identifiers. This area defines standards for conducting electronic document interchange (EDI) health transactions. This area is not covered in this book.

- **Standards for Privacy**—The HIPAA Privacy Rule creates national standards to protect personal health information and also grants patients greater access to their own medical records. When you visit your doctor's office, you'll notice that more forms are required than there used to be.

- **Standards for Security**—The HIPAA Security Rule has the largest impact for people working within information security. This rule sets standards for the security of electronic health information. It requires that *covered entities* (as described in the following section) safeguard the confidentiality of *electronic protected health information (ePHI)*.

Who Is Affected by HIPAA?

You are required to comply with HIPAA regulations if you meet the definition of a covered entity. A *covered entity* is a health plan, health-care clearinghouse, or health-care provider that conducts certain financial and administrative transactions electronically. Examples of these transactions are billing for services, eligibility verification, or enrollment. Covered entities are further defined as follows:

- A *health plan* is an individual or group plan that provides, or pays the cost of, medical care.

- A *health-care clearinghouse* is an organization that processes health-care transactions on behalf of providers and insurers.

- A *health-care provider* is a person or organization that is trained and licensed to give health care.

If you are not sure whether you are a covered entity, answer these two questions:

- Do you furnish, bill, or receive payment for health care?
- Do you conduct covered transactions electronically?

If you answer yes to both questions, you are a covered entity.

What Are the Penalties for Noncompliance?

Both civil and criminal penalties can be imposed if you do not comply with HIPAA regulations. Complaints regarding noncompliance are sent to the U.S. Department of Health and Human Services (HHS). If HHS chooses to pursue criminal penalties, the case is handed to the U.S. Department of Justice for investigation.

Table 2-1 describes the civil penalties for noncompliance. The Secretary of HHS can reduce the fine if a violation is not due to willful neglect and has been corrected within 30 days.

Table 2-1 *Civil Penalties for HIPAA Noncompliance*

Monetary	Prison	Offenses
$100	None	Single violation of a provision. This amount can be multiplied for violating multiple provisions.
$25,000	None	Multiple violations of the same provision, made during the same calendar year.

Table 2-2 describes the criminal penalties for noncompliance.

Table 2-2 *Criminal Penalties for HIPAA Noncompliance (Maximum)*

Monetary	Prison	Offenses
Up to $50,000	Up to one year	Wrongful disclosure of individually identifiable health information
Up to $100,000	Up to five years	Wrongful disclosure of individually identifiable health information committed under false pretenses
Up to $250,000	Up to ten years	Wrongful disclosure of individually identifiable health information committed under false pretenses, with the intent to sell, transfer, or use for commercial advantage, personal gain, or malicious harm

HIPAA Security Rule

The Security Rule is composed of three sections, called *safeguards*. Each of the safeguards contains a list of standards that a covered entity needs to comply with. Each of the standards is composed of implementation specifications that might be required or addressable. The three sections are as follows:

- **Administrative Safeguards**—Consist primarily of policies and procedures for managing, developing, and implementing security measures to protect ePHI

- **Physical Safeguards**—Consist of measures, policies, and procedures for protecting the buildings, equipment, and information systems from physical hazards and unauthorized intrusions

- **Technical Safeguards**—Consist of the technology used to protect ePHI, as well as the policies and procedures involved

---

NOTE   An *addressable implementation specification* is one in which the covered entity has flexibility regarding compliance. This means that you can implement the standard as written, implement an alternate security measure, or use a combination of both. Additionally, the covered entity can elect not to address the standard. In this case, though, you must document why it would not be reasonable or appropriate to implement it.

An example of an addressable implementation specification is when a physician is the only worker in a small medical office. An addressable specification that requires security awareness training for all employees would be addressed by documenting that there is no one to provide training to.

Required implementation specifications are those in which you must meet the requirements that are listed. You still have a degree of flexibility, however, in that you decide what is reasonable given the size of your business and your budget.

Administrative Safeguards—Sec. 164.308

The following nine administrative safeguard standards are in place:

- **Security management process**—Covered entities must implement policies and procedures to prevent, contain, and correct security violations. This standard includes the requirement to conduct a thorough assessment of the potential risks and vulnerabilities of ePHI. It also requires you to implement security measures to reduce the risks and vulnerabilities to a reasonable and appropriate level. When you discover personnel who are failing to comply with the security policies, you are required to apply appropriate penalties. Finally, within this standard, you are required to implement policies to regularly review records of information systems activity, such as audit logs, access reports, and security incident reports. Security event correlation systems and SIM products, such as CS-MARS, can assist in complying with this requirement.

- **Assigned security responsibility**—All covered entities must assign a security official or officer who is responsible for the development and implementation of the Security Rule's required policies and procedures.

- **Workforce security**—This is an addressable standard, rather than a required implementation. All covered entities must implement policies and procedures to ensure that all members of the workforce have appropriate access to ePHI. The specifications of this standard include implementing procedures for the authorization or supervision of workforce members who work with ePHI, as well as procedures to determine whether the workforce member's access is appropriate and to outline termination procedures.

- **Information access management**—In this standard, covered entities are required to implement policies and procedures to provide isolation between portions of the organization that provide clearinghouse functions from portions that do not. Additionally, this standard contains two addressable specifications. The first of these is to implement policies and procedures for granting access to ePHI data. The second is to implement policies and procedures to document, review, and modify user access rights to workstations, programs, transactions, or processes.

- **Security awareness and training**—This standard is composed of addressable specifications. Covered entities must implement a security awareness and training program for all members of the workforce. This includes specifications for security reminders, protection against malicious software, login monitoring, and password management.

- **Security incident procedures**—Covered entities are required to have a documented policy for responding to security incidents, including mitigation of known harmful effects. This standard also requires that security incidents and outcomes are documented.

- **Contingency plan**—This standard consists of both required and addressable implementation specifications. All covered entities are required to have policies and procedures for creating and maintaining retrievable exact copies of ePHI, as well as a plan for recovering from a disaster and restoration of lost data. Policies and procedures are also required to protect the security of ePHI when the organization is operating in an emergency mode. The addressable portions of this standard are for testing and revisioning of the contingency plans, as well as assessing the criticality of specific applications and data in support of the other contingency plans.

- **Evaluation**—All covered entities must perform periodic evaluations to determine how well the organization is complying with the requirements of the Security Rule, and to determine any environmental or operational changes that affect the security of ePHI.

- **Business associate contracts**—This standard requires that a contract be in place for business associate relationships to obtain satisfactory assurances that the business associate will apply appropriate safeguards to protecting information.

Physical Safeguards—Sec. 164.310

Four physical safeguard standards are in place. These standards are physical measures, policies, and procedures to protect a covered entity's buildings, equipment, and electronic information systems from both natural and environmental hazards, and unauthorized intrusions. The four physical safeguard standards are as follows:

- **Facility access controls**—This is an addressable standard. Each covered entity needs to implement policies and procedures to limit physical access to electronic information systems and the facilities in which they are housed. The implementation specifications within this standard include establishing a policy and procedure for contingency operations, restoration of lost data, and emergency mode operations. The standard also contains a specification for policies and procedures for a physical security plan, physical and software program access controls, and maintenance records.

- **Workstation use**—Covered entities must document the functions to be performed, how the functions are performed, and the physical surroundings of workstations with access to ePHI.

- **Workstation security**—Covered entities must ensure that only authorized users have access to workstations that contain ePHI.

- **Device and media controls**—This standard contains both addressable and required implementation specifications. In this standard, covered entities are required to implement policies and procedures that govern the receipt and transfer of hardware and electronic media that contain ePHI. This means that you are required to implement policies and procedures that address the final disposition of computers and media that have stored ePHI. It also means that you must implement procedures for making sure that ePHI is removed from media before that media can be reused. The addressable specifications include both maintenance of records of the movements of hardware and electronic media and data backup and storage of ePHI before equipment is moved.

Technical Safeguards—Sec. 164.312

This set of safeguards covers policies and procedures governing the use of technology to protect ePHI. The following five technical safeguards are in place:

- **Access control**—Covered entities are required to allow access to only those people or software programs that have been granted rights. Within this standard are two required and two addressable implementation specifications. The first requirement is for each user to be assigned a unique name or number for identifying and tracking identity. The second requirement is to establish and implement procedures for obtaining emergency access to ePHI. The addressable specifications are to implement an automatic logoff system when an electronic session is inactive for a predetermined period of time, and encryption and decryption of ePHI.

- **Audit controls**—Covered entities must implement mechanisms that record and examine activity in information systems that contain or use ePHI.

- **Integrity**—Covered entities need to address how they verify that ePHI has not been altered or destroyed in an unauthorized manner.

- **Person or entity authentication**—Each covered entity must implement procedures to verify that a person or entity seeking access to ePHI is actually the person she claims to be.

- **Transmission security**—Covered entities must address two implementation specifications showing that protections against unauthorized access to ePHI while it is being transmitted over an electronic communications network have been implemented. The two addressable specifications are for both integrity controls, meaning that data has not been modified, and encryption of data when appropriate.

HIPAA Security Rule and Security Monitoring

The HIPAA Security Rule covers a lot of different topics. How do the implementation specifications with the administrative, physical, and technical standards impact your security monitoring solution? The following set of commonly asked questions should help clarify the impact.

What Should I Monitor with CS-MARS?

The administrative safeguard standards don't specify technical or physical measures, but they do have requirements that are solved with a centralized logging system.

The information systems activity review requires monitoring of system activity, including audit logs, access reports, and security incident reports. These types of systems can often send logs to a monitoring server for correlation and reporting. You should note that built-in support often isn't within CS-MARS for alerting and reporting on these types of custom activities, but CS-MARS provides the capability to create custom reports, queries, and event types to fit your needs.

Within the security awareness and training standard are a couple of addressable implementation specifications for which you can use CS-MARS. Because CS-MARS supports logs from some antivirus vendors, as well as host intrusion protection software, it works well for the protection from malicious software specification. Additionally, you can use CS-MARS to monitor login attempts for operating systems, databases, and some applications.

The security incident procedures standard requires covered entities to respond and report on security incidents. This is the core capability of CS-MARS. You should consider sending all security device logs to it to identify security incidents. As you investigate incidents within CS-MARS, you'll be presented with options for mitigating the incidents.

How Much Effort and Money Do I Need to Put Toward Implementing These Safeguards?

The HIPAA Security Rule does not specify exact methods of complying with the safeguards. Many possible ways of meeting a requirement exist. Some of these are very expensive and provide a very strong level of security. Others are less costly and provide a lower level of security. HIPAA leaves this choice to the covered entity. You should choose how to implement the measures based on what is feasible for your organization. A large national health-care plan should have stronger controls than a small health-care provider because the larger organization has more resources to work with.

How Long Do I Need to Retain Security Logs?

This is a question that each organization needs to determine for itself. HIPAA does not impose any requirements for data retention. However, it does require that your **policies and procedures** for the security standards be retained for at least six years. This does not necessarily mean that the actual logs need to be retained for the same period of time. Your organization needs to make that determination based on its needs. Many covered entities have elected to retain security logs for one to two years. This is probably a reasonable period because it allows you adequate time to investigate claims of privacy violations while not imposing overwhelming storage costs.

Are There Other Things to Consider?

Yes. A requirement of the administrative safeguard standards is a regular evaluation of your network security, based on the standards implemented under the Security Rule. As this evaluation is performed, whether you choose to perform it internally or through an external security firm, security incidents will be created because of the various scans that are performed. This record, combined with written documentation, will be proof that you have complied with the evaluation requirement, and will show a reasonable effort toward complying with the Security Rule.

When Do We Have to Comply with the Security Rule?

You need to comply now. Most covered entities were required to comply with the Security Rule by April 21, 2005. Small health plans were given an additional year to comply.

Gramm-Leach-Bliley Act of 1999 (GLB Act)

The GLB Act is also known as the Financial Modernization Act of 1999. The GLB Act was passed into law in 1999 as Public Law 106-102, and is a set of federal legislation that includes provisions to protect consumers' personal financial information that is held by financial institutions.

The three principal parts of the GLB Act are as follows:

- **The Financial Privacy Rule**—Governs the collection and disclosure of personal financial information by financial institutions. It also applies to companies that are not financial institutions, but have received such information.

- **The Safeguards Rule**—Requires financial institutions to design, implement, and maintain adequate safeguards to protect individual financial information. It applies to both financial institutions and other companies that have received financial information, such as collection agencies.

- **Pretexting Provisions**—Provisions of the GLB Act provide protections for consumers from individuals and companies that obtain their personal financial information under false pretenses.

The first two parts apply to financial institutions. Eight federal agencies and the individual states are given authority to administer and enforce these rules. Banks, credit unions, securities firms, insurance companies, consumer loan companies, and tax preparers are all considered to be financial institutions. In addition, nontraditional financial institutions are also impacted, including places such as real estate settlement services, collection agencies, credit counseling services, and financial planners.

Who Is Affected by the GLB Act?

You must comply with the requirements of the GLB Act if your company is classified as a financial institution by the Federal Trade Commission (FTC) and is significantly engaged in financial activities for individuals. A financial institution can be any company that provides financial services, such as loans, financial advice, investment services, or insurance. For the purposes of the GLB Act, the FTC also has jurisdiction over other financial institutions that are not covered by federal banking agencies, the Securities and Exchange Commission, the Commodities Futures Trading Commission, and state insurance agencies. These other institutions include nonbank mortgage lenders, loan brokers, financial and investment advisers, tax preparers, providers of real estate settlement services, and debt collectors.

The GLB Act does not apply to information collected about business activities. Only information collected about individuals is covered.

What Are the Penalties for Noncompliance with GLB?

Section 505 of the GLB Act grants authority to sanction financial institutions for violations. The agencies, which already regulate the financial institutions, are also responsible for sanctioning those same institutions they regulate. Each agency uses a different set of standards for violations. In addition to the financial sanctions the agencies can impose, Sections 521 and 523 also provide criminal penalties for people who gain access to protected financial information through fraudulent means. Criminal sentences can be up to five years, or up to ten years when a history of illegal activity can be shown.

The Federal Deposit Insurance Corporation (FDIC), as one example, can impose penalties ranging from $5,000 to $1,000,000 per day on banks that violate the GLB Act.

The GLB Act Safeguards Rule

The GLB Act Safeguards Rule, which is enforced by the FTC, requires financial institutions to have a security plan for safeguarding the confidentiality and integrity of personal consumer information. The Federal Trade Commission published *Standards for Safeguarding Customer Information; Final Rule* on May 23, 2002, as required by Section 501(b) of the GLB Act. The Final Rule establishes standards relating to technical, physical, and administrative safeguards subject to the FTC's jurisdiction. The effective date of the rule, or the date by which financial institutions must comply, was May 23, 2003.

The Safeguards Final Rule requires financial institutions to develop a written information security plan that describes their plan to protect customer information. The plan must be appropriate to the financial institution's size and complexity, in addition to the scope of its activities and the sensitivity of the customers' information it handles. Each financial institution must address each of the following overall requirements:

- **Designate security personnel**—The first step toward complying with the Final Rule is to designate a person or group of people responsible for coordinating the safeguards. The Final Rule allows a lot of flexibility with all requirements. Each financial institution needs to determine how it can best balance security with feasibility. With this first requirement, some institutions might choose to designate a single security officer, while other larger institutions might assign this responsibility to a team of personnel.

- **Assessment of risks**—The second step is to identify and assess the risks to customer information in each relevant area of the company's operation, and to evaluate the effectiveness of all current safeguards.

- **Design and implement a safeguards program**—After evaluating the effectiveness of the current safeguards, determine how to improve security. Create written security policies and procedures, and implement the updated safeguards.

- **Monitor and test**—Implement a monitoring system to watch for effectiveness of the safeguards. Regularly test the safeguards with internal or external security assessments.

- **Select providers and implement safeguards**—Select service providers and contract with them to implement additional safeguards.

- **Evaluate and adjust**—Regularly evaluate and adjust the safeguards program based on the results of the monitoring system and security assessments. Take into consideration any changes in the business operations or arrangements, and any other relevant information, such as new network or application vulnerabilities.

Each area of the financial institution's operation must be considered when developing and implementing the safeguards. The Safeguards Rule suggests that these three areas are particularly important to information security. The sections that follow address the practices to be considered.

Employee Management and Training

Your employees must be properly screened during the hiring process. This helps ensure that you are hiring ethical individuals who can be trusted to handle sensitive information. Additionally, an ongoing training program helps remind your employees that confidentiality and security are important. The following list outlines the FTC's recommendations:

- Check references of new employees who will have access to customer information.

- Require all employees to sign an agreement to follow your security and confidentiality policies.

- Provide security training to all employees. Each employee should know how to take basic steps to maintain the security, confidentiality, and integrity of customer information.

- Remind all employees of the organization's security and confidentiality policies. Consider posting reminders on posters, screen savers, and other locations.

- Limit access to customer information to employees who have a need to know.

- Impose disciplinary measures when an employee violates customer privacy rules.

Information Systems

Information systems include the design and implementation of the network and all software in use. It also includes storage, transmission, retrieval, and disposal of information systems and data.

The FTC offers the following suggestions on maintaining security throughout the life cycle of customer information:

- **Store records in a secure facility**—Limit physical access to the systems to authorized employees. In particular, pay attention to Internet connectivity of systems that contain customer information. A system that stores customer information should be isolated from direct Internet connectivity. Electronic banking, or similar activities, obviously require access to the data, but a security design should be implemented so that no connectivity exists between the Internet and the system storing the data. Also, all connectivity from any other system must require at least password authentication. If possible, implement stronger authentication mechanisms.

  Make sure that backup media is stored securely. Backups should not be stored in the same location as the systems being protected. Instead, store the backups in an offsite location, or some other physically secure area.

- **Make use of secure data communications any time you collect or transmit customer information**—Use clear instructions and simple security tools to accomplish this. Specifically, when credit card or any other financial information is collected or transmitted, as you will do on an e-banking website, use Secure Socket Layer (SSL) encryption or other encryption technologies. Warn customers against sending sensitive information using electronic mail, and when any information must be transmitted by electronic mail to a customer, ensure that messages are password-protected so that only authorized people have access.

- **Dispose of customer information in a secure manner**—Make sure that all paper records are shredded rather than simply disposed of in a trash receptacle. Consider contracting with a records disposal company.

  Make sure that electronic media is securely erased or destroyed prior to disposal. Promptly dispose of all outdated customer information.

Managing System Failures

To effectively manage security, you must include the prevention, detection, and response to attacks, intrusions, and other system failures. These system failures can include such things as virus infections, worm outbreaks, and botnets, as well as targeted attacks by people attempting to steal or otherwise compromise your customers' information. This includes both external attacks and those that originate inside your network.

NOTE   A *botnet* is a group of computers running programs that allow them to be controlled under a common command and control infrastructure. Botnets are a major problem on the Internet today. The bots, or compromised computers, can be infected and controlled through a variety of means. Internet Relay Chat (IRC) is commonly thought of as the channel through which bots are controlled, because it was the original method of controlling them; however, today's botnets can be controlled in an almost limitless fashion.

With a botnet, a single individual can instruct hundreds, or even hundreds of thousands, of computers to all function as he desires. Usually, this is with malicious intent. Botnets have been instrumental in distributed denial of service (DDoS) attacks, often as part of a blackmail scheme to force a company to pay large sums of cash to avoid being attacked. They've also been used to harvest financial and other personal information from corporate and government networks to be used in identity theft. Much of the spam you see in your e-mail inbox is sent from botnets.

Maintaining up-to-date applications and controls is a key factor in reducing the vulnerability to system failures. Follow these suggestions:

- Follow a written contingency plan to address any breaches of physical, administrative, or technical safeguards.

- Keep current with software applications by regularly obtaining and installing patches or new versions to mitigate software vulnerabilities.

- Use antivirus software that updates automatically.

- Maintain up-to-date firewalls, particularly if you use broadband Internet access at any locations or if you allow employees to access your network from offsite locations.

- Provide centralized management and monitoring products for employees, and keep them notified of updates regarding security breaches or risks.

Additionally, you might want to explore the use of host-based intrusion prevention software as protection against botnet infestation, and as protection against new attacks that have not yet been protected against by traditional systems such as antivirus software. These new attacks are often referred to as *zero-day attacks*.

You should take steps to preserve the confidentiality, security, and integrity of customer information in the event of a system failure. As an example, you should regularly back up applications and data.

Additionally, make sure that access to customer data is restricted to only those employees who need it. Use tools to verify the identity of users before allowing access to the information. Consider using passwords combined with personal identifiers, or use a one-time password (OTP) system.

When customer information has been lost, damaged, or otherwise compromised, be sure to promptly notify the customers.

The GLB Safeguards Rule and Security Monitoring

The requirements for security monitoring within the Safeguards Final Rule are relatively vague. This is because of the flexibility financial institutions have in deciding what makes the most sense for their organization. All financial institutions are required to monitor and test their controls, but how this is done is not described.

What you should think about is how your monitoring solution can provide the monitoring needs, and how it can be used to demonstrate due diligence in other areas. An obvious use for a monitoring solution is to analyze and store security event logs from firewalls and intrusion detection systems. You can also direct application logs to it, in addition to authentication successes or failures. By combining, or correlating, the information from each of these systems, a security analyst can locate attempted or successful attacks earlier than possible without this correlation. Doing this also improves the ability to determine the scope and severity of a system failure, which results in faster response and mitigation as well as reduced costs.

The Sarbanes-Oxley Act of 2002 (SOX)

In 2001, it became apparent that Enron Corporation's executives had been lying to the public in its financial statements to falsely give the impression of a healthy, growing company, while at the same time secretly selling off their own shares. Just a year prior, Enron's stock was selling at $90 per share. *Forbes Magazine* had listed Enron as one of the "100 Best Companies to work for in America." While Enron's executives were forecasting massive growth, and telling the world that they expected Enron stock to be trading at over $130–140 within one year, they were secretly selling stock worth tens of millions of dollars.

Enron's stock values continued to drop, but all the while, its executives continued to forecast a bright future. Investors were encouraged to continue buying stock, even though values were dropping. When it became apparent that corporate corruption and financial fraud were committed, Enron stock dropped below $1 per share, and Enron filed for bankruptcy in both Europe and the United States. The financial well-being of thousands of investors and employees was devastated. Enron employees lost their life savings, pensions, and children's college savings plans.

The aftermath of this collapse was huge. Criminal charges were filed against many people, and the cases are still in the courts. It was obvious that laws needed to be changed to help prevent similar corporate abuses in the future. The Sarbanes-Oxley Act was signed in July 2002 as a direct response to the Enron scandal and similar scandals at Tyco International and WorldCom. WorldCom announced in June 2002 that it had overstated its earnings by more than $3.8 billion over five quarters.

Sarbanes-Oxley (SOX or SarbOx) is a U.S. federal law (Public Law 107-204) also known as the Public Company Accounting Reform and Investor Protection Act of 2002. SOX covers issues such as establishing a public company accounting oversight board, auditor independence, corporate responsibility, and enhanced financial disclosure.

The major provisions of Sarbanes-Oxley are as follows:

- The chief executive officers and chief financial officers must certify the accuracy of financial reports.
- Personal loans to any executive officers or directors are banned.
- Accelerated reporting of trades by company insiders is required.
- During pension fund blackout periods, inside trades are prohibited.
- Chief executive officer and chief financial officer compensation and profits must be reported publicly.
- Auditor independence is established.
- Criminal and civil penalties are imposed for violations of securities laws.
- Significantly longer jail sentences and larger financial penalties are imposed for corporate executives who knowingly and willfully misstate financial statements.
- Audit firms are prohibited from providing certain "value-added" services to their clients that are unrelated to their audit work.
- Publicly traded companies must furnish independent annual audit reports on the existence and condition of internal controls as they relate to financial reporting.

Who Is Affected by Sarbanes-Oxley?

Any company that is publicly traded is required to comply with the requirements stated within the Sarbanes-Oxley Act. Compliance was required by 2004, but most companies are still working to comply with the requirements.

What Are the Penalties for Noncompliance with Sarbanes-Oxley?

Both civil and criminal penalties can be imposed on companies and company officers. Maximum civil penalties for willfully and knowingly violating the provisions can be as high as $5,000,000. Maximum criminal penalties include up to 20 years of imprisonment.

Sarbanes-Oxley Internal Controls

Section 302 of SOX requires that a set of controls be implemented to ensure the accuracy of information in financial disclosures. The officers who sign the financial disclosures must certify that they are responsible for establishing and maintaining internal controls and have designed internal controls to ensure that information relating to the company and subsidiaries is made known to the officers. The officers must evaluate the effectiveness of internal controls within 90 days of submitting a report, and have presented their conclusions in the report.

This section causes great concern among company officers. The executive and financial officers of a company don't typically have direct responsibility for the information that exists in their databases and documents. However, they are required to sign for the internal controls of the information with personal liability attached.

Section 404 of SOX requires company management to produce an internal control report as part of each annual Exchange Act report. The report must affirm the responsibility of management for establishing and maintaining an adequate internal control structure and procedures for financial reporting. The report must also contain an assessment of the effectiveness of the internal controls, as of the end of the most recent fiscal year.

The Public Company Accounting Oversight Board (PCAOB) was tasked with issuing guidelines for companies to use as a reference. The PCAOB suggested using Committee of Sponsoring Organizations (COSO) or Control Objectives for Information and related Technology (COBIT) framework for guidelines on controls, auditing, and other technology issues. In general, most companies have chosen COSO.

Section 802 of SOX requires that pertinent audit records be maintained for at least seven years. This requirement is to allow investigators adequate time to examine any questions that might come up in an audit.

Payment Card Industry Data Security Standard (PCI-DSS)

In June 2001, Visa USA implemented the Cardholder Information Security Program (CISP). The goal of CISP was to assure Visa credit card customers that their account information was safe whenever they use their card for a purchase, regardless of whether it's through telephone, across the Internet, through the mail, or in person. In 2004, the CISP requirements were incorporated into a new industry standard called the Payment Card Industry Data Security Standard (PCI-DSS). The PCI-DSS is now a requirement by all major credit card companies, including Visa, MasterCard, Discover, Diner's Club, and American Express.

In September 2006, version 1.1 of the PCI-DSS was released, with updated requirements. The most noticeable difference between version 1.0 and 1.1 is in the categorization of various merchant levels. Effective with the release is a change in who controls the standard. Although Visa USA owned version 1.0, the PCI Security Standards Council (PCI SSC) now owns the standard and all its supporting documents.

Unlike the other regulations in this chapter, which allow a large amount of discretion and variability in how a company complies with requirements, the PCI-DSS is very strict and detailed.

Who Is Affected by the PCI Data Security Standard?

All merchants, members, and service providers that store, process, or transmit credit card information are required to comply with the PCI-DSS. Compliance is mandatory regardless of whether the business is a traditional retail store, an Internet e-commerce store, or a mail/ telephone order business.

NOTE	All entities that store, process, or transmit cardholder data are subject to PCI Data Security Standards. These requirements are not limited to retail stores. Colleges and universities, hospitals, veterinary clinics, and restaurants are all subject to these requirements.

Four different levels of merchant currently exist, each with slightly different requirements. Table 2-3 describes the current definitions of merchant levels, as determined by PCI SSC.

Table 2-3   *Merchant Levels Defined*

Merchant Level	Description
1	Any merchant processing over 6,000,000 Visa transactions per year.
	Any merchant who has suffered an attack or hack that resulted in account data compromise.
	Any merchant that Visa determines should be Level 1, for any reason.
	Any merchant that any other credit card company has determined should be Level 1.
2	Any merchant processing from 1,000,000 to 6,000,000 transactions per year.
3	Any merchant processing from 20,000 to 1,000,000 e-commerce transactions per year.
4	Any merchant processing fewer than 20,000 e-commerce transactions per year, and all other merchants processing up to 1,000,000 Visa transactions per year.

What Are the Penalties for Noncompliance with PCI-DSS?

If you fail to comply with the data security standards contained within CISP/PCI, the credit card company might issue a fine on your banking member, impose restrictions on your company, or both.

One requirement of PCI-DSS is that the merchant or service provider must immediately report any suspected or confirmed loss or theft of any material or data that might contain cardholder data. The merchant must also take immediate action to investigate the incident and limit the exposure of the compromise.

If a merchant fails to immediately report a suspected or confirmed security breach, the member institution can be fined up to $100,000 per incident. If, at the time of the compromise, the merchant was not compliant with the PCI-DSS requirements, the fine can increase to $500,000 per incident.

As an incentive toward compliance, PCI-DSS provides Safe Harbor to protect the merchant, member, or service provider. This means that if at the time of a compromise, the merchant, member, or service provider was fully compliant with the PCI-DSS requirements, and the incident was reported immediately, the provider is protected from fines and compliance exposure by the credit card company.

The PCI Data Security Standard

Twelve requirements within the PCI Data Security Standard fall within seven categories, which are outlined in Table 2-4 and described in detail in the sections that follow.

Table 2-4   *PCI-DSS Requirements and Categories*

Category	Requirement
Build and Maintain a Secure Network	Requirement 1: Install and maintain a firewall configuration to protect data.
	Requirement 2: Do not use vendor-supplied defaults for system passwords and other security parameters.
Protect Cardholder Data	Requirement 3: Protect stored data.
	Requirement 4: Encrypt transmission of cardholder and sensitive information across public networks.
Maintain a Vulnerability Management Program	Requirement 5: Use and regularly update antivirus software and programs.
	Requirement 6: Develop and maintain secure systems and applications.
Implement Strong Access Control Measures	Requirement 7: Restrict access to data by business need-to-know.
	Requirement 8: Assign a unique ID to each person with computer access.
Implement Strong Access Control Measures	Requirement 9: Restrict physical access to cardholder data.
Regularly Monitor and Test Networks	Requirement 10: Track and monitor all accesses to network resources and cardholder data.
	Requirement 11: Regularly test security systems and processes.
Maintain an Information Security Policy	Requirement 12: Maintain a policy that addresses information security for employees and contractors.

Build and Maintain a Secure Network

The most important part of securing credit card data is a secure network. PCI-DSS outlines a minimum set of technologies it requires before a network is considered secure.

Requirement 1: Install and Maintain a Firewall Configuration to Protect Data

You must establish firewall configuration standards that include such things as

- A formal change control process for approving and testing all external network connections and changes to the firewall configuration.

- A current network diagram showing all connections to cardholder data, including wireless networks.

- Requirements for a firewall to be deployed at each Internet connection and between any demilitarized zone (DMZ) and the intranet.

- Descriptions of groups, roles, and responsibilities for logical management of network components.

- Documented lists of all services and ports necessary for business.

- Justification and documentation for any available protocols besides HTTP and SSL (HTTPS), Secure Shell (SSH), and VPN.

- Justification and documentation for any risky protocols in use, such as FTP, Telnet, or any cleartext protocol. The justification must include the reason for using the protocol and all measures taken to secure its use.

- Periodic review of firewall and router rules.

- Configuration standards for routers.

Build a firewall configuration that denies all traffic from untrusted networks except for the following:

- Web protocols such as HTTP and HTTPS.

- System administration protocols such as SSH and VPN.

- Other protocols needed for business. Typically, these other protocols inherently use secure transport. An example might be Transport Layer Security–encrypted (TLS-encrypted) e-mail, or proprietary communications required by a PC-based banking or financial software application.

Build a firewall configuration that restricts connections between publicly accessible servers and any system components that contain cardholder data, including connections from wireless networks. The configuration should include the following:

- Ingress filters to restrict inbound Internet traffic to systems within the DMZ.

- Restricting inbound and outbound traffic to HTTP (TCP port 80) and HTTPS (TCP port 443).

- Not allowing internal addresses to pass from the Internet to the DMZ.
- Stateful inspection, which is also known as dynamic packet filtering. This type of firewall maintains an internal table in memory to track the state of connections.
- Placing the database in an internal network zone that is separate from the DMZ.
- Restricting outbound connections to those that are necessary for the payment card environment.
- Securing and synchronizing router configuration files.
- Denying all inbound and outbound traffic not explicitly permitted.
- Installation of perimeter firewalls between any wireless networks and the payment card environment.
- Installation of personal firewall software on mobile or employee-owned personal computers that access the organization's network.

Prohibit any direct public access between external networks and any systems that store cardholder information, such as databases, by doing the following:

- Implementing a DMZ to filter and screen all traffic, to prohibit direct routes for inbound and outbound traffic.
- Restricting outbound traffic from payment card applications to IP addresses within the DMZ.

Implement IP masquerading to prevent internal addresses from being translated and revealed on the Internet. Use technologies that utilize private IP address space (RFC 1918) such as network address translation and port address translation.

Requirement 2: Do Not Use Vendor-Supplied Defaults for System Passwords and Other Security Parameters

Numerous resources exist on the Internet for discovering vendor-default passwords for administrative access to systems. Always change the vendor-supplied defaults before installing a system on the network. This should include passwords and Simple Network Management Protocol (SNMP) community strings, as well as elimination of unnecessary accounts. For wireless environments, be sure to change defaults for Wired Equivalent Privacy (WEP) keys, default service set identifiers (SSIDs), and passwords. Additionally, disable SSID broadcasts and, when possible, deploy WiFi protected access (WPA) technology for encryption and authentication.

Develop configuration standards for all system components, making sure to address known security vulnerabilities and industry best practices as follows:

- Implement only one primary function per server. For example, a Domain Name System (DNS) server and a web server should not exist on the same computer system. Likewise, a web server and a database should not reside on the same system.

- Disable all unnecessary and insecure services and protocols.
- Configure system security parameters to prevent misuse.
- Remove all unnecessary functionality, such as scripts, drivers, features, subsystems, and file systems. This would include removal of unused web servers that are often installed by default when a new operating system is installed. An example of this is when Microsoft IIS is installed by default on a Windows server, or when Apache Web Server is installed by default on a Linux server.

Encrypt all nonconsole administrative access. Use technologies such as SSH, VPN, or SSL/TLS for web-based administration.

Protect Cardholder Data

Security is more than simply protecting the perimeter. You also need to consider how to protect data at rest. This means that you need to think about possible ways data that is stored by various systems might be compromised, either through the network or by someone with physical access to a system. It also means protecting data that resides on backup media.

Requirement 3: Protect Stored Data

Encryption of stored data is the ultimate protection. This is because even if a system is otherwise compromised, the data is inaccessible without also breaking the encryption in use.

Keep cardholder information storage to a minimum. Develop a data retention and disposal policy. Place limits on data retention to those required for business reasons or legal/ regulatory reasons.

Do not store sensitive authentication information, even if it is encrypted. The following list outlines key PCI-DSS requirements:

- Do not store the full contents of any track from the magnetic strip.
- Do not store the card validation code. On most cards, this is the three-digit security number on the back of a credit card or the four-digit security number on the front of other cards.
- Do not store the personal identification number (PIN) verification value.

Mask account numbers when displayed. The first six and last four digits are the maximum allowed to be displayed. This does not apply to employees who have a business need to view the entire number.

Render sensitive cardholder data unreadable anywhere it is stored, including when stored on backup media and portable media using any of these approaches. At a minimum, the account number must be rendered unreadable. Methods for making information unreadable include the following:

- One-way hashes, such as Secure Hash Algorithm 1 (SHA-1).
- Truncation.
- Index tokens and packet assemblers/disassemblers (PADs), with the PADs being securely stored. A PAD refers to a key that is usually used only once to decrypt a line of text.
- Strong cryptology, such as Triple DES (3DES) 128-bit or Advanced Encryption Standard (AES) 256-bit encryption.

Protect encryption keys from misuse or disclosure by doing the following:

- Restricting access to keys to the fewest number of custodians possible.
- Storing keys securely in the fewest possible locations and forms.

Fully document all key management processes and follow these guidelines:

- Generate strong keys.
- Secure key distribution.
- Secure key storage.
- Implement periodic key changes.
- Destroy old keys.
- Split knowledge and control of keys so that it requires two or three people to reconstruct an entire key.
- Prevent unauthorized substitution of keys.
- Replace known or suspected compromised keys.
- Revoke old or invalid keys.
- Require key custodians to sign a form specifying that they understand and accept their key custodian requirements.

Requirement 4: Encrypt Transmission of Cardholder and Sensitive Information Across Public Networks

All traffic transmitted across the Internet must be encrypted to prevent hackers from gaining unauthorized access to data.

Use strong cryptography and encryption techniques (at least 128-bit) such as SSL, Point-to-Point Tunneling Protocol (PPTP), and IPsec to safeguard cardholder data during transmission across public networks.

Never send cardholder information through unencrypted electronic mail.

Maintain a Vulnerability Management Program

Vulnerability management means several things. It means keeping track of your software and operating systems, and tracking vulnerability announcements that are related to them. It also means developing and enforcing policies that keep systems patched to minimize the security impact of vulnerabilities.

Requirement 5: Use and Regularly Update Antivirus Software and Programs

Because, in recent years, most vulnerabilities and viruses enter the network from employees' e-mail activities, all e-mail systems and desktops must feature antivirus software.

Deploy antivirus software on all systems commonly affected by viruses.

Ensure that all antivirus mechanisms are current, actively running, and capable of generating audit logs. You should consider a network admission control (NAC) system that can perform posture checking of computers to verify and enforce your antivirus policies.

Requirement 6: Develop and Maintain Secure Systems and Applications

Hackers use security vulnerabilities to find ways of gaining unauthorized access to systems. Many vulnerabilities are fixed through vendor-supplied security patches, and all systems should have current patches installed to protect against exploitation. In-house–developed applications should be developed using secure coding techniques.

Within one month of release, all security patches should be installed on affected systems.

Establish a process to identify newly discovered vulnerabilities. Update your standards to address the new vulnerability issues.

Develop software applications based on industry best practices, and include information security throughout the development process. Include the following procedures and guidelines:

- Test all security patches, system software, and software configuration changes before deployment.
- Separate development and test environments from production environments.
- Separate duties between development and test environments and production environments.
- Production data cannot be used for testing and development. For example, real credit card numbers cannot be used when testing applications.
- Remove test data and accounts before production systems become active.

- Remove custom application accounts, usernames, and passwords before applications become active or are released to customers.
- Review custom code prior to release to production or customers to identify potential coding vulnerabilities.

Follow change control procedures for all system and software configuration changes. The procedures should include the following:

- Documentation of impact
- Management sign-off by appropriate parties
- Testing that verifies operational functionality
- Back-out procedures

Develop web applications and software based on secure coding guidelines, such as the Open Web Application Security Project guidelines. Cover prevention of common coding vulnerabilities in software development processes to include the following:

- Unvalidated input
- Broken access control, such as the malicious use of user IDs
- Broken authentication/session management
- Cross-site scripting (XSS) attacks
- Buffer overflows
- Injection flaws, such as Structured Query Language (SQL) injection attacks
- Improper error handling
- Insecure storage
- Denial of service
- Insecure configuration management

Implement Strong Access Control Measures

Strong access controls means considering what data and resources different groups of users need access to. Determine the best way of restricting access to the information, and then use strong authentication practices to guarantee the identity of the users.

Requirement 7: Restrict Access to Data by Business Need-to-Know

Limit access to computing resources and cardholder information to only those individuals whose job requires such access.

Establish a mechanism for systems with multiple users that restricts access based on a user's need to know, and is set to deny all others unless specifically allowed.

Requirement 8: Assign a Unique ID to Each Person with Computer Access

By requiring each user to have a unique ID, you can enforce restrictions on who can access sensitive or critical data, and you can track when the access occurs.

PCI-DSS requires that you verify the identity a user offers. This means that you should use a password, one-time password or token, public-key infrastructure (PKI), or biometrics.

Remote access should be authenticated using a two-factor method by employees, administrators, and contractors.

Make sure that all passwords that are transmitted or stored on a system are encrypted.

Ensure proper user authentication and password management for all nonconsumer users as follows:

- Control the addition, deletion, and modification of user accounts and credentials.
- Verify user identity before performing password changes or resets.
- Set first-time passwords to a unique per-user value and require that they be changed upon first use.
- Immediately revoke access from terminated users.
- Remove inactive user accounts at least every 90 days.
- Enable accounts used by vendors for remote maintenance only during the time needed.
- Distribute the password policy and procedures to all users who have access to cardholder information.
- Do not use group, shared, or generic accounts and passwords.
- Change user passwords at least every 90 days.
- Require a minimum password length of seven characters.
- Require both numeric and alphabetic characters in passwords.
- Do not allow a user to reuse a password that has been one of his last four passwords.
- Limit repeated login attempts by locking out a user who attempts to log in multiple times. You should allow no more than six attempts before locking out the user.
- Set the lockout duration to 30 minutes, or until an administrator has reenabled the account.
- If a session has been idle for more than 15 minutes, require the user to enter the password to reactivate the session.
- Authenticate all accesses to a database that contains cardholder information.

Implement Strong Access Control Measures

All the electronic security in the world is mostly useless if unauthorized personnel have physical access to systems that contain sensitive information.

Requirement 9: Restrict Physical Access to Cardholder Data

Regardless of electronic data security measures you might take to safeguard cardholder data, if someone with malicious intent is able to gain physical access to systems that contain sensitive data, that person can obtain the sensitive data. For this reason, adequate physical security measures must be taken.

Use appropriate entry controls to limit and monitor physical access to facilities and systems that store cardholder information as follows:

- Use cameras to monitor sensitive areas. Audit this data, and correlate it with other entries. Store the information for at least three months, unless otherwise restricted or directed by law.

- Restrict physical access to publicly accessible network jacks.

- Restrict physical access to wireless access points, gateways, and handheld devices. Consider where network routers, switches, and access points are placed. These are commonly seen in retail locations in or near public restrooms, where an attacker can physically access and potentially modify the configurations of devices, or even connect a rogue access point.

- Develop procedures to help employees easily identify whether someone is an employee or visitor.

- Make sure that all visitors are authorized before entering sensitive areas, have been given a physical token or badge, and are made to surrender the token or badge upon leaving. Many companies also use special color-changing badges so that anyone attempting to reuse a badge on a different day is obvious.

- Use a visitor log to retain a physical audit log of visitors. Store the visitor logs for at least three months, unless otherwise restricted or directed by law.

- Store media backups in a secure offsite location.

- Physically secure all paper and electronic media that contains cardholder information.

- Maintain strict control over the distribution, either internal or external, of any kind of media that contains cardholder information. Media should be labeled as confidential and sent through a secure courier or other method that allows accurate tracking.

- Ensure that management approves all media that is moved from a secure area.

- Maintain strict control over the storage of any media that contains cardholder information. Make sure that you properly inventory and securely store all media.

- Destroy media that contains cardholder information when it is no longer needed for business or legal reasons.

Regularly Monitor and Test Networks

If you don't monitor your security and system logs with a quality correlation tool, you will not be able to adequately identify when someone attempts to compromise or succeeds in compromising your systems. Additionally, you should hire a qualified company to verify that your security controls are functioning as designed, and that no unexpected vulnerabilities exist in your security infrastructure.

Requirement 10: Track and Monitor All Accesses to Network Resources and Cardholder Data

Logging mechanisms are key to being able to track user activities. Various systems all have individual logging capabilities, and you must be able to accurately parse and correlate the different log files. When something goes wrong, or an auditor asks for access logs that show attempted accesses to cardholder data, the ability to quickly extract the needed information from the logs will be critical. Additionally, when a suspected compromise has occurred, the ability to quickly report and act to contain the compromise will be determined by the capabilities of your logging and correlation solution.

Establish a process for linking all access to systems, especially with administrative privileges, to individual users.

Implement automated audit trails to reconstruct the following events, for all system components:

- All individual user accesses to cardholder data
- All actions taken by any individual with administrator or root privileges
- Access to all audit trails
- Invalid access attempts
- Use of authentication and identification mechanisms
- Initialization of audit logs
- Creation and deletion of system components

Record at least the following audit trail entries for each event, for all system components:

- User identification
- Type of event
- Date and time
- Success or failure indication
- Origination of event
- Identity or name of affected data, system, or resource

Synchronize all critical system clocks and times. You should make use of Network Time Protocol (NTP), wherever available, on all systems that generate logs, whether they are servers, workstations, security devices, or network devices. It is *critical* that time be synchronized among all your network and security devices and with your event-logging and -correlation solution. NTP is the most widely supported time synchronization system. You should be diligent in making sure that all devices are configured to use it.

Secure audit trails so they cannot be altered. You should adhere to the following guidelines:

- Limit viewing of audit trails to those with a business need.
- Protect audit files from unauthorized modifications.
- Promptly back up audit files to a centralized repository or logging server that is difficult to alter.
- Use file integrity monitoring/change software on logs to ensure that existing log files are not modified without generating new alerts.

Review logs for all system components at least once per day. Log reviews should include those servers that perform security functions, such as network IDSs and authentication servers.

Retain your audit histories for a period that is consistent with its effective use, as well as legal regulations. Audit histories usually cover a period of least one year, with at least three months available online.

Requirement 11: Regularly Test Security Systems and Processes

A network can be secure one day, but open to new vulnerabilities the next. Hackers continually expose new vulnerabilities in applications, operating systems, and network devices. In addition to regularly updating and patching systems, you also need to frequently test the security you've implemented.

Test security controls, limitations, network connections, and restrictions routinely to make sure that they can adequately identify or stop unauthorized access attempts. If wireless networking is deployed, a wireless scanner should be used to identify all installed wireless devices.

Run internal and external network vulnerability scans at least quarterly and after any significant change in the network. Be aware that PCI-DSS requires that external vulnerability scans be performed by a scan vendor qualified by the payment card industry.

Perform penetration testing on network infrastructure and applications at least once per year, and after any significant change in the network.

Use network IDSs, host-based IDSs, or IPSs to monitor network traffic and alert personnel to suspected compromises. Maintain the IDS/IPS engines and any signatures to current levels.

Deploy file integrity monitoring to alert personnel to unauthorized modifications of critical system or content files, and perform critical file comparisons at least daily.

Maintain an Information Security Policy

A written security policy, whether it's a single policy or a group of multiple policies, should be maintained. Additionally, the policy needs to be signed by an officer of your company.

Requirement 12: Maintain a Policy That Addresses Information Security for Employees and Contractors

A strong security policy sets the security tone for the entire company and lets employees know what is expected of them. It also lets employees know what actions might occur should they violate security policies. All employees should be aware of the sensitivity of cardholder information and their responsibilities for protecting it.

Establish, maintain, publish, and distribute a security policy that addresses all parts of the PCI-DSS requirements and includes an annual review of the policies.

Develop daily operational security procedures that are consistent with these specifications.

Develop usage policies for critical employee-facing technologies, such as wireless or remote access, to define proper usage of these technologies for employees and contractors. Ensure that these usage policies require the following:

- Explicit management approval.
- Authentication for use of the technology.
- A list of all such devices and personnel with access.
- Labeling of devices with owner, contact information, and purpose.
- Acceptable uses of the technology.
- Acceptable network locations for the technology.
- A list of company-approved products.
- Automatic disconnect of modem sessions after a specific period of inactivity.
- Activation of modems for vendors only when needed, with immediate deactivation after use.
- When accessing cardholder information remotely, through a modem, disable local storage of cardholder information onto local hard drives, floppy disks, or other media. Also, disable cut-and-paste and print functions during remote access.

Ensure that the security policy and procedures clearly define information security responsibilities for all employees and contractors.

Assign to an individual or team the following responsibilities:

- Establish, document, and distribute security policies and procedures.
- Monitor and analyze security alerts and information, and distribute to appropriate personnel.
- Establish, document, and distribute security incident response and escalation procedures to ensure timely and effective handling of all situations.
- Administer user accounts, including additions, deletions, and modifications.
- Monitor and control all access to data.

Compliance Validation Requirements

Depending on your merchant level, certain requirements exist for validating your compliance with the PCI-DSS standards. These include quarterly and annual assessments or scans that must be documented and provided to the credit card companies. Table 2-5 lists the requirements for each merchant level.

Table 2-5 *Merchant-Level Compliance Validation Requirements*

Level	Validation Action	Validated By
1	Annual onsite PCI security assessment	Qualified security assessor or internal audit if signed by officer of the company
	Quarterly network scan	Approved scanning vendor
2 and 3	Annual PCI self-assessment questionnaire	Merchant
	Quarterly network scan	Approved scanning vendor
4	Annual PCI self-assessment questionnaire	Merchant
	Quarterly network scan	Approved scanning vendor

Summary

This chapter covered a lot of material. It can get overwhelming when you consider the requirements being imposed on your company or organization by government privacy regulations and private industry policies. Where do you start? Is it achievable? How much is it going to cost?

A common item, seen in all the regulations and policies, is the requirement for a system that provides logging, correlation, and reporting capabilities. CS-MARS is an ideal choice, and it can help you achieve your compliance goals at a reasonable cost and with a relatively mild learning curve.

## CHAPTER 3

CS-MARS Deployment Scenarios

Before you can deploy a Cisco Security Monitoring, Analysis, and Response System (CS-MARS), you must first understand the various ways that you can deploy it. This means deciding how many MARS appliances you need, where to place them, and which devices you want to log to them. Many companies need only a single appliance. Others, though, need to deploy several appliances, using a centralized MARS appliance, called a *global controller (GC)*, to manage the entire deployment.

This chapter describes the various options you have, including the following:

- **Deployment types**—You can deploy a single CS-MARS appliance as a standalone controller if that fits your needs. Otherwise, you can deploy a global controller that manages an environment that uses several remote CS-MARS appliances, which are called *local controllers*.

- **Size of your deployment**—Determine which CS-MARS deployment model and appliance types fit your needs for volume of events, reporting performance, and data retention policy requirements.

Deployment Types

The simplest and most common way to deploy CS-MARS is by using a *standalone controller*. This means that you use a single CS-MARS appliance that collects events from your security and network devices or software.

The other deployment option is to use a *GC*. This means that you deploy two or more *local controllers (LC)*, each of which is configured to interact with a GC. Your network and security devices are configured to send events to the LCs, and management of the CS-MARS appliances occurs either on the LC or on the GC.

You should understand that monitored devices and software can never send events directly to a GC.

Each of these deployment models has advantages and disadvantages. When selecting one of these deployment models, you must understand your network and have a good idea of the volume of events that need to be collected and processed.

Local and Standalone Controllers

No difference in hardware or software exists between a local controller and a standalone controller. A standalone controller is a MARS-20R, MARS-20, MARS-50, MARS-100e, MARS-100, MARS-110R, MARS-110, MARS-200, or MARS-210 that operates as a complete CS-MARS system. An LC is the same model that is configured to communicate with a global controller.

Table 3-1 shows the capabilities of each of the CS-MARS local and standalone controllers.

Table 3-1   *CS-MARS Local and Standalone Controllers*

Model	Events per Second	NetFlow Events per Second	Storage	RAID Level	Size, Rack Units (RU)
MARS-20R	50	1500	120 GB	None	1
MARS-20	500	15,000	120 GB	None	1
MARS-50	1000	30,000	240 GB	0	1
MARS-100e	3000	75,000	750 GB	1+0	3
MARS-100	5000	150,000	750 GB	1+0	3
MARS-110r	4500	75,000	1.5 TB	1+0	2
MARS-110	7500	150,000	1.5 TB	1+0	2
MARS-200	10,000	300,000	1 TB	1+0	4
MARS-210	15,000	300,000	2 TB	1+0	2

Each MARS appliance fits into a 19-inch rack. They each run a hardened installation of Linux and have two Ethernet interfaces.

When determining which MARS appliance fits your needs, you should closely study the information presented in Table 3-1. MARS appliances are sized by the number of events that that particular model can process without dropping information. The number of devices that can send events to the MARS appliance is unlimited. However, in a flood condition, such as when a network worm has infected your network, or when your network is the target of a denial of service (DoS) attack, you will see a significant spike in numbers of events that your network and security devices or software is sending to the monitoring console. As you increase the number of devices that report to MARS, the potential for event traffic also increases.

Additionally, you need to consider the available storage on each appliance, especially as you determine the length of time that security incidents and events need to be immediately available on the MARS appliance. This time period varies from customer to customer; it also varies according to what industry your company is in and which regulatory requirements you need to meet. Take note that the MARS-100 and larger appliances all have Redundant Array of Independent Disks (RAID) arrays to decrease the chance of a hard drive failure causing loss of data or functionality. These appliances also have hot-swappable hard drives.

Global Controllers

There are three different models of GC. The MARS-GC and MARS-GCM share the same hardware platform, while the MARS-GC2 is an entirely different platform. The MARS-GC and GCM differ in that the GCM is a restricted version, available for a lower price. Table 3-2 provides a comparison of the models.

Table 3-2   *CS-MARS Global Controllers*

Model	Manages	Max LC	Storage	RAID Level	Size, RU
MARS-GCM	MARS-20R, 20, and 50	5	1 TB	1+0	4
MARS-GC	All	Unlimited	1 TB	1+0	4
MARS-GC2	All	Unlimited	2 TB	1+0	2

A global controller acts as the central console for a network that requires multiple local controllers. It also provides a variety of additional capabilities, including the following:

- Global authentication, across all local controllers
- Unified rule and report generation
- Simplified software maintenance
- Reduction of traffic across WAN links
- Faster user interface

Typically, three scenarios encourage you to deploy a global controller, as follows:

- **Volume of events is more than a single controller can handle**—If your network is sending more events than a single controller can handle, you can add a second local controller and point some traffic to the first controller and some to the second. By doing this, you are able to scale appliance capabilities linearly. For example, two MARS-200 appliances, reporting to a MARS-GC, can receive and process approximately 20,000 events per second (EPS) and up to 600,000 netflows per second (NPS).

- **Network consists of a remote site, connected across a WAN**—It often doesn't make good business sense to send syslog and Simple Network Management Protocol (SNMP) events across slow and expensive WAN links to a centralized logging server, or MARS. Many times, a single centralized MARS is sufficient to handle the volume of events, but this causes degradation in performance on your slow network links. In this case, as illustrated in Figure 3-1, smaller MARS models deployed at remote sites keep the bulk of the information at the remote sites, while also allowing centralized reporting and monitoring. As the MARS global controller needs information from the local controller, it requests it automatically.

Figure 3-1 *Global Controller Deployment with Remote Sites*

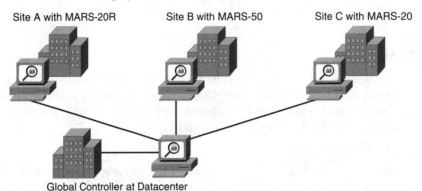

- **Network is spread across multiple business units, each with its own logging requirements**—Often it make sense to place appropriately sized MARS local controllers so that each LC monitors a business unit or organization within your company. Splitting reporting devices across multiple MARS local controllers allows you to provide separate role-based monitoring for each of the monitored organizations or business units. This means, for example, if your company is ACME Corporations, and it is composed of ACME Widgets, ACME Gadgets, and ACME Finance, that each of these separate organizations can have its own monitoring console by logging in to its specific local controller. Additionally, ACME Corporation can maintain a global security operations center (SOC) that has overall monitoring and reporting over each of the separate organizations. Figure 3-2 illustrates this example. You should be aware that, to accurately portray the network topology and correctly correlate events, all devices in one location should report to the same LC. For example, you would not want all intrusion prevention system (IPS) devices to report to one LC and all firewalls to another.

Figure 3-2 *Global Controller Deployment Across Business Units*

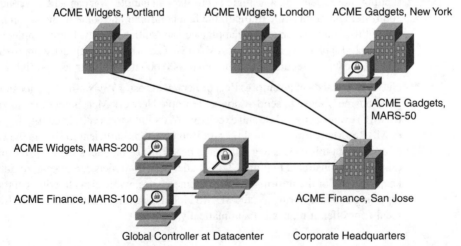

Sizing a CS-MARS Deployment

After you have chosen a deployment model, it is time to decide which CS-MARS appliance or appliances best fit your needs. Table 3-1 provided an overall view of the EPS and NPS of each of the models. Selecting the appropriate size appliance is perhaps the most difficult task.

Each reporting device can send a certain number of events per second, based on the software it is running and the platform it is running on. For CS-MARS sizing purposes, you can elect to calculate the properly sized appliance based on the maximum number of events each device is capable of sending, or you can examine your existing logs to determine how many events you are already receiving.

If you use the maximum possible EPS, you will automatically prepare yourself for flood conditions. However, you'll also most likely spend a bit more money than you need to. As an example, if you look at a Cisco PIX 535 firewall, you see that it can send as many as 15,000 EPS by itself. A Cisco PIX 515 can send as many as 1500 EPS. A Cisco Firewall Services Module can send 25,000 EPS. Using these types of numbers quickly builds the case for a MARS global controller with multiple local controllers. However, is this model right for your network? Just because a device can send this many events, does that mean you should plan for it? Not necessarily. How many events you're likely to see depends on many factors, including the following:

- The speed of your Internet connection. Slower Internet connections usually see fewer events than faster ones.

- The logging level of your reporting devices.

- Your overall security posture. If your firewalls are configured in a stringent manner, unexpected flood conditions might be less likely to occur.

Table 3-3 shows an approximate number of events that various reporting devices can potentially send to CS-MARS (or any other logging system) under flood conditions.

Table 3-3 *Maximum Events per Second*

Reporting Device Type	Maximum EPS
Cisco ASA-5520 firewall	10,000
Cisco ASA-5540 firewall	20,000
Cisco PIX 515 firewall	1500
Cisco PIX 535 firewall	15,000
Cisco Firewall Services Module	25,000
Windows XP, 2000, NT operating system logs	300
Snort IDS	1000
Cisco IPS	1300

continues

Table 3-3　*Maximum Events per Second (Continued)*

Reporting Device Type	Maximum EPS
Check Point FW-1	3500
Cisco IOS switch	200
Cisco IOS router (with ACLs)	300
NetScreen VPN	1000
Cisco VPN-3000 concentrator	500

As shown in Table 3-3, if you use the maximum possible number of EPS a device can send, you could exceed the capabilities of a single CS-MARS appliance with a small number of devices, even though it's extremely unlikely for this to occur in a typical network. For this reason, it usually makes more sense to calculate how many events you actually see on your own network, and then take into consideration what the maximum number is for determining how a network flood could affect you.

Special Considerations for Cisco IPSs

Organizations running Cisco Intrusion Prevention System (IPS) have additional factors to consider when sizing a MARS deployment. Cisco IPS sensors, whether running on an appliance (IPS-4200 series), Catalyst 6500 module (IPSM-2), network module, or ASA security services module, or within Cisco IOS Software (IOS IPS), use Security Device Event Exchange (SDEE) for communications with a monitoring device or software. SDEE is much like Secure HTTP (HTTPS). It typically runs on TCP port 443 and is encrypted with Transport Layer Security/Secure Socket Layer (TLS SSL). Instead of traditional HTTP-formatted pages, though, information is in Extensible Markup Language (XML) format.

SDEE features a pull mechanism, where the monitoring system (MARS) connects to the IPS sensor over TCP port 443 and downloads the IPS events. This method has several advantages over more traditional logging mechanisms. Some of the key advantages include the following:

- Guaranteed delivery of events
- Ability to filter which events to pull
- Ability to retrieve older events that still exist in the event store

Traditional logging mechanisms, such as syslog and SNMP, do not have these benefits. Both typically run on User Datagram Protocol (UDP), which does not provide guaranteed delivery. Because both are push mechanisms, the logging system cannot be selective in what it receives, nor can it retrieve events again when they have already been sent once.

The challenge that SDEE provides to MARS is the necessity for MARS to connect to the IPS and retrieve the events. MARS appliances have threads allocated to this process, but the number of threads varies by MARS model, and each thread is limited to the number of events it can pull per second.

Table 3-4 details the numbers of threads available on each MARS appliance, as well as the total number of IPS EPS that that appliance is capable of receiving from Cisco IPS sensors.

Table 3-4 *Cisco IPS Sensor Sizing*

Model	Threads	Total Cisco IPS EPS
MARS-20R	1	50
MARS-20	1	100
MARS-50	2	200
MARS-100E	5	500
MARS-100	10	1000
MARS-110R	5	500
MARS-110	10	1000
MARS-200	20	2000
MARS-210	20	2000

Each thread within MARS is capable of approximately 100 EPS. All threads run in parallel to each other, meaning that more threads typically equals more performance.

If your organization has two IPS sensors, and you are using a MARS-200 for monitoring, you can retrieve about 200 EPS, because you're using only two threads. However, if you have 20 or more devices, all reporting to a single MARS-200, you can retrieve 2000 EPS from the sensors.

It is rare to see the limit of 100 EPS being reached on a Cisco IPS sensor. The sensors automatically summarize events when IPS signatures fire multiple times. This effectively prevents the sensor from flooding its monitoring system, or MARS.

Determining Your Events per Second

Although the numbers presented in Table 3-3 might not be realistic in your network, they do give you an idea of which types of devices tend to send the most events. The "noisiest" devices on your network are likely in this order:

1 Internet-facing firewalls

2 Other firewalls

3 Intrusion detection systems/intrusion prevention systems (IDS/IPS)

4 Virtual Private Network (VPN) devices

5 Routers

6 Switches

7 Other devices, such as databases, operating systems, antivirus software, desktop and server protection software (such as Cisco Security Agent), and so on

This list of noisiest devices might be completely different from what is found in your environment; it is shown only as an average.

Most organizations already use a syslog server for collecting raw events from security devices. These existing logs can be useful in sizing your CS-MARS deployment.

Begin with your Internet-facing firewalls. To get a rough idea of the EPS being generated, select a log file from your firewalls that spans one or more days. Follow these steps to determine the average EPS from these devices in a 24-hour period:

Step 1 Gather the logs for one or more 24-hour periods.

Step 2 Count the number of lines in the file or files.

Step 3 Divide the number of lines by the number of 24-hour periods the file contains.

Step 4 Divide this number by 86,400.

The number you get will be the average number of EPS in that 24-hour (or longer) period.

The average number of events you calculate provides a good starting point for determining the CS-MARS appliance you need. Understand, though, that you have just calculated a 24-hour average instead of an average during peak hours. For a better estimate, look at a snapshot of logs from a busy time of day, or use a tool that can analyze your logs for you and show peak periods. After calculating the number of events for your Internet-facing firewall, calculate the average for your other firewalls and IDSs/IPSs you'll be taking logs from.

NOTE Log files on a syslog server are usually far too large for any text editor to open. The easiest way to count the number of lines in a large file is with the Linux/UNIX command-line tool **grep** or with the Windows **find** command.

The **grep** tool, normally used for searching for text within a file, is simple to use. You can also use the **grep** tool to display a count of the number of lines that contain a string in a file. In this example, we are searching the file called logfile for the number of lines that contain an empty string. The following syntax matches on every line in the file:

```
grep -c "" logfile
```

For Windows syslog servers, you can use the **find** command with the following syntax:

```
find /c /v "someweirdstring" logfile
```

With **find**, you are telling Windows to display the count of the number of lines that do not contain the string "someweirdstring".

If you can count all lines in all syslog files for each device you'll be monitoring, this will be the most accurate. However, most organizations don't have these files readily available.

After you've determined the overall average number of EPS, you should attempt to determine your peak event periods, especially if your traffic tends to vary by time of day or day of week.

The same formula used for the overall average can work for hourly averages. Just don't divide by 86,400 if you're looking only at a single hour. There are 60 seconds per minute and 60 minutes per hour. So, if you have a log file with a single hour of data, divide the number of lines by 3600 to reach the average EPS for that period of time.

Determining Your Storage Requirements

CS-MARS processes events in the following order:

1 Receive, or retrieve, events from monitored device. Each individual log entry is considered a single event.

2 Sessionize the events by correlating on all events, from all monitored devices, that are part of the same traffic flow. This is done by correlating on time stamps of events, source IP address, destination IP address, source port and protocol, and destination port and protocol.

3 Process sessions through the rules engine.

4 Verify the accuracy and validity of the apparent incidents.

5 Record and display incidents.

As events, sessions, and incidents are received or created, they are marked with a unique identifying number and then written to the onboard Oracle database. On an hourly basis, information from the previous hour is compressed and written to an archive server, if you've configured one. The CS-MARS appliances have a finite amount of storage available, and as the available space is filled, old events, sessions, and incidents are purged. Reporting on data that resides in the onboard database is quick and easy. Reporting on data that has been purged from the database, and that exists only on the archive server, is time-consuming. Chapter 7, "Archiving and Disaster Recovery," goes into detail about the archiving functionality.

Table 3-5 shows the usable storage on each of the CS-MARS appliances. Note that available storage is not the same as the total storage on the appliance.

Table 3-5   *CS-MARS Usable Storage*

Model	Total Storage	Available Storage
MARS-20R	120 GB	77 GB
MARS-20	120 GB	77 GB
MARS-50	240 GB	155 GB
MARS-100E	750 GB	565 GB
MARS-100	750 GB	565 GB
MARS-200	1000 GB	795 GB
MARS-110R	1500 GB	866 GB
MARS-110	1500 GB	866 GB
MARS-210	2000 GB	1221 GB

The amount of time that events can be stored on a CS-MARS appliance depends on both the rate of events, or average EPS, as well as the average event size. It might not seem like much of a difference, but a typical SNMP trap, as you might see from a third-party intrusion detection system, might be only about 200 bytes, while a typical syslog entry from many devices will be about 300 bytes. If verbose logging is enabled on a Cisco IPS sensor, events can grow to 500 bytes or so. This is a difference of 2 1/2 times the size of an SNMP trap, meaning that much less data can be historically stored.

A good average event size for most networks is 300 bytes. Use this number when calculating your storage capabilities unless you have determined a different number for your network.

Use the following formula to calculate the number of days you can store events on a CS-MARS appliance before they are purged:

Days = Usable storage / (Event size * EPS * 86,400)

For example, If ACME Finance is collecting 45 EPS on average on a CS-MARS-100E appliance, and the average event size is 300 bytes, the calculation is as follows:

Usable storage = 565,000,000,000 bytes (565 GB)
Event size = 300 bytes
EPS = 45
Days (calculated) = 484 days

ACME Finance can store nearly 1 1/2 years of event data on its MARS-100E. If the company's policy is to keep event data for one year, the MARS-100E is a decent choice. If, however, it is required to store for two years, ACME Finance needs a MARS-200 instead.

Considerations for Reporting Performance

When reports are generated on CS-MARS, the processing required for the reports is given a lower priority than that given for event, session, and incident processing. For this reason, a CS-MARS appliance that is working at an EPS level that is close to the maximum for that appliance will process reports slowly, especially when compared to a lightly loaded appliance.

You must determine whether reporting performance improvements that you might see on a larger MARS appliance are worth the additional cost of the appliance. As you increase the load on the appliance, you will see on-demand reporting begin to run slower. Consider deploying a faster CS-MARS appliance if your actual EPS is nearing 50–60 percent of the rated EPS.

As you move from the lower-end MARS appliances to the larger appliances, you move to faster processors. Additionally, on the MARS-100E and higher models, the appliances use multiprocessor system boards. This dramatically improves performance.

You will also see performance improvements when deploying a global controller. This is because the actual event processing occurs on the various LCs, while correlation and user interface handling occur on the GC.

Considerations for Future Growth and Flood Conditions

While you are determining the correct CS-MARS model and deployment option, consider how your network will react in a flood condition. When your network is under a DoS attack, a worm is loose on your network, or some other serious incident occurs, you want to be able to use MARS to determine the following:

- What is happening
- Where it is happening
- How you can mitigate the problems

If your MARS appliance is overwhelmed by the volume of traffic it is receiving, you might not have all the information you need to do your job.

Make sure that you give yourself capacity to deal with unexpected conditions. Also, consider that after you begin using CS-MARS, you'll likely decide that other devices or software would provide useful information if it was also logging to your MARS appliance. You can initially decide to deploy MARS to provide centralized monitoring and reporting of your firewalls and IDSs only. However, after a month or so, you might realize that by adding authentication servers to MARS, you can correlate between logged-in usernames and the IP addresses that show up in your logs. You might also decide that by monitoring your Oracle database servers, you can satisfy requirements that a compliance auditor has asked about.

Ideally, when sizing your MARS deployment, you should aim for using no more than 50–60 percent of the capacity of the appliance to allow room for growth and the ability to deal with flood conditions.

Planning for Topology Awareness

One of the features that make CS-MARS unique in the Security Information Management (SIM) marketplace is its capability to understand your network's topology. Topology awareness is what allows sessionization to work. It also creates the capability for MARS to recommend mitigation actions to you, based on which devices on your network are capable of stopping or preventing an attack.

Planning for topology awareness means that you should consider where, on your network, you could get better, more accurate information by configuring more monitored devices. As an example, consider the following scenario:

> An Internet-facing firewall is continually bombarded with malicious traffic. Most of this is blocked because of the default policies on your firewalls. For example, Slammer worm traffic continually assaults your firewalls by trying to establish connections on TCP port 445. Your firewall does what it is supposed to, and denies the traffic while sending an event to CS-MARS.

If only the firewall is alerting to MARS, you are getting massive amounts of messages that essentially say "Stopped TCP 445 traffic." A savvy security analyst might look at this and understand that it is Slammer worm traffic. He can also usually begin looking for a way to remove these events from his MARS console. This tuning of events potentially removes traffic that might be interesting next month when some new attack is launched.

A better solution might be to place an intrusion detection system outside the Internet-facing firewall. Because MARS understands where various devices are installed, and because IDSs can classify various attacks, you can provide auto-tuning by installing what can be thought of as a security probe.

When the Slammer worm traffic passes the IDS, the traffic is classified as Slammer worm. The TCP port 445 traffic that is denied by the firewall is also alerted on. CS-MARS, in its initial correlation, or sessionization, sees the combined events as the Slammer worm being stopped by the MARS appliance. As long as the firewall has denied the traffic, MARS will automatically remove these events from the MARS Dashboard, while still keeping them available for analysis later. The automatic tuning of security incidents comes at a cost, though, of more security events being processed by MARS.

CS-MARS Sizing Case Studies

The case studies that follow should help you determine which deployment model and appliances will suit your network best.

Retail Chain Example

ACME Gizmos Outlet Stores has four datacenters. They are located in Portland, Las Vegas, Phoenix, and San Francisco. Each datacenter acts as a hub for regional outlet stores. The individual retail stores all have digital subscriber line (DSL) or other broadband connectivity to the Internet, and are VPN-attached to their datacenters.

All ingoing and outgoing Internet connectivity is through the main datacenter in San Francisco, which uses a Cisco ASA-5540 firewall. Each retail store uses a Cisco ASA-5505 firewall to provide the high-speed VPN connectivity back to its regional datacenter, and there are 400 total stores, distributed somewhat equally across the four datacenters. A combination of Cisco IPSs and Snort IDSs are deployed throughout the four datacenters. The switching infrastructure is all Cisco Catalyst switches.

The only IP connectivity from store to store is voice traffic. All data connectivity between stores is blocked.

The average events per second is 5 EPS per store, 500 EPS at the San Francisco datacenter, and 100 EPS at the other three datacenters.

ACME Gizmos determines that it is seeing a total of nearly 3000 EPS in normal traffic conditions. The company wants to leave room for growth, which means that the MARS-100E and MARS-100 are both too small for its needs. A MARS-200 would be more than sufficient because the broadband access to the stores allows centralized storage and correlation of all security events.

State Government Example

The State of Jefferson Department of Information Services (DIS) provides computing and network services to all state agencies, acting much like an Internet service provider (ISP) to the other agencies.

Agencies are headquartered at the State Capitol Mall, generally, with major agencies connected through Gigabit Ethernet. DIS is deploying MARS primarily to watch over the statewide backbone and to provide centralized monitoring of the DIS employee network.

The DIS datacenter has Check Point firewalls and Cisco Firewall Services Modules installed. Cisco Security Agent is deployed on all Windows web and application servers. DIS administrators have determined that their network is generating nearly 4000 EPS. They are also interested in aiding other state agencies in deploying MARS.

DIS decides that deploying a MARS GC, along with a MARS-200, will provide it with the capacity it needs today, and also puts the infrastructure in place to allow additional MARS appliances as other state agencies deploy their own. DIS will be able to have a statewide view of security across all agencies, while also allowing each agency to see only its own local controllers.

Healthcare Example

ACME Regional Healthcare System is a small hospital that provides care for a large rural area. ACME Healthcare has not standardized on any single security or network vendor, and has chosen CS-MARS because of its capability to monitor a multivendor environment.

ACME Healthcare uses NetScreen firewalls, Symantec IDSs, Cisco VPN concentrators, Symantec antivirus software, and Cisco routers and switches.

On average, ACME Healthcare's log servers collect approximately 2.6 million events per day. The company's chief security officer has determined that for compliance with HIPAA requirements, ACME should maintain logs for a minimum of 18 months.

A level of 2.6 million events per day averages to approximately 30 EPS. The average event size is slightly less than 300 bytes.

At 30 EPS, any MARS appliance would be satisfactory, but because of the company's data retention policy, it needs to look at a larger model. ACME Healthcare decides that the most cost effective option that meets its needs is the MARS-100E. With 565 GB of usable storage, the MARS-100E can store more than two years of event data, and can satisfy the company's regulatory requirements.

Summary

Properly sizing a CS-MARS deployment is key to a happy, useful deployment. By following the recommendations in this chapter, you will satisfy your needs for the following:

- A speedy, responsive user interface
- The ability to monitor and correlate various security and network devices throughout your network
- Data retention of events that meets your requirements

Remember to allow room to grow in addition to room for flood conditions. Your network and security needs typically grow significantly each year, and your monitoring needs will grow as well.

CS-MARS Operations and Forensics

## CHAPTER 4

Securing CS-MARS

A Security Information Management (SIM) system can contain a tremendous amount of sensitive information. This is because it receives event logs from security systems throughout a network. These logs potentially contain information that can be used to target attacks at sensitive systems. For example, intrusion detection system (IDS) logs can contain actual packets seen on the network. Some of these packets can be decoded with freely available packet analyzers to find usernames and passwords that your employees might be using to access websites, e-mail systems, and network devices.

Although security people always encourage users to select unique passwords for company networks, the reality is that many users tend to reuse passwords both for work and home activities. If an employee has decided to use his work network password as his personal web-based e-mail password, if an attacker discovers the cleartext authentication for web e-mail, he has also discovered an account on your network in which to begin nefarious activities.

As a topology-aware SIM product, the Cisco Security Monitoring, Analysis, and Response System (CS-MARS) often contains even more sensitive information. The most accurate method of maintaining the network topology awareness within MARS is by discovering each network device. This involves configuring access information for MARS to authenticate to the devices, retrieve interface information, and periodically rediscover it. From within the user interfaces, both the command-line interface (CLI) and web user interface, device authentication information is masked to prevent anyone from using the console to gain unauthorized information. However, if an attacker gains access to the base operating system, or gains physical access to the appliance, he could use that access to retrieve all information contained on the hard drives, which could include device authentication information. He can also use that access to install back doors to allow remote access at any time.

This chapter describes recommendations for securing MARS appliances, both physically and electronically. It also provides detailed insight into the TCP and User Datagram Protocol (UDP) ports that MARS requires for communication with other MARS appliances, in addition to monitored security, network, and other devices.

Physical Security

You cannot properly address network security without also addressing physical security. This is evident with common sense and in the various regulations addressed in Chapter 2, "Regulatory Challenges in Depth." All the network security in the world is worthless if someone with malicious intent can gain physical access to the target.

Make sure that the hosts on your security management network, and MARS specifically, reside in a protected facility. At the very least, they should be locked in a room that is inaccessible to the public and staff without a specific business need. Ideally, security management resides in a datacenter that exercises strong controls. Staff with access rights to the facility need to have a security badge and need to sign in, either on paper or electronically, before entering. In Chapter 2, the Payment Card Industry (PCI) data security standard has good recommendations that datacenters everywhere should attempt to adhere to, even if your facility is not affected by PCI requirements.

Inherent Security of MARS Appliances

Management access to all MARS appliances is through Secure Socket Layer (SSL)–encrypted web access (HTTPS) and Secure Shell (SSH). These protocols, using TCP/443 and TCP/22, respectively, are inherently secure because they use encryption, authentication, and authorization. Unencrypted protocols that serve similar functions, such as HTTP and Telnet, are both disabled on the MARS appliance and cannot be enabled.

MARS appliances are hardened Linux servers that run a variety of services, including Oracle, Apache HTTP Server, and more. With each software update, the various services and drivers on MARS are updated with new versions or patches to mitigate against any newly discovered vulnerabilities. Additionally, unnecessary or unused services are disabled to prevent them from being potential weaknesses in the security of the appliances.

This hardening of the operating system provides a good starting level of security. However, it is not enough. You need to take into consideration the sensitivity of the information contained on the MARS appliances when considering how secure the appliances should be. You should have a well-defined written plan for preventing MARS from being used as an attack vector on your network. This includes placing the appliance in a part of your network that is protected from the rest of the network by a firewall and an IDS.

Without protecting MARS with a firewall and IDS or intrusion prevention system (IPS), a hacker can try to find vulnerabilities, either in the management protocols or in other protocols that are used to monitor security or network devices. The additional protections provided by the firewall or IDS/IPS allow you to limit the exposure to attacks while also creating an audit trail of attempted attacks.

As an example, consider SSH, the command-line method of administering MARS remotely. In the past, a number of vulnerabilities have appeared in the OpenSSH application, which provides this service for MARS. No known vulnerabilities exist in the SSH service that MARS uses at this time. However, at some time in the future, a new vulnerability might be found. For this reason, it makes sense to restrict the capability of computers to establish an SSH connection to MARS unless they are connected to a specific network or set of networks at your location. A stateful inspection firewall is the ideal device for providing these limits. A network IDS or IPS that is regularly updated with new signatures can detect when someone is attempting to use a known vulnerability to compromise the MARS appliance.

Another example, also using SSH, involves a brute-force password attack against the MARS appliance. In this attack, an attacker repeatedly uses a dictionary of passwords, using a script, to attempt to crack the password that administers the MARS appliance. MARS is especially vulnerable to this type of attack because the administrator's username is a well-known value—pnadmin—and this is the only username that can use SSH. This example is mitigated using the same methods as the first example. First, placing MARS on a protected network, with a stateful inspection firewall separating it from the rest of your network, allows you to limit connection attempts to a limited number of devices or networks on your company's network. Additionally, a network IDS or IPS can detect multiple login attempts, whether by SSH or web-based. The detection by an IDS can notify the appropriate personnel, or an IPS can prevent further attempts.

Security Management Network

As a best practice, you should create a network as a security management network if you don't already have one. This network should contain various servers used for administering and monitoring the security of your network. The entire network should be protected by a firewall and IDS/IPS. Access to it should be tightly restricted, and any remote access to it should be through a Virtual Private Network (VPN).

Examples of hosts that should reside on this network include the following:

- MARS global controller (GC)
- MARS local controller (LC), if practical
- MARS archive server
- Firewall management consoles, such as Cisco Security Manager or Check Point SmartCenter
- IDS/IPS/HIPS management consoles
- Any existing syslog servers
- Vulnerability scanning hosts

The systems that reside on your management networks are some of the most sensitive in your organization. They often contain the keys to the kingdom, and for this reason, the management networks are targets of attackers. After an attacker has compromised a host on a management network, an open freeway often exists to other systems because of the trust assigned to hosts on the management network.

Don't cut corners on network hardware that you use on your security management network. Install switches that support security features. You might want to consider configuring features such as private VLANs, which provide isolation between hosts on the same network. Other switch security features, such as the capability to prevent VLAN hopping, should also be considered.

MARS Communications Requirements

Before you can protect MARS with a firewall, you first need to understand which TCP and UDP ports MARS requires to operate properly, and which of these carry outbound or inbound traffic. Table 4-1 provides a summary of all communications when MARS and the various monitored devices are all configured with default ports. Many or all of these can be changed, and you might need to modify this table for your installation.

Table 4-1   *MARS TCP and UDP Ports*

Port	Description	Direction
TCP/21	Used by MARS to retrieve switch and router configuration files from centralized servers. FTP uses additional TCP ports (usually TCP/20), and most firewalls allow this to occur automatically.	Outbound
TCP/22	Used for management access to MARS LCs and GCs.	Inbound
	Used by MARS to connect to devices when learning topology or investigating hosts.	Outbound
TCP/23	MARS uses Telnet as one method to connect to some network devices when learning topology or investigating hosts.	Outbound
TCP/25	Used by MARS to e-mail reports and alerts.	Outbound
UDP/53	Used by MARS to look up host name–to–IP address resolution.	Outbound
TCP/53	Used by MARS to look up host name–to–IP address resolution.	Outbound
TCP/80	Used by MARS to communicate with Cisco routers for Distributed Threat Mitigation (DTM).	Outbound
	Used by MARS to receive some events, including web logs from iPlanet and Apache web servers, as well as NetCache.	Inbound
UDP/123	Used by MARS to synchronize time with Network Time Protocol (NTP) servers.	Outbound
TCP/137	Used by MARS to pull events from Windows systems.	Outbound
UDP/161	Used for Simple Network Management Protocol (SNMP) communications from MARS to monitored devices that use SNMP as the access method.	Outbound

Table 4-1 *MARS TCP and UDP Ports (Continued)*

Port	Description	Direction
UDP/162	Used by MARS to receive SNMP traps from monitored devices that are configured to use traps for logging.	Inbound
TCP/443	Used for management access to MARS LCs and GCs.	Inbound
	Used by MARS to pull security events from Cisco IDS 4.*x* and IPS 5.*x* sensors and Cisco IOS IPS.	Outbound
	Used by MARS GCs and LCs for communications between appliances.	Inbound and Outbound
TCP/445	Used by MARS to pull events from Windows systems.	Outbound
UDP/514	Used by MARS to receive syslog messages from monitored devices.	Inbound
UDP/2049	Used by MARS to write archive data using Network File System (NFS).	Outbound
UDP/2055	Used by MARS to receive NetFlow data from monitored devices.	Inbound
TCP/8444	Used for communications between MARS GC and LC appliances.	Inbound and Outbound
TCP/18184	Used by MARS to pull event logs from Check Point firewalls.	Outbound
TCP/18190	Used by MARS to retrieve configuration settings from Check Point firewalls.	Outbound
TCP/18210	Used by MARS to retrieve certificates from Check Point firewalls or management consoles.	Outbound
All TCP/ UDP	Used for vulnerability assessment scanning by MARS if enabled.	Outbound

Network Security Recommendations

As you can see, depending on your environment and the location of hosts, a complex set of rules can be required on your firewall. Don't let the complexity prevent you from properly configuring the firewall, however. A little work initially can mean a better, more secure monitoring solution.

The following sections discuss issues regarding firewall protection for MARS and network-based IPSs and IDSs. The suggestions given are a good place to begin, but they by no means work in every network. For example, the TCP and UDP ports described in the preceding sections are only defaults. You can configure most of these services, which are common in many networks, to use other ports. Check Point firewalls, for example, are commonly configured to use different ports than the defaults of TCP ports 18184, 18190, and 18210.

Ingress Firewall Rules

To simplify the work involved, you should define some network object groups on your firewall. If you're not familiar with this term, think of object groups as variables that you can use while configuring the firewall to make life easier. Rather than referring to a large list of IP addresses or TCP/UDP ports, you can simply refer to a name instead. The following examples use an object group called CORP_NET, which consists of all IP addresses used on your organization's network.

Ingress traffic refers to traffic that is inbound to a firewall (toward CS-MARS) from a less trusted network. Figure 4-1 shows both ingress traffic and *egress traffic*, or traffic that leaves CS-MARS to go toward the less trusted network.

Figure 4-1 *Ingress and Egress Traffic*

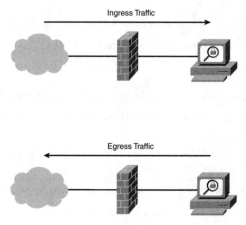

The following ingress rules are a good starting point for most companies:

Step 1   Permit syslog and SNMP trap traffic (UDP 162 and 514) from security operations (SecOps).

Step 2   Permit NetFlow traffic (UDP 2049) from SecOps.

Step 3   Permit HTTPS (TCP 443) from SecOps if a large number of people will be accessing the web console of MARS to run ad hoc reports. Otherwise, permit HTTPS to a restricted range of addresses.

Step 4   Permit SSH (TCP 22) to a very restricted set of addresses. If the security management network has its own VPN gateway, which might be a function of the firewall, you might want to require administrators to establish a VPN connection before permitting SSH.

Step 5   Permit HTTP (TCP 80) from any monitored web servers running iPlanet or Apache. If you're using NetCache appliances, permit HTTP from it as well.

Step 6   If your MARS deployment consists of multiple MARS LCs that communicate to a centralized MARS GC, permit required management traffic between those systems (TCP 443 and 8444).

Step 7   Deny all other traffic.

Egress Firewall Rules

Egress firewall rules refer to filters that restrict traffic from the protected network to less trusted networks. Ideal security would restrict outbound traffic to only those ports that are necessary for proper functioning of the MARS appliance. However, in real life, this might be unmanageable. You need to determine the proper balance between security and manageability.

For example, a strict default egress policy might make sense for your company's public-facing web server. Hopefully, connectivity from the Internet to your web server (ingress rule) is permitted only on either TCP 80 or 443, depending on whether your web server uses encrypted HTTP. The egress policy should deny all traffic that originates from the web server to hosts on the Internet. In other words, someone should never be allowed to browse the Internet from your web server, to download files from the web server, or to have other communications from the web server to the Internet. By applying a proper egress rule on the firewall that denies it, an attacker is also denied that same communications path. In most instances where a web server, or any other server, is compromised by a hacker, the hacker's next steps include copying files to the web server. This is either to deface websites, install root kits, or retrieve the software needed to further hack into the network. Strict egress filters raise the difficulty level, often to a level that exceeds the capabilities of the hacker.

Depending on your environment and which MARS features you're using, strict egress filters might be unmanageable. However, you should evaluate them to see whether they are workable in your environment.

The following list of egress filters serves as a good starter set for most networks:

Step 1 Permit traffic required for name resolution to CORP_NET—for example, Domain Name System (DNS) and Server Message Block (SMB) for Windows hosts (TCP and UDP 53, TCP 137 and 445) to CORP_NET.

Step 2 Permit Network Time Protocol (NTP) to specified NTP servers, either on your network or internetwork.

Step 3 Permit device discovery traffic on CORP_NET for routers and switches—for example, Telnet (TCP 23), SSH (TCP 22), and SNMP (UDP 161).

Step 4 Permit HTTPS to CORP_NET to allow MARS to discover Cisco IDS/IPS sensors as well as to allow event retrieval from Cisco IDSs/IPSs and Cisco routers running IOS IPS, and to allow communications between MARS LCs and GCs. If possible, restrict this range to a subset of CORP_NET.

Step 5 Permit FTP (TCP 21) to a centralized FTP server that contains configuration files of routers and switches, if you want to take advantage of this feature.

Step 6 Permit Simple Mail Transfer Protocol (SMTP) (TCP 25) to allow MARS to e-mail reports and alerts to your SMTP gateway.

Step 7 Permit NFS (UDP 2049) if your MARS archive server resides on a different network (not recommended).

Step 8 Permit TCP 8444 to allow communications between MARS LCs and GCs, if they reside in different locations.

Step 9 Deny all other traffic.

If you want to take advantage of the MARS internal vulnerability assessment capabilities, the preceding list of rules *will not work*. Instead, use the following egress filter list:

Step 1 Permit all TCP and UDP traffic sourced from CS-MARS or a third-party vulnerability scanner.

Step 2 Permit NTP traffic to defined NTP servers, if they do not exist locally on SecOps.

Step 3 Deny all other traffic.

In day-to-day use of MARS, when you choose to get more information about a specific host, the internal vulnerability assessment feature of MARS initiates a port scan of the host. You cannot accurately define an egress rule list that permits the vulnerability assessment to take place while also restricting outbound ports. If you already use a supported third-party vulnerability assessment tool, such as QualysGuard, you do not need to use the internal tool. Otherwise, using the tool can greatly improve the accuracy of information presented to you by MARS.

Network-Based IDS and IPS Issues

A network-based IPS offers an additional level of protection to complement that provided by a stateful inspection firewall. An IPS is closely related to an IDS. At first glance, the most obvious difference between the two is how they are deployed.

An IDS examines copies of network traffic, looking for malicious traffic patterns. It then identifies them and can sometimes be configured to take an automated response action, such as resetting TCP connections or configuring another network device to block traffic from an attacker.

NOTE   It is important to remember that an IDS detects malicious traffic after it has already happened. Although automated response actions can take place, it is usually too late to stop the attack.

As shown in Figure 4-2, an IDS is typically deployed beside a traffic flow. It receives copies of network traffic from the network switches, hubs, taps, or routers. Because it does not sit in the flow of traffic, it does not break anything that MARS requires.

Figure 4-2   *Intrusion Detection System*

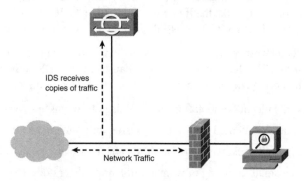

IDS receives
copies of traffic

Network Traffic

An IDS often issues a large number of alerts based on traffic generated from MARS, especially if you're using the internal vulnerability assessment feature. You need to tune your IDS so that it does not alert on the vulnerability scans that originate from MARS. You might want to adjust the IDS tuning so that scans from MARS to your CORP_NET are ignored, but scans directed to the Internet trigger an alert. It is generally considered a bad practice to automatically scan hosts outside your own network; the practice might even be illegal. Make sure that MARS is not configured to scan anything that is not on your own network. Your firewall egress rules should not allow this either. However, in the case of a misconfiguration, your IDS can alert the appropriate personnel so that the configuration errors can be corrected.

An IPS sits in the path of network traffic (see Figure 4-3), usually as a transparent device (like a bridge), and watches for many of the same behaviors as an IDS. A major difference between the two, though, is the capability of the IPS to act instantly when malicious traffic is seen.

Figure 4-3 *Intrusion Prevention System*

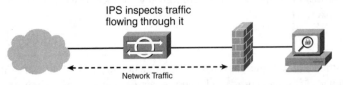

NOTE In addition to the automated actions an IDS can take, an IPS can also prevent the malicious traffic from passing through it.

Because traffic must pass through an IPS, the IPS can prevent MARS from functioning properly if it is misconfigured. Take time to closely watch alerts generated by your IPS and tune it appropriately. Like the IDS, you should tune the IPS to allow vulnerability scanning to occur from MARS to CORP_NET, while preventing it from scanning the Internet.

Some of the newest types of IPSs, such as the Cisco IPS, have a feature called *traffic normalization*. This feature, in particular, causes the MARS vulnerability assessment to fail. Traffic normalization enables several functions, including the following:

- Prevents illegal combinations of TCP flags from passing, or removes the illegal flags
- Prevents fragmented traffic from passing, or rebuilds it so that it is not fragmented
- Changes all packets in a traffic flow to have the same time to live (TTL)

This is just a small sampling of what a traffic normalizer does. In general, you can think of it as an engine that takes traffic that does not conform to standards, and either prevents the traffic from passing through the IPS or makes it conform to standards first.

By itself, traffic normalization breaks a large amount of attacks and reconnaissance activities. It also stops vulnerability assessment tools from being able to accurately determine information such as the operating system that a target host is running.

| NOTE | Cisco IPS 5.*x* and 6.*x* software, by default, does not generate alerts on most traffic normalization signatures. To properly tune the software, you need to enable alerts on that family of signatures. |

If you're protecting your security management network with an IPS that supports traffic normalization, you need to tune it to either ignore the scans from MARS and Qualys (or other vulnerability scanners) or disable the traffic normalization capabilities.

Summary

MARS contains sensitive information that you need to protect from malicious users. You must protect MARS with a firewall that is properly configured to allow necessary inbound and outbound traffic.

A network-based IDS or IPS can provide increased levels of security, but adds a level of complexity.

## CHAPTER 5

Rules, Reports, and Queries

One of the most important things to understand about the Cisco Security Monitoring, Analysis, and Response System (CS-MARS) is how rules, reports, and queries are related. When you create reports, you need to first understand what you are looking for. Creating useful rules is an important part of operating a MARS appliance. Rules and queries allow you to look at the data in a structured, intelligent fashion. This is what lays the groundwork for everything else in this book.

This chapter discusses built-in reports that are already installed on your CS-MARS appliance and shows you how to create reports that you might need to satisfy your organization's requirements. This chapter also discusses the relationships between reports and rules, and describes how you can configure alerts based on rule matches. You also learn how to create scheduled reports.

Throughout the MARS interface, you are presented with opportunities to create reports, although it might not be apparent immediately. Figure 5-1 shows a common icon, the letter *q* on a dog-eared rectangle, that provides you with an easy way to drill down to specific information. This is one way to quickly create a report.

Figure 5-1 *Query Icon*

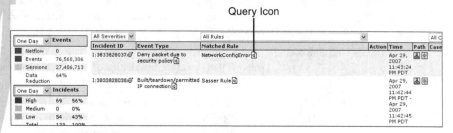

Built-In Reports

Many reports are already built in to the MARS appliance. Table 5-1 shows a list of the default report groups. Report groups are categories of reports that make it easier to locate the report you're looking for. Table 5-2 shows some of the default reports or queries. In the interest of space, the entire list is not shown in this book.

Table 5-1 *Report Groups*

Report Group	Description
Access	Reports related to authentication success or failure, whether to a network or a host.
All Events - Aggregate View	Network Address Translation (NAT) reports, as well as "Top" reports, such as Top Destination Ports, Top Event Types, Top Sources, and so on.
All Exploits - Aggregate View	Reports of Attacks Prevented, Attacks Seen, Top Sources, and Destinations for Attacks.
COBIT DS3.3 - Monitoring and Reporting	Reports related to Control Objectives for Information and related Technology (COBIT) framework DS3.3. Consists of reports on performance and capacity of devices.
COBIT DS5.10: Security Violations	Reports related to COBIT framework DS5.10. Consists of reports on various security violations.
COBIT DS5.19: Malicious Software	Reports related to COBIT framework DS5.19. Consists of reports on virus and worm activity, as well as spyware.
COBIT DS5.20: Firewall control	Reports related to COBIT framework DS5.20. Consists of reports on firewall traffic, including Top Ports, Top Destinations, and Top Sources.
COBIT DS5.2: Authentication and Access	Reports related to COBIT framework DS5.2. Consists of reports on user and administrator logins to hosts.
COBIT DS5.4: User Account Changes	Reports related to COBIT framework DS5.4. Consists of reports on user and group modifications on hosts.
COBIT DS5.7: Security Surveillance	Reports related to COBIT framework DS5.7. Consists of reports on Top Event Types and Top Reporting Devices.
COBIT DS9.4: Configuration Control	Reports related to COBIT framework DS9.4. Consists of reports on configuration changes on hosts and network devices.
COBIT DS9.5: Unauthorized Software	Reports related to COBIT framework DS9.5. Consists of reports that detect the installation of undesirable software, such as chat, file sharing, and spyware.
CS-MARS Distributed Threat Mitigation (Cisco DTM)	Reports on the status and activities of CS-MARS dynamically pushing Cisco intrusion prevention system (IPS) signatures to routers as a result of detected malicious activity.
CS-MARS Incident Response	Mitigation reports. This consists of reports on the success or failure of CS-MARS to mitigate incidents through DTM or the shutting off of user switch ports.
CS-MARS Issue	Reports on errors within CS-MARS, including information on certificates, connectivity, and resource utilization.

Table 5-1   *Report Groups (Continued)*

Report Group	Description
Client Exploits, Virus, Worm, and Malware	Reports that show hosts that have been compromised by a worm, virus, or other malicious software.
Configuration Changes	Reports that show configuration changes on hosts and network devices.
Configuration Issue	Reports that indicate possible configuration problems on hosts and network devices.
Database Server Activity	Reports that show modifications, authentications, and other activity on Oracle databases.
Host Activity	Reports that show various activities occurring on monitored hosts, such as registry changes, privileged access, and user/ group changes.
Network Attacks and DoS	Reports showing increases in network traffic that can indicate a denial of service (DoS) attack.
New Malware Outbreak (Cisco ICS)	Reports that show Cisco Incident Control System statistics, including new virus or worm detection, automatic deployment of outbreak prevention, and hosts involved in the outbreak.
Operational Issue	Reports showing information useful in troubleshooting network devices, such as connectivity errors and interface errors and utilization.
Reconnaissance	Reports showing reconnaissance activities, including various types of scans.
Resource Issue	Reports that show device utilization information where safe thresholds have been exceeded.
Resource Usage	Reports that show general device utilization information.
Restricted Network Traffic	Reports showing where certain types of network traffic have been restricted, including file sharing, chat, spyware, and recreational Internet usage.
SOX 302(a)(4)(A)	Reports related to Sarbanes-Oxley requirement for establishing and maintaining internal controls.
SOX 302(a)(4)	Reports related to Sarbanes-Oxley requirement for documentation of the effectiveness of internal controls.
Security Posture Compliance (Cisco NAC)	Reports related to authentication and host posture checking as reported by Cisco Network Admission Control (NAC) Framework.
Server Exploits	Reports that show attempted and successful attacks against servers.

Table 5-2 *Some of the Default Reports*

Default Report	Description
Activity: AAA-Based Access - All Events (Total View)	This report details authentication, authorization, and accounting (AAA) access to the network or specific devices.
Activity: AAA-Based Access Failure - All Events (Total View)	This report details all failed AAA authentications. AAA typically refers to authentications made through radius or Terminal Access Controller Access Control System (TACACS) mechanisms.
Activity: Accounts Locked - All Events (Total View)	This report details events that indicate that excessive login attempts have caused an account to be locked.
Activity: Accounts Locked - Top Hosts (Total View)	This report ranks the hosts with locked accounts.
Activity: All - NAT Connections (Total View)	This report lists nondenied network address translations as reported to CS-MARS.
Activity: All - Top Destination Ports (Peak View)	This report ranks destination ports by amount of usage.
Attacks: All - All Events (Total View)	This report shows all events reported to CS-MARS.
Attacks: All - Top Destinations (Total View)	This report ranks destination hosts by amount of traffic destined for them.
Attacks: All - Top Event Type Groups (Total View)	This report ranks event types by the number of times each event type has been reported.
Attacks: All - Top Rules Fired (Peak View)	This report ranks rules by the number of times each has fired.
Attacks: All - Top Sources (Peak View)	This report ranks sources of attacks.
Operational Issues: Network - Top Reporting Devices (Total View)	This report ranks reporting devices by number of events that indicate a potential problem with the device.
Operational Issues: Server - All Events (Total View)	This report lists details of events that can indicate problems with servers.
Operational Issues: Server - Top Reporting Devices (Total View)	This report ranks servers by the number of potential problems as reported to CS-MARS.

The information you're looking for is often readily available in one of the built-in reports or queries. Additionally, all the default reports can be modified to suit your needs. You should not modify the default reports, but instead make a duplicate of one when you want to modify it. In the current software version, it is not obvious how to clone or copy a report. Find the report you want to modify on the Query page instead of the Report page. Modify it however you like, and then click the **Save As Report** button. This creates a copy with a different name, and whatever changes you want.

Understanding the Reporting Interface

The following sections describe how to quickly and easily create reports. Using a number of sample scenarios, you learn the various methods of creating reports.

Reporting Methods

Throughout this chapter, you learn about the different methods of reporting on data. Each of these methods uses the query interface, which can be used directly, or can be prepopulated with initial query criteria.

The different reporting methods include the following:

- **Inline query**—This type of query allows you to run a query immediately, using whichever filtering criteria you desire. The default time period for an inline query is 10 minutes, but can be modified to any period of time. If the amount of data the query uses is too large, you must run the query as a batch, or you can select the method of running the query.

- **Batch query**—This type of query is similar to an inline query. However, instead of running the query immediately, it is run at a lower priority, and you are notified through e-mail when it is finished.

- **Real-time query**—A real-time query does not use a set period of time. Instead, it displays data, in real time, as the events are reported to MARS. Real-time queries can be useful for troubleshooting network and security devices.

- **Reports**—A report is a stored query and can be run on demand or on a scheduled basis. Reports are also used to populate the graphs that appear on the Dashboard and on the Network Status and My Reports pages.

The Query Interface

CS-MARS has an easy-to-use query interface, as shown in Figure 5-2. The interface allows you to build a query, whether simple or complex, in a straightforward manner without needing to learn SQL or any programming language. To modify a query parameter, simply click the text below one of the headers. For example, to look for data relating to traffic from a specific IP address, click **Any** in the Source IP column.

Figure 5-2 *CS-MARS Query Interface*

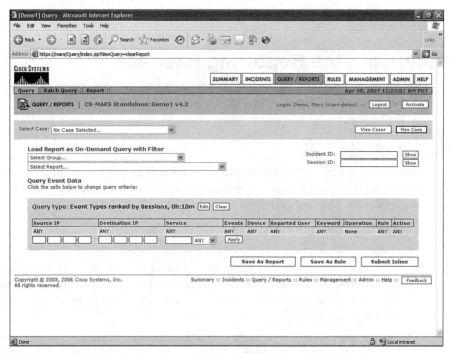

In Figure 5-3, the source IP has been selected. Notice the options for selecting a source. From the drop-down menu on the right, you can select predefined hosts, networks, or devices. At the lower left, you can enter single IP addresses or ranges of addresses. You can also include an IP in the search or specifically exclude it by clicking the arrow button with != on it. != means *not equal to*.

Figure 5-3   *Source IP Options*

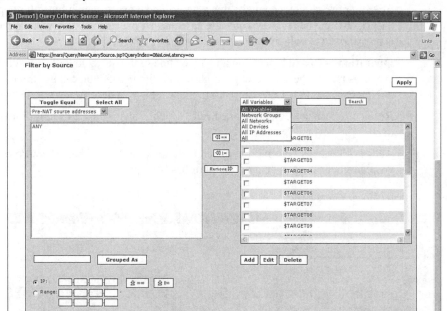

Here is a summary of what each of the query selections from the query interface shown in Figure 5-2 means:

- **Source IP**—Enter source IP addresses or networks. Addresses can be included or specifically excluded from the query.

- **Destination IP**—Enter the destination IP addresses or networks. Addresses can be included or specifically excluded from the query.

- **Service**—This field lets you select predefined services, as are typically indicated by the TCP or User Datagram Protocol (UDP) destination ports they use. If you do not want to choose a predefined service (such as HTTP, Simple Mail Transfer Protocol [SMTP], or Domain Name System [DNS]), you can enter the port numbers manually.

- **Events**—This field lets you select event categories to look for in your query, for example, "AOL IM Login."

- **Device**—This field lets you filter by CS-MARS reporting device.

- **Reported User**—You can select usernames that are reported by an authentication server, if CS-MARS is configured to receive logs from an authentication server, such as Remote Authentication Dial-In User Service (RADIUS) or a Windows domain.

- **Keyword**—Type in the text you're looking for that appears within an event log. Note, from Figure 5-4, you can make this a multiline keyword search by adding operators (AND, OR, and NOT). Keywords are case insensitive, and the only wildcard available is an asterisk (*), which represents any number of characters.

- **Operation**—This field lets you add a new line to the query to look for additional events as part of the same query. As shown in Figure 5-5, you can use three operators (AND, OR, and FOLLOWED-BY) to make a query a description of a behavior.

- **Rule**—You can select a predefined rule, which is also a single or multiline query in itself.

- **Action**—This lets you filter on different actions CS-MARS has taken. For example, you can filter on when an administrator has been paged.

Figure 5-4 *Keyword Match Within a Query*

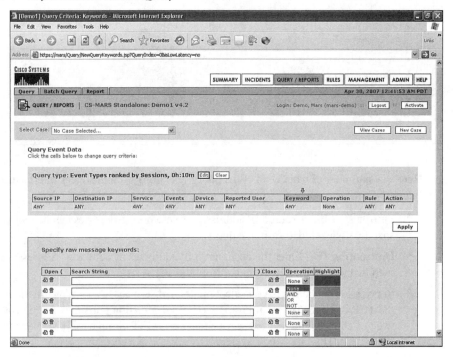

Figure 5-5 *Create a Multiple-Line Query with the Operation Field*

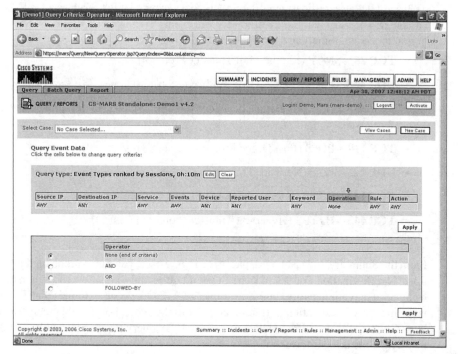

As you see in the sections that follow, this query interface can be prepopulated with information, making it easier for you to define queries.

Creating an On-Demand Report

In the first scenario, you learn one method to build an on-demand report. Throughout MARS, you'll find that you have numerous ways to do things, and building queries is no different.

Scenario:

On the ACME Gadgets network, you have determined that TCP port 80 is the most commonly used destination port. Your manager has asked you to find out which user is the top web surfer and what websites are most popular.

NOTE   TCP and UDP use destination port numbers to determine which services are accessed on a computer. The most commonly used services use well-known port numbers. Some of the port numbers commonly used include the following:

- **TCP 25**—SMTP (Simple Mail Transfer Protocol)

- **UDP and TCP 53**—DNS (Domain Name System)

- **TCP 80**—HTTP (Hypertext Transfer Protocol), which is better known as the World Wide Web

- **TCP 110**—POP3 (Post Office Protocol version 3)

- **UDP 123**—NTP (Network Time Protocol)

- **TCP 143**—IMAP (Internet Message Access Protocol)

- **TCP 443**—HTTPS (Hypertext Transfer Protocol [Secure])

From the Summary, or Dashboard, page (see Figure 5-6), you find a graph on the lower left titled Top Destination Ports. Click the **Legend** button and look at the top destination port being used on your network. In this example, ACME Gadgets determines that TCP port 80 is the most used destination port number. Next to the actual port number, click the Query icon. Clicking this icon prepopulates a query on the Query page and provides options to modify the resulting information.

Figure 5-6   *Top Destination Report*

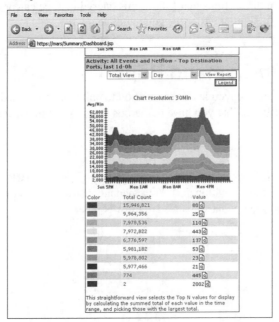

In this example, you've been asked to identify which host uses TCP port 80 the most. By clicking the Query icon next to port 80 on this Dashboard report, you can prepopulate a query. In Figure 5-7, you can see several options, providing you with several ways to drill down further into the data:

- Result Format
- Order/Rank By (session count or bytes)
- Filter by Time (optionally, you can select real-time events only)
- Use Only Firing Events (indicates how many results to return; the default is 5000)

Figure 5-7   *Prepopulated Query*

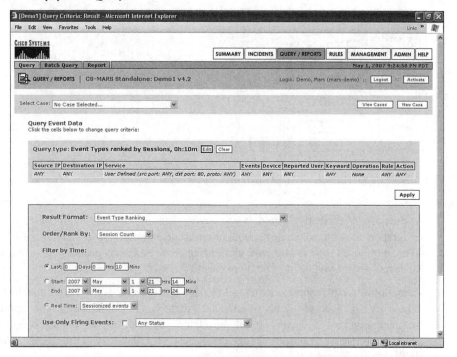

Because you are trying to see who is surfing the web the most, you might want to select **Source IP Address Ranking** as the result format, as demonstrated in Figure 5-8. Be sure to look at the time used by the query. Figure 5-7 showed that the default time period for a query is only 10 minutes. You will probably want to increase this to a longer period of time. An hour or two, or even several days or weeks, is a better period for your query. Just be aware that the longer the time period, the longer it will take for the query to run.

Figure 5-8 *Result Format Options*

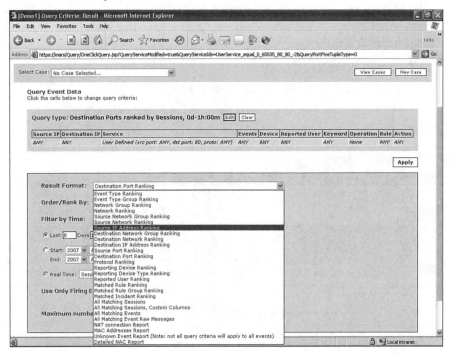

As the query is currently written, if you were to submit the query at this time, you would see a report showing which hosts, both internal and external to your network, use TCP port 80 most often, as reported by your monitoring devices. This is probably good enough. However, what if you want to be more exact?

Many firewalls can report each time a web page is requested. Is this better than just a count of how often TCP port 80 is accessed? That's up to you to decide, but if other applications are running on port 80, it can certainly be a better indicator of your web users. To filter out other port 80 traffic, you must change the event type. Click **Any** in the Events column, as highlighted in Figure 5-9.

Figure 5-10 shows the Filter by Event Type page. You can see three boxes. In the top box, you can select only certain event severities. The box in the lower-left corner shows the currently selected event types. Currently it shows ANY. The box in the lower-right corner is the list of possible events and event groups you can select from.

Figure 5-9   *Events Field on the Reports Page*

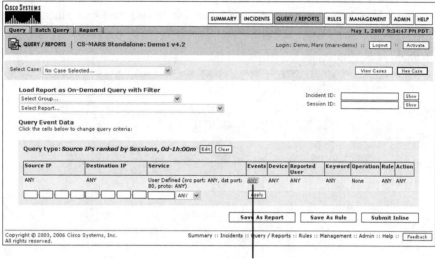

Filter by Event Type

Figure 5-10   *Filter by Event Type*

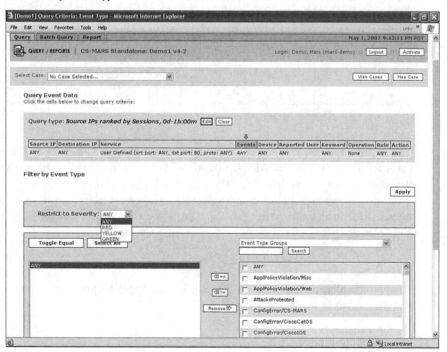

Remove the ANY from the box on the lower left. Then search for **Accessed a specified URL or FTP site** from the specified event type drop-down box on the lower right, and move this selection from the right to the left by clicking the <<== button (as shown in Figure 5-11). Click the **Apply** button.

Figure 5-11 *Event Type to Filter on Is Selected*

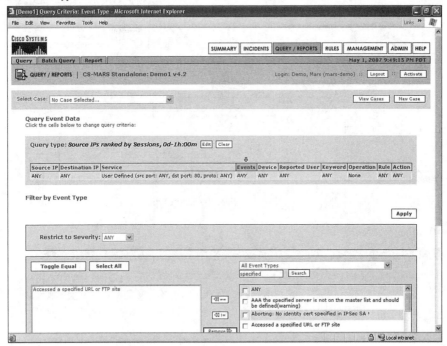

NOTE	Many thousands of event types are cataloged on the appliance. You can view the entire list of event types by clicking the **MANAGEMENT** button at the top of the page. Event types categorize various events that different monitored devices send to MARS. For example, logs from different manufacturers' firewalls all look different from each other, even though the logs might mean the same thing. Event types group events that mean the same thing into a single category that is used by rules, queries, and reports.

After you complete the event type filter and click the **Apply** button, you are presented with these three options, as shown in Figure 5-12:

- Save As Report
- Save As Rule
- Submit Inline

Figure 5-12 *Event Reporting Options*

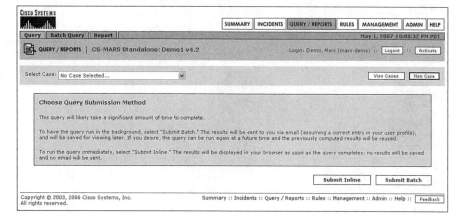

Instead of seeing Submit Inline, you might see Submit Batch. If you see this, MARS is telling you that the query will likely take some time to complete, and that the query should run in the background so that it does not take needed CPU cycles from regular event processing. You might also see a button that is simply labeled Submit. If you click this button, you are presented with a choice to Submit Inline or Submit Batch, as shown in Figure 5-13. You can have a little control over what options are provided to you by selecting a smaller or larger time period to search through.

Figure 5-13 *Choose Query Submission Method*

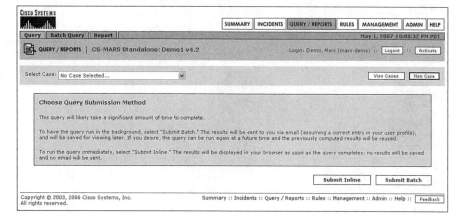

NOTE When a query is submitted inline, MARS runs the query immediately and shows you the results on the page when it is finished. You do not receive an e-mail with the results, and the results are not saved, unless you attach the query to a case (as you see in Chapter 6, "Incident Investigation and Forensics").

When a query is submitted as a batch, processing takes place at a lower priority, in the background. You receive an e-mail message with the results when it is finished—as long as you have a valid e-mail address in your MARS profile. You can also rerun the query to see previously computed results.

When a query is submitted as a rule, it becomes a rule that functions like any other rule. In other words, you can have it appear on the Dashboard page, as an incident, when it is fired.

When a query is submitted as a report, you are prompted to provide more information, including the frequency in which the report should run. You can e-mail the results to others and to yourself, and it is available as an on-demand report. Additionally, you can place a small graph with the results on your My Reports page.

For your purposes, submitting inline might be the best option. Figure 5-14 shows the results for this query.

Figure 5-14 *Results of Query*

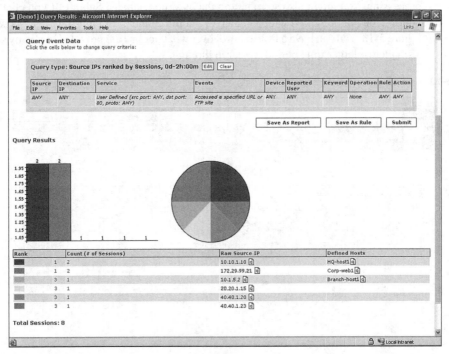

In the example shown in Figure 5-14, you can see the IP addresses of the hosts that surf the web most, but you cannot see which websites they access. MARS can provide you with different views of the data to make it more interesting. If you click the **Edit** button, you can rerun the query.

Because you want to see which URLs are being accessed, you should change the report format to All Matching Event Raw Messages, as shown in Figure 5-15.

Figure 5-15 *Change Query to All Matching Event Raw Messages*

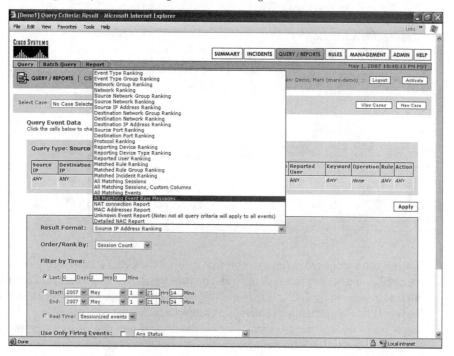

Click the **Apply** button and then the **Submit Inline** button. Try comparing this format with what is shown when you change the report format to All Matching Events. When the format is All Matching Events, you can click an IP address to see the DNS-resolved host name, as shown in Figure 5-16.

Figure 5-16 *Report Results*

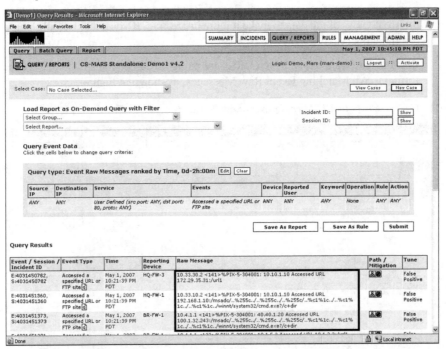

You might have noticed in this example that many of the URLs accessed contain strings that are similar, and have numbers, letters, and percent signs (%). These are encoded strings that attempt to exploit a vulnerability in an early version of Microsoft Internet Information Server (IIS). This particular vulnerability allows a malicious web surfer to trick the web server into accessing files that exist outside the defined web page directories, including Windows system files. Attackers commonly attempt to access important system files, such as cmd.exe, which provides a command-line shell to the attacker. In a real network, this could consist of only a few hosts that exist within a cast of millions. You need to drill down further and see only the hosts that are attempting to access this URL. In this case, you use string matching and attempt to find source IP addresses that are submitting a URL string with "cmd.exe" in the request.

In the top portion of the reporting interface, in the Keyword column, click **Any**. You are then presented with the page shown in Figure 5-17.

Figure 5-17 *Keyword Query*

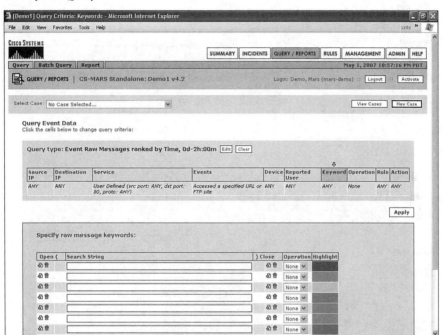

The keyword query presents you with a few options. You can select Boolean options such as AND, OR, and NOT, and you can select a color code for matches. In the Search String field, enter **cmd.exe** in the top line and click the **Apply** button. For simplicity, keep the result format as it is and then click the **Submit Inline** button. Figure 5-18 shows the results.

Now you see only events that contain "cmd.exe," and the keyword is highlighted on each line. It is easy and quick to create these types of reports. In addition to clicking the **Submit Inline** button, you can also save a report you've created. This allows you to have reports run automatically at predefined times, or simply to have the report available to run whenever it is needed.

Figure 5-18 *Keyword Result*

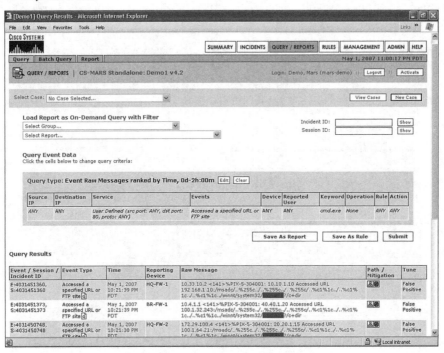

This was a quick example that showed both the most-often-accessed web servers and the hosts accessing the servers. This example also showed how to use the keyword functionality to further refine a query. Additionally, the results could have been filtered further, by filtering for specific source or destination IP addresses, or even by reporting device. For example, if all you are concerned about is web traffic that accesses the Internet (rather than your company's intranet), you might want to look only at events from your perimeter firewall.

Even more information is readily available by doing the following things:

- Clicking the Path icons to quickly locate hosts
- Clicking IP addresses to resolve names

Batch Reports and the Report Wizard

The following sections show you how to create a report that is automatically generated at regular intervals, such as daily, weekly, or hourly. Additionally, you can predefine reports to be available on demand.

Scenario:

A new proxy server has been placed on the network. Your organization's policy specifies that all web and FTP traffic must use this proxy. Your manager needs a report that identifies potential violators of this policy. Your internal network uses IP addresses in the range of 10.0.0.1 through 10.0.0.255, which is also commonly listed as 10.0.0.0/24. The reporting interface of CS-MARS can help you locate hosts that are not properly configured to use the proxy server, because it is already receiving logs from the firewalls and routers. Configuring a report in which hosts in the 10.0.0.0/24 subnet are accessing the web directly, rather than through the proxy, is simple.

With CS-MARS, you can create a report by doing one of the following:

- Defining the query first, and then saving the query as a report
- Defining the report parameters first, such as e-mail recipients, frequency of running the report, and report format, and then defining the query

When the goal is to create a report that can be used repeatedly, many people choose the second option; however, it is certainly a personal preference. You might find it easier to define the query first. Neither way is more correct.

To begin by defining the report parameters first, click the **QUERY/REPORTS** button, and then click the **Report** tab. Figure 5-19 shows the Report page. Several reports show up on this page already, and you can search through them manually or by selecting a report group with a drop-down menu.

Figure 5-19 *Report Page*

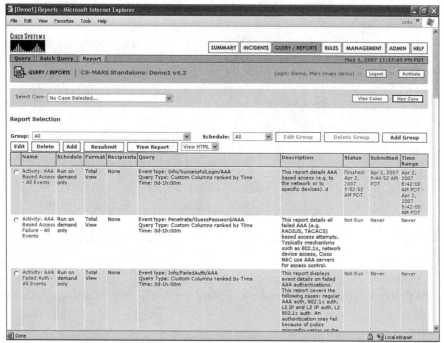

Click the **Add** button to launch the Report Wizard. Enter a name and description for the report. Make sure that the name is somewhat descriptive. Best practice would dictate giving a name that makes it easy to separate the custom reports from the built-in reports. If you have several users on the system, you might want to break it out further by adding your initials and the date the report was created, such as the following report name shown in Figure 5-20:

CUSTOM-JDOE: HOSTS NOT USING PROXY 2MAY2007

Then click the **Next** button.

NOTE   Including a description is mandatory. Do not skip this step! Be sure to enter something that is intuitive and useful.

Figure 5-20 *Accessing the Report Wizard*

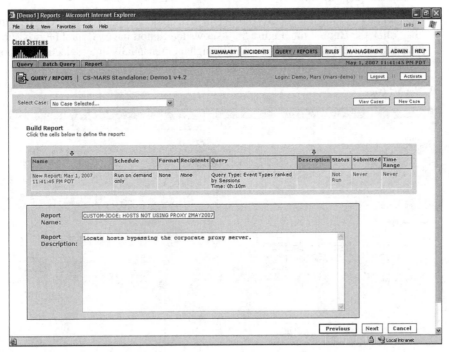

In the following step, illustrated in Figure 5-21, you have to define the schedule. Here, you select how often to run the report and select the view it uses. You probably don't want to have to remember to log in to MARS every morning and run the report manually. Instead, you would like this report to arrive in your e-mail inbox every morning at 7:00.

Four different View Type options appear at the bottom of the screen:

- **Total View**—Values displayed in the report will be the total number of times the condition occurs.

- **Peak View**—Values displayed in the report will be the peak number of times the condition occurred during the time period.

- **Recent View**—Values displayed in the graphs will be total view, but a table of data, showing both the total view and the recent view (totals of the past hour), is provided. This can be useful when looking for anomalous behavior.

- **CSV**—Values from the total view are provided in a comma-separated values file that can be downloaded to your computer.

Choose the view you want, and then click the **Next** button when you're finished with these parameters.

Figure 5-21 *Schedule and View*

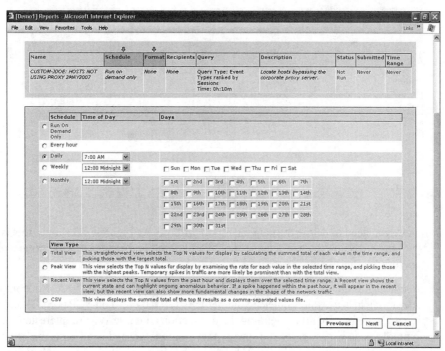

Because you want to have the report in your e-mail inbox, you need to select your username in the Recipients page shown in Figure 5-22. By default, the right box displays user groups.

Select the drop-down menu to change this to **All Users** or one of the other options. You might want to select a group to receive this report, such as administrators or operators.

A user must be defined as a MARS user to receive an e-mailed report. You do not have the option to enter an e-mail address by itself. If you do not want the user to be able to access the MARS interface, you can create the user as Notification Only.

Click the **Next** button when finished.

Figure 5-22 *Choose Recipients*

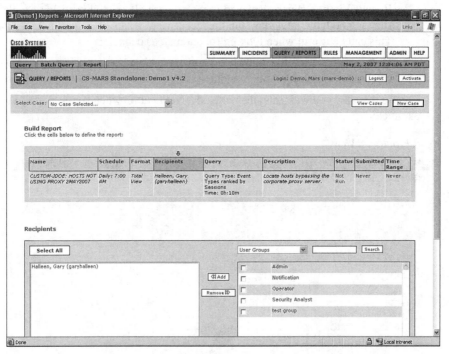

Now, you need to define the data the report will use. As Figure 5-23 shows, this is defined with the query interface. The page should look familiar, because it is the same query tool you used earlier.

According to the parameters outlined for this scenario, you are interested in computers attempting to access sites outside your network (10.0.0.0/24) on TCP ports 21 and 80. This is easy to define. Begin by defining the destination addresses you're interested in. The **!=** symbols mean *not equal to*. You specify that you're interested in all hosts that are not in the range of 10.0.0.1 through 10.0.0.255. Click **ANY** in the Destination IP column, and define the addresses as shown in Figure 5-24. Click the **Apply** button.

Figure 5-23 *Report: Query Interface*

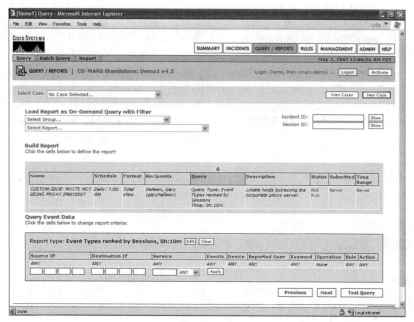

Figure 5-24 *Destination Address*

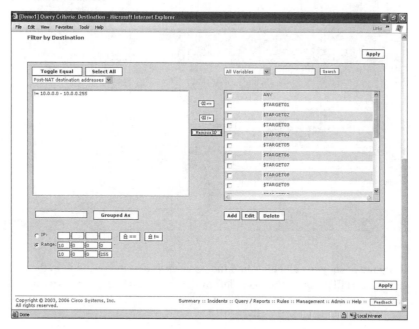

TIP   As you can see from the Grouped As field in Figure 5-24, you can also create groups. If you have a larger network, consisting of multiple IP address ranges, you can benefit by grouping addresses into a logical name, such as Corp Network, which might use IP addresses 10.0.0.0/24, and Factory Network, which might use 192.168.0.0/16.

Grouping addresses allows you to easily refer to this group of addresses throughout the MARS interface and also allows easy handling of discontiguous network ranges. Although you can define address groups from this page, you can also create or modify address groups by clicking the **MANAGEMENT** button, and then clicking **IP Management**.

The query is partially complete, as you can see from Figure 5-25. Next, you need to define the service. Click **ANY** in the Service column.

Figure 5-25 *Partially Completed Query*

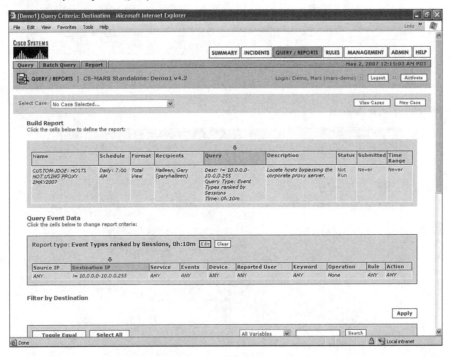

In Figure 5-26, you can either find the services you're interested in in the right window (FTP and HTTP), or, at the lower left of the page, you can enter source and destination ports, as well as protocol.

Figure 5-26 *Select Services*

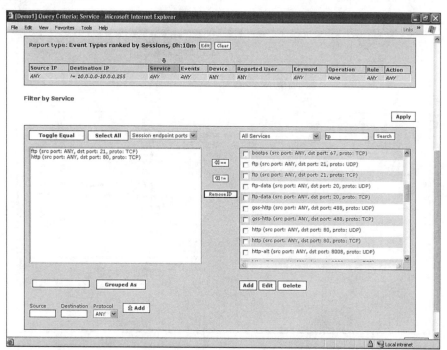

If you manually specify ports, you need to enter **80** and **21** under Destination, and select TCP as the protocol. Click the **Apply** button.

Next, specify the event types you're interested in. This is the same as you did in the first scenario. Without defining this, you'll see any event that uses TCP port 80 or 21 with a destination outside your network. Because you're interested only in web and FTP traffic that violates policy, you should select the event just as you did in the previous example, by selecting the **Accessed a specified URL or FTP site** check box, as illustrated in Figure 5-27. Click the **Apply** button.

The next page, shown in Figure 5-28, gives you a summary of your report. Look for mistakes, and make changes here.

Figure 5-27 *Select Event Types*

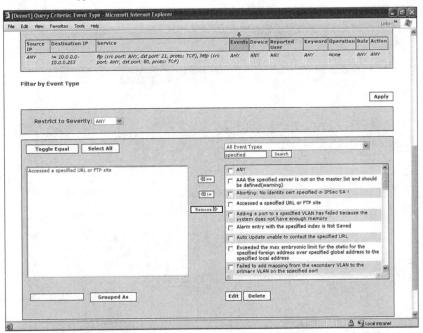

Figure 5-28 *Report Progress Summary*

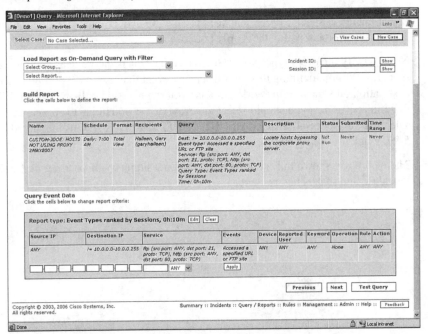

One change you might need to make is to filter your proxy server from the source addresses of the report. Otherwise, the report will probably show the proxy server as one of the violations. On the other hand, you might want to see the connections from the proxy server to use as a comparison.

From this page, you can either click the **Test Query** button or the **Next** button. In most cases, you should test to make sure that the report is giving you the information you're looking for.

If you test the query, you will see the results of running your query, just the same as running a query inline. See Figure 5-29 for an example.

Figure 5-29 *Test Query Results*

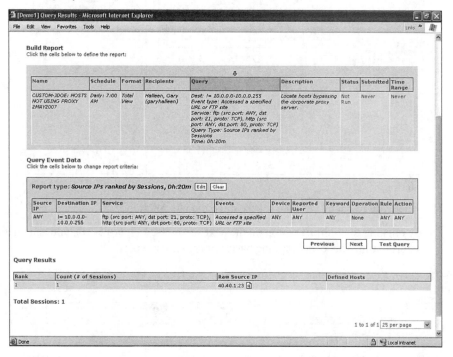

Make sure to select the report format you would like and the time interval you're interested in. In this example, as Figure 5-30 shows, you're interested in a 24-hour time interval and **Source IP Address Ranking** for the format.

Figure 5-30 *Setting Report Format and Time Interval*

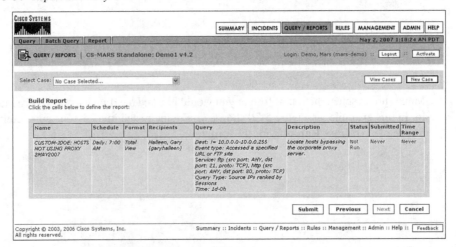

When you're happy with the report, click the **Next** button.

By clicking the **Submit** button on the next screen (see Figure 5-31), you can queue the report to run. This concludes the basics of creating a report.

Figure 5-31 *Report Summary*

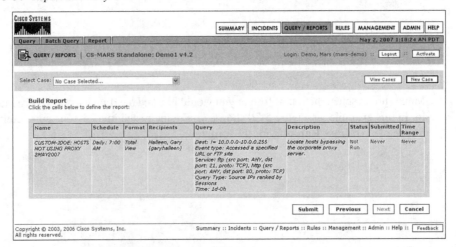

The report you've created now appears in the following locations:

- From the Query screen, in the Select Report drop-down menu, as shown in Figure 5-32

- From the Query screen, in the Select Group drop-down menu, after you select **User Reports**

- From the Report screen, in alphabetical order, or in the Group User Reports drop-down menu

Figure 5-32 *The Report Appears in the Drop-Down Menu*

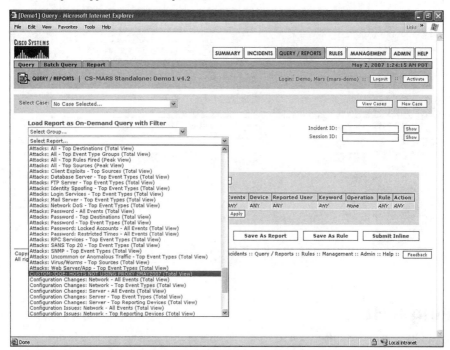

To run the report on demand, in addition to the schedule, you can do the following things:

- Select the report from the Query page and click the **Submit Inline** button

- Select the report from the Report page and click the **Resubmit** button

This new report can also be available through the My Reports interface on the Dashboard. This can be useful when you would like to create a page to quickly glance at and have easy access to data.

To add this new report to My Reports, click the **Edit** button by the My Reports section on the left side of the Dashboard. This opens a window with all eligible reports, as illustrated in Figure 5-33. Select the check box next to your new report and click the **Submit** button.

Figure 5-33 *My Reports*

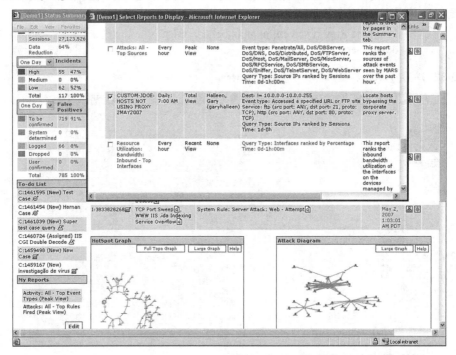

Creating a Rule

Often, you don't just want to see the results of queries and reports. Instead, you want to define a behavior that MARS should watch for. When it occurs, you want to be notified. This is precisely what rules are for.

This next scenario shows you how to create a rule.

Scenario:

This scenario is similar to the previous one, but it exempts a single host from the requirement to use the proxy server. In this case, the CEO does not want to access the proxy, and wants access to the Internet directly. The CEO uses a static IP address of 10.10.10.10. You want MARS to ignore the CEO's access, but whenever another user attempts to access a website directly, you want MARS to display the attempt on the Dashboard, as an incident.

About Rules

A *rule* is a description or definition of a behavior that you want to take some type of action on when it is seen. For example, a rule defines what a successful web attack looks like. When you see one on your network, you want it to appear on the MARS Dashboard. You also might want someone to be notified when it occurs.

Rules are defined using the query engine, in a similar manner as reports. Like reports, rules can be created in the following ways:

- Through a Rules Wizard, by clicking the **RULES** and then the **Add** button. This defines certain parameters, such as name and description of the rule first, and then builds the query.
- Through the Query page, by defining a query and then saving it as a rule.

Rules can be simple or they can be based on complex, multiple-line queries that define a sequence of events.

NOTE   The following variables commonly represent source or destination IP addresses:

- **$Target01 through $Target20**—The same variable in another field or offset signifies that the address is the same IP address.
- **ANY**—Any IP address is valid.
- **SAME**—Signifies that the IP address for each count is the same IP address. This variable is local to its offset. In other words, in a multiline rule, SAME in a destination IP address means that the address is the same as other lines in the destination IP address.
- **DISTINCT**—Signifies that the IP address for each count is a unique IP address. This variable is local to its offset.

Creating the Rule

Because you have already created a report that fits most of your needs for the rule, it is easiest to begin with that report.

Go to the Query/Reports page, and select the custom report you created in the previous section, as illustrated in Figure 5-34.

Figure 5-34 *My Reports*

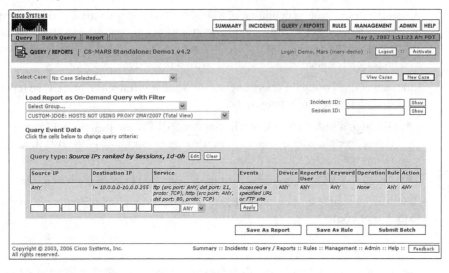

Click the **Save As Rule** button in the lower-right corner.

Enter a rule name and an intuitive description, as illustrated in Figure 5-35. Other MARS users can see this as the incident name if the rule fires.

Figure 5-35 *Rule Name and Description*

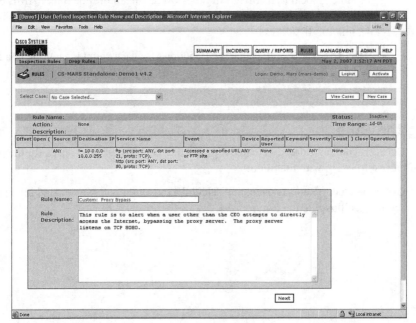

After clicking the **Next** button, the source IP address screen appears, as shown in Figure 5-36. The CEO uses 10.10.10.10 and needs to be excluded. Enter it here as an exclusion, by clicking the not equal to button (**!=**), as highlighted in Figure 5-36. Click the **Next** button when you are finished.

Figure 5-36 *Source IP Screen*

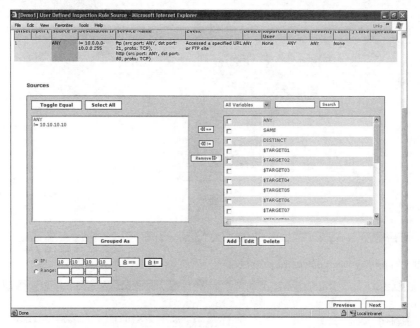

You can leave the following fields alone (do this by clicking **Next** through them): Destination IP, Service Name, Event, Device, Reported User, and Keywords. When you reach the Severity/Counts screen, as illustrated in Figure 5-37, leave Severity set to **ANY** and enter **1** in the Counts box. Click the **Next** button.

Finally, a box appears asking whether you are done applying rule conditions. If you need multiple lines for your query, click the **No** button here. Otherwise, click the **Yes** button, as illustrated in Figure 5-38.

Figure 5-37 *Severity and Count*

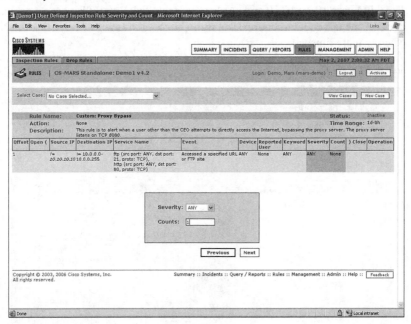

Figure 5-38 *Confirming Definition of Rule Conditions*

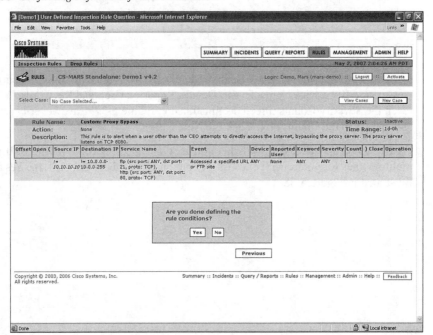

The next page, as shown in Figure 5-39, allows you to set alerting actions, if you want to use them. The following alerting actions are available:

- **E-mail**—Send a minimal e-mail message to the recipient.
- **E-mail with XML content**—Send an e-mail message with XML content and details about the incident.
- **Page**—Use the built-in modem in the MARS appliance to send an alphanumeric page.
- **Syslog**—A message is forwarded to a syslog server.
- **SNMP Trap**—A Simple Network Management Protocol (SNMP) trap is forwarded to a server.
- **SMS**—A notification is sent, using the network, to a Short Message Service (SMS) system. This sends short (160 characters or less) text messages to mobile phones and personal digital assistants.
- **Distributed Threat Mitigation**—DTM is a method of pushing an IPS signature to a Cisco router so that it can block malicious traffic that is detected by MARS.

Figure 5-39 *Attach an Action to the Rule (Optional)*

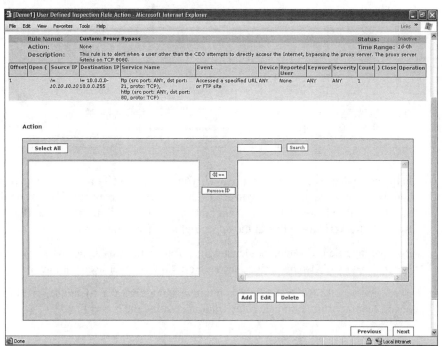

An action is not required. By its nature, a rule that fires will create an incident and populate it into the Dashboard and the incident table. An action is something you want to happen in addition to the incident creation. For example, you use an action if you want someone paged or an e-mail message sent.

If you want to use an action, click the **Add** button, and then, as shown in Figure 5-40, provide a name and select the action you want to use. If it doesn't appear, you have the option to create an action.

Figure 5-40 *Define Actions*

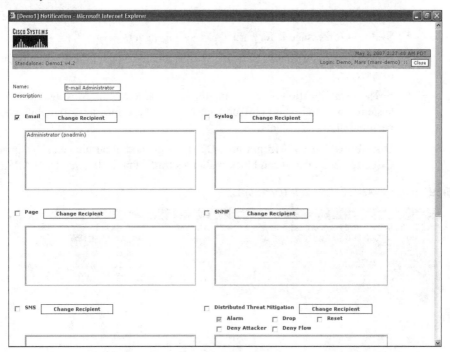

On the next page, as shown in Figure 5-41, you need to specify the time range that the rule should evaluate. The time range you used in the report is probably too long. You might want to set this to 10 minutes. Click the **Next** button and then the **Submit** button. Don't forget to also click the **Activate** button at the upper-right corner of the screen.

Now that the rule is created, incidents will appear on the Dashboard whenever this rule is triggered. You will also be notified through e-mail whenever users violate this policy.

As you can see, the Rules interface is intuitive and allows you to quickly create reports, convert them to rules, or create rules without creating the report first.

Figure 5-41 *Modify Time Range of Rule*

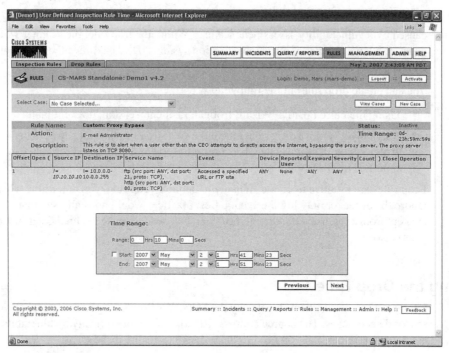

Creating Drop Rules

So far in this chapter, you've learned about queries, reports, and rules. The following sections cover a special kind of rule, the drop rule. A *drop rule* is an exception rule—a rule that MARS uses to ignore a behavior that would otherwise trigger an incident.

Scenario:

MARS is detecting network and host scans sourced from one of your internal hosts. Upon further investigation, you've determined that this is a dedicated vulnerability assessment system. It actively scans hosts on your network, watching for unauthorized systems and services. Because this is an authorized scanning server, you need to configure MARS to ignore the scans.

About Drop Rules

MARS uses drop rules to exempt certain traffic from triggering a rule. For example, MARS will likely alert on your SMTP relay server and claim it is a host sending spam. MARS thinks this because your SMTP server is sending out more e-mails than a typical host sends. In reality, this is normal behavior for your SMTP server, but MARS doesn't know it is normal for that particular host. You can use a drop rule to exempt your SMTP server from the event type that defines a spammer.

Another example of when to use a drop rule would be to eliminate noise on your console caused by a vulnerability assessment scanner. Without a drop rule, the scanner would generate a large amount of intrusion detection system (IDS) and firewall events that would certainly trigger rules on MARS.

You can create drop rules in the following ways:

- Using the False Positive Wizard from an incident, session, or event table.

- Manually creating a drop rule, much like creating a regular rule, by clicking the **Drop Rules** tab on the Rules page. It is useful to remember that any drop rule can be modified in this manner also.

Drop rules are intuitive to create. When you define a drop rule, you determine whether to ignore the events or only log the events. Best practices would normally say that all events are kept from a forensics standpoint; however, you need to make the final determination for your network.

Creating the Drop Rule

Figure 5-42 shows incidents created by the TCP SYN Port Sweep rule firing when your IPS sensor detects scans. The source address, 10.0.0.63, is your company's vulnerability assessment scanner, and you need to tune MARS to ignore these scans.

Figure 5-42 *Scans from Vulnerability Assessment System*

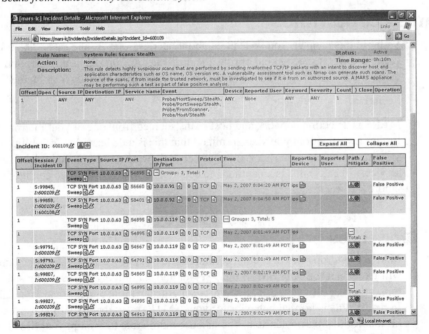

As described earlier, you have a couple of ways to create the drop rule, but the easiest is usually to use the False Positive Wizard. To use the wizard, click the **False Positive** link on the far right of any incident, session, or event page, as shown in Figure 5-42.

After clicking the **False Positive** link, you are asked to tune it further by event or source/ destination IP address, as illustrated in Figure 5-43. Because the host at 10.0.0.63 will be scanning multiple hosts on your network, you should select the event type of **TCP SYN Port Sweep** and set filtering events from 10.0.0.63 to **ANY**. Click the **Tune** button when you've selected this.

Figure 5-43   *Granular Filters*

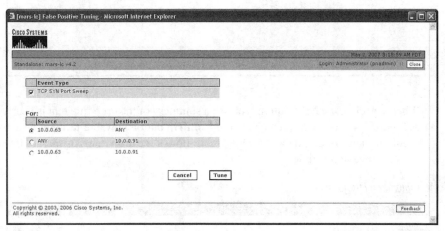

Now, you need to determine whether to have MARS keep the matched events. From the dialog box shown in Figure 5-44, you can choose to drop the events or log them to the database. We recommend that you log them to the database unless you have a good reason not to. Dropping them means that you will never be able to run reports or queries on those events, while logging them to the database keeps the events available for reports and queries. Both options prevent rules from firing and creating incidents.

In this example, you should log the events to the database. Because the vulnerability assessment scanner is performing a security function, and might be part of a compliance requirement, logging the events to the database lets you prove to an auditor that you are meeting the requirements. You can always run a query or report to demonstrate when scans occurred.

Figure 5-44 *Drop or Log the Events*

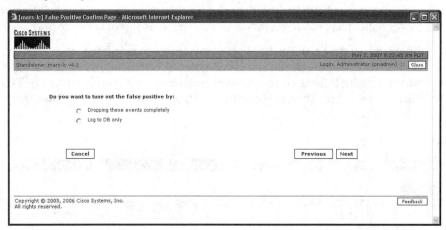

When you click the **Next** button, you see a summary of the drop rule that is nearly created, as Figure 5-45 shows. You can click the **Confirm** button now, but it might be a good idea to edit the name or give a more usable description of the drop rule. Any part of the drop rule can be edited at this time.

Figure 5-45 *Completed Drop Rule*

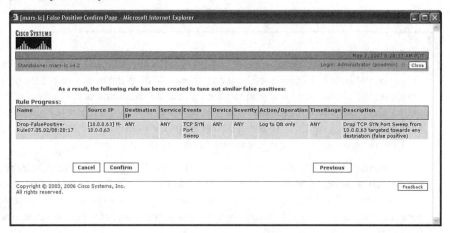

Depending on the type of drop rule created, you might need to widen the scope of hosts involved or filter by monitored device, for example. Click the **Confirm** button when you are finished.

If you ever need to edit a drop rule, or you want to manually create one instead of using the wizard, simply click the **RULES** button and, then click the **Drop Rules** tab (see Figure 5-46) .

Figure 5-46 *Drop Rules Page*

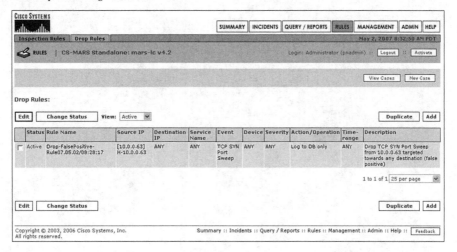

Summary

In this chapter, you learned about the basic building blocks of CS-MARS—the strong, easy-to-use query engine. Queries are used throughout MARS—when writing reports, investigating incidents, writing rules and drop rules, and more.

A good understanding of the capabilities of queries can make your life simpler and unlock the potential of CS-MARS in your organization.

## CHAPTER 6

Incident Investigation and Forensics

When a serious incident occurs, you need to know what to do. A serious incident will eventually occur with all organizations, and it could take many forms. For example, it might be any of the following:

- Sensitive financial information about your company or employees is stolen and posted to a hacker blog.

- An e-mail worm attacks your e-mail system, resulting in degraded network performance.

- An employee is inadvertently sharing all his Word documents on Limewire, Kazaa, or some other peer-to-peer (P2P) file-sharing network.

- You are notified by a motion picture association that someone on your network is downloading and distributing copyrighted material.

- Your e-commerce website falls victim to a distributed denial of service (DDoS) attack. In a DDoS attack, tens or hundreds of thousands of hosts all simultaneously attack your site, rendering it inaccessible to legitimate users.

The following six steps can help you properly handle an incident:

Step 1   **Preparation**—It is always too late if an organization waits until an incident occurs to learn how a device can capture packet data or run debugging commands. The first step in incident handling is to learn about your equipment and tools and have a plan.

Step 2   **Identification**—You must identify the incident. This step highlights one of the strengths of the Cisco Security Monitoring, Analysis, and Response System (CS-MARS). Through its capability to use both built-in and user-defined rules, as well as the capability to detect anomalous traffic, MARS enables you to rapidly identify and respond to new incidents. This chapter can help you understand what you should do when you discover an incident.

Step 3   **Containment**—To contain an incident means to use a control, temporarily or permanently, to isolate or stop a security incident. Additionally, containment includes collection of available forensic data. This could mean unplugging a network cable or disabling a switch port.

It could also mean changing a firewall rule to prevent a host from communicating across the firewall. Containment, or mitigation, as it is called within CS-MARS, is a task MARS can greatly assist you with and can contain a compromised device, giving you time to identify what occurred. This chapter describes the types of mitigation that you can accomplish with MARS and its importance to your incident-handling plan.

Step 4   **Eradication**—You must repair the compromised system to the state it was in prior to being attacked. It is often difficult, or even impossible, to fully repair the compromised system. Many organizations instead rebuild the system from scratch and restore only the necessary data. Eradication is a time-intensive step, and it should be performed only after all forensic data has been captured. In fact, you should consider replacing the compromised system with a new system, especially if you will be pursuing legal channels against the attacker. This chapter covers forensics and replay, but it is beyond the scope of this book to detail eradication in general.

Step 5   **Recovery**—In this step, the replacement or cleaned system is placed back into service. This should be done carefully, and controls should be in place to identify any further attempts to attack the system. MARS should have rules defined to watch for these attacks. Again, it is beyond the scope of this book to detail placing the system into service, but it is important to understand the process.

Step 6   **Lessons learned**—In this step, you look over the incident and make note of what you have learned. This is a time to reconsider your security controls, policies, and procedures and answer the following questions:

— Do you need to change anything to prevent a recurrence or similar compromise in the future?

— How much did it cost to troubleshoot and correct the incident?

— Did your organization sustain damage to its reputation?

Discuss the incident with your staff and management, if necessary, and then document the entire process. This can help you operate better the next time an incident occurs.

This book is not intended to be your guide to developing an incident-handling plan. However, it is useful for demonstrating how CS-MARS can give you better access to the information you need when an incident occurs. You can find excellent references to the preceding steps at the SysAdmin, Audit, Network, Security (SANS) Institute and the National Institute of Standards and Technology (NIST). Here are a few Internet links:

- **NIST's Computer Security Incident Handling Guide**—http://csrc.nist.gov/ publications/nistpubs/800-61/sp800-61.pdf

- **U.S. Security Awareness**—http://www.ussecurityawareness.org/highres/incident- response.html

The most important step in the preceding list on incident handling is the first step— preparation. Preparation allows rapid, orderly processes, and is a sign of the maturity of an organization's view on security. Step 6—Lessons learned—helps your organization grow and prepare for the next incident.

MARS directly relates to both Step 2, Identification, and Step 3, Containment, in the incident-handling process.

NOTE   You can find more information about incident handling from the National Institute of Standards and Technology (NIST) in Special Publication 800-61, as previously referenced. These steps are considered by many to be the standard procedure for incident handling.

Incident Handling and Forensic Techniques

This section walks you through a sample incident using the Identification and Containment steps of incident handling.

ACME Widgets has had a suspicious incident appear on the MARS Dashboard. According to MARS, a Windows RPC DCOM Overflow attack has occurred (see Figure 6-1).

Figure 6-1 *Suspicious Incident, as It Appears on MARS Dashboard*

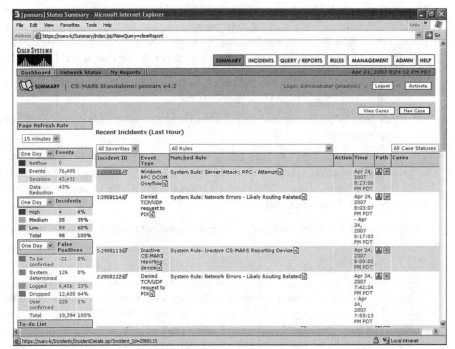

Initial Incident Investigation

It is often a good idea to create a case, especially when you are investigating what appears to be a serious security incident. After a case is opened, you can return to it and attach more incidents or change the status.

To create a case, drill down into the incident by clicking the incident ID. Then, click the **New Case** button, which appears in the upper-right corner of the screen, as illustrated in Figure 6-2.

Figure 6-2   *Drilling into an Incident*

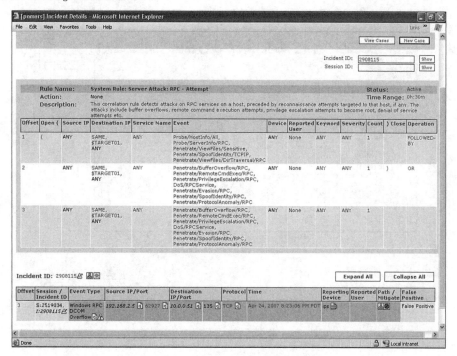

As you open a case, you select a case severity level, or importance—Red, Yellow, or Green, as demonstrated in Figure 6-3—and can assign the case to an individual with comments.

If someone else should be assigned to this case, you can assign it to that person by selecting his or her name from the drop-down list. The names are automatically populated from the MARS user database.

NOTE   Shared logins should be avoided. Make sure that each MARS user has a unique login ID and password.

Try to be clear and concise in your notes. This can help you later when you review the incident, or if you need to work with law enforcement.

Figure 6-3 *Create a Case*

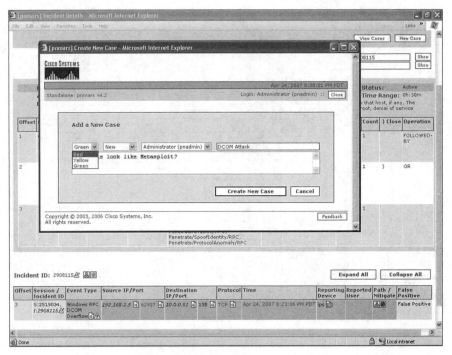

After you have created the case, it is time to begin investigating the incident. You might want to think about whether your actions will alert the attacker that he has been detected. For example, if the attack is in progress or the attacker is capturing keystrokes, pinging, or performing a host lookup, using common Domain Name System (DNS) tools such as nslookup or dig might signal the attacker that he is being investigated. If you have not yet isolated the compromised system, and the attacker learns he has been seen, he might attempt to erase his tracks or even destroy the compromised system.

Figure 6-4 shows the series of sessions and incidents that are related to the incident you're looking at. It appears that this incident is isolated, but a couple other instances of this incident have occurred. This is apparent from the offset of 3 that appears next to the incident ID. From this screen, if you click an IP address, MARS automatically performs a DNS lookup on that IP address. If you're dealing with a sophisticated attacker, this could signal him that he's been seen. This shouldn't prevent you from performing the lookup, but at least be aware of the possibilities and use discretion as it pertains to your circumstances.

Figure 6-4   *Tracking Affected IP Addresses*

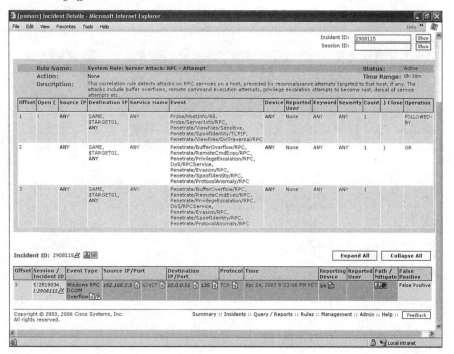

When the incident occurs, MARS performs some additional forensic duties automatically. It attempts to determine where on the network this host resides, and which security or network devices sit between this host and the attacking host. Additionally, MARS attempts to determine what the operating system version and patch level are and which listening applications are running on the suspect TCP or User Datagram Protocol (UDP) port. All this information is used to determine whether an attack was successful, or even if the host is vulnerable to this type of attack. Log messages from other reporting hosts are correlated to determine whether the attack traffic was blocked within the path of the attack.

If you click the destination IP address of this incident, you see that the target host is a Cisco Security Agent (CSA) Management Center, as Figure 6-5 shows.

Figure 6-5   *Host Information by Clicking IP Address*

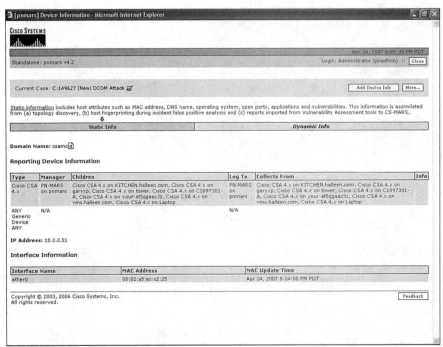

You can click the source IP address, as well, to get information on the attacker. Additionally, you can access useful information by clicking the port numbers. For example, if you click the destination port number of this incident, as shown in Figure 6-6, you can find out that TCP port 135 is commonly used for "Microsoft_RPC_DCE_Endpoint_ Resolution" and has also been associated with the MSBlaster worm.

Referring to Figure 6-4 again, you now know that there was at least one attempt to communicate with the CSA Management Center, with Microsoft's endpoint resolution protocol, and your Cisco intrusion prevention system (IPS) sensor identified this traffic as malicious. The source address of the attacker was 192.168.2.5, which sits outside one of your firewalls.

Figure 6-6   *Port Information*

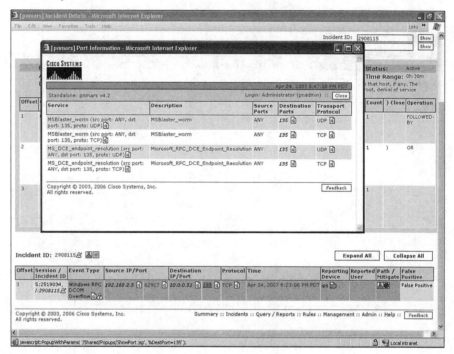

Viewing Incident Details

MARS offers several graphical views that can assist you in understanding, or even mitigating, the incident. On the Incident Details page, shown previously in Figure 6-4, if you look next to the incident ID, you can see two icons. The icon that looks like a star provides a logical view of the incident, and also provides the capability to step through the incident, one event at a time. The other icon provides the same information, displayed in a physical view. Figure 6-7 shows the logical view provided in the attack diagram.

Figure 6-7 *Logical View Shown in Attack Diagram*

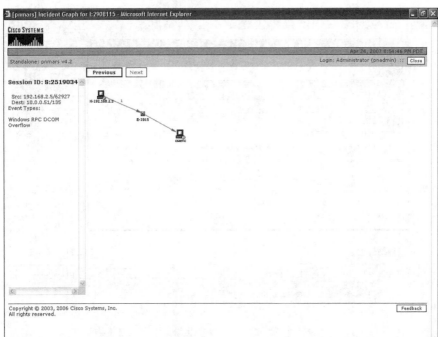

Notice that you can click the **Next** and **Previous** buttons to step through an incident one session at a time. Hosts are color coded in all the graphical views. The host that is being attacked is shown in red, while the host that is attacking is shown in brown. The following list explains the color codes used:

- **Brown host**—This host's behavior indicates that it might be an attacker.

- **Red host**—This host appears to be under attack. It is the victim.

- **Purple host**—This host has performed as both the attacker and the victim. This might be a compromised host.

Figures 6-8 and 6-9 show the physical views of the incident. This is accessed by clicking the other icon next to the incident ID on the Incident Details page in Figure 6-4. Initially, you see the topology view in Figure 6-8, which shows only the hosts involved in the attack, as well as subnets and other devices within the path of the attack. However, by clicking the **Toggle Topology** button, you can see the attack overlaid with other devices near the incident, as illustrated in Figure 6-9.

Figure 6-8   *Physical View Shown on Incident Graph*

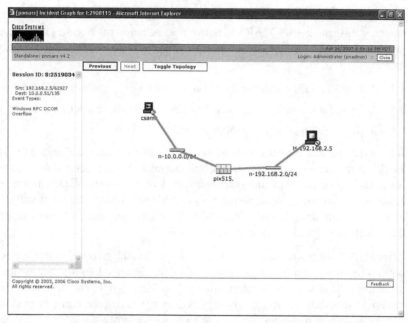

Figure 6-9   *Incident Graph After Toggling Topology*

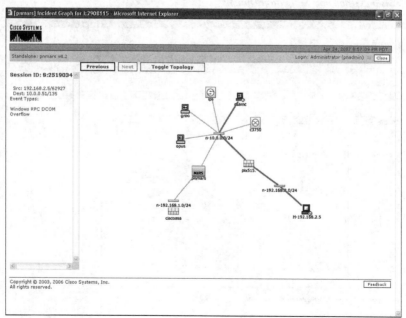

The third way to graphically view the incident is to click the **Path/Mitigate** button near the right edge on each line of the Incident ID table, as illustrated in Figure 6-4.

Clicking this icon causes MARS to perform some behind-the-scenes investigation. If possible, MARS determines which monitored devices can block the attack in the future. For example:

- A firewall might restrict access from the attacker to one or more hosts or networks.
- A router might have an access control list applied to restrict access.
- A switch can have a port disabled.

If the attacking host is internal to your network, and is connected to one of the switches that MARS is monitoring, MARS attempts to determine the attacker's MAC address. MARS regularly queries switches and routers on your network to maintain this information, which exists in the content addressable memory (CAM) and Address Resolution Protocol (ARP) tables in your network devices. When MARS has this information, it can locate the host and the switch port to which the host is connected.

After MARS has evaluated the Layer 2 and Layer 3 paths involved in this attack, it presents options for mitigation. You should understand that MARS does not automatically mitigate an attack. Instead, it provides information to you. Figures 6-10 and 6-11 show the mitigation screen presented in this attack. MARS has determined that the best way to stop the attack, or prevent it from recurring, is to create an access control list entry on the PIX firewall.

Figure 6-10 *Session Graph and Mitigation Options*

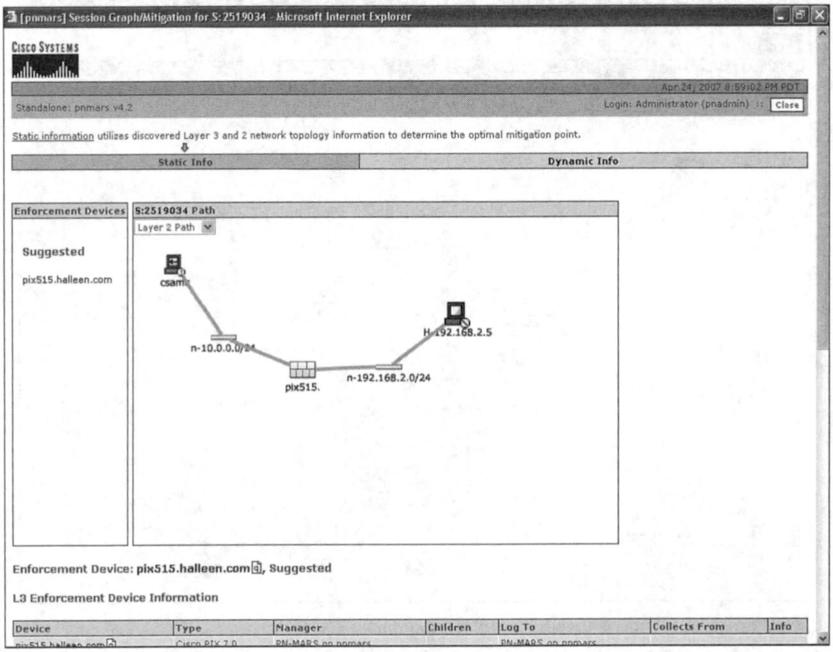

Figure 6-11 *Session Graph and Mitigation Options, Continued*

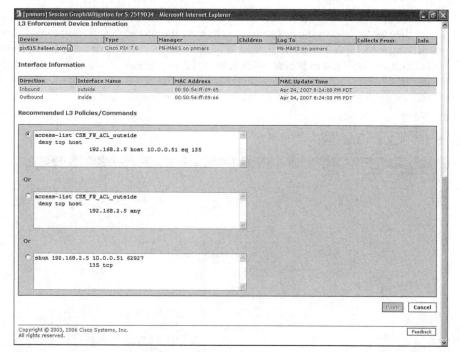

Occasionally, you might also be presented with the option to disable the switch port that the attacker is connected to. In fact, you can click a red **Push** button to instantly disable the port.

CAUTION   *Be wary of simply clicking the **Push** button!* MARS might have made a mistake in determining the switch port. Avoid potential network outages by double-checking your switch connectivity. The port that MARS has determined might be a trunk port connecting to a different switch that is *not* monitored by MARS. Disabling the port, in that case, can interrupt network access of all hosts on the other switch.

This is not a common occurrence, but you should always be careful.

If you would like to change the view, you can select among Layer 2, Layer 3, and Full Topology views. Additionally, if multiple mitigation devices appear on the left panel, you can select them to see different recommendations for mitigation. However, only the Layer 2 mitigation enables the **Push** button.

Viewing Raw Log Messages

In addition to viewing the incident with one or more of the visual tools, you often want to see the raw log messages, as they came from the monitored device. You can do this by clicking the icon that looks like a sheet of paper with 0s and 1s on it in the Reporting Device column, as displayed in Figure 6-4. Figure 6-12 displays the raw logs from our sample incident. You can see that the reporting device is a Cisco IPS sensor. The raw data you view includes both the packet that triggered the event notification and the alert from the IPS sensor.

Figure 6-12 *View Raw Log Messages*

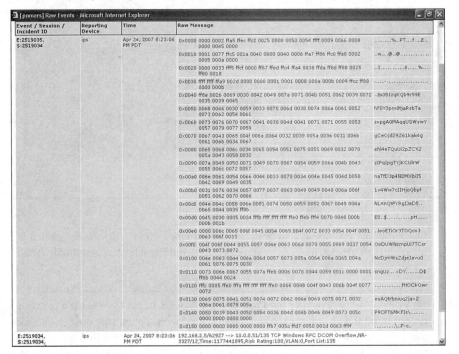

NOTE   Notice that after you have opened a case, it remains open through all MARS screens. This allows you to add information or incidents whenever needed. You need to close the case when you are finished with it.

Tracking Other Attacker Activities

You might find it useful to run one or more reports to see what other activities the attacker has been up to. To do this, click the **Query** icon (the icon with a *q* in it) next to the attacker's IP address (in the Source IP/Port column) in MARS, as displayed in Figure 6-4. This prepopulates a query for you. The query, Event Types Ranked by Sessions, filtered to include only the attacker's source IP address, might be enlightening, as you can see from Figures 6-13 and 6-14. You might also want to run the query Destination IPs Ranked by Session to see which hosts that attacker has also been communicating with.

Figure 6-13 *Results for a Query Filtered by Attacker Source IP Address: Part I*

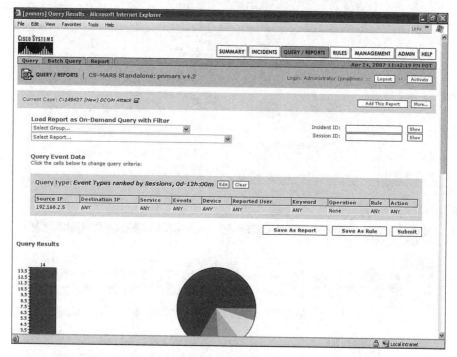

Each time you find a report or query that looks useful, click the **Add This Report** button that appears at the upper-right corner of this page (refer to Figure 6-13) to attach that report to the case you opened earlier. Each query or report that you attach to a case is easily accessible later. In addition, if you see more incidents that seem to be related, be sure to add them to the same case. At any time, you can click the case number at the top of the page to pull up a summary of everything that's attached to the case, as demonstrated in Figure 6-15.

Figure 6-14 *Results for a Query Filtered by Attacker Source IP Address: Part II*

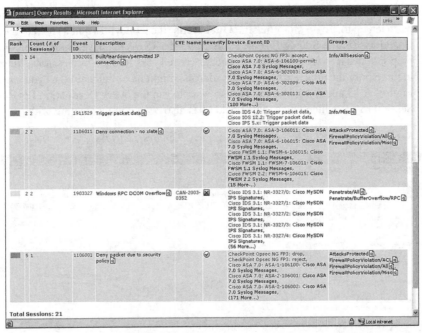

Figure 6-15 *Case Summary*

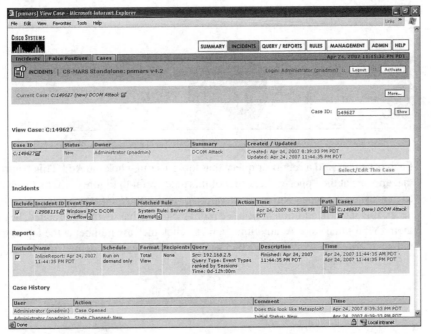

Determining What an Event Means

If you aren't sure what an event means, click the event title in the Incident ID table. A description of the event will be shown, as shown in Figures 6-16, 6-17, and 6-18, explaining what the event means, which hosts are likely to be affected by it, and which security products supported by MARS can detect it.

Figure 6-16 *Event Type Details*

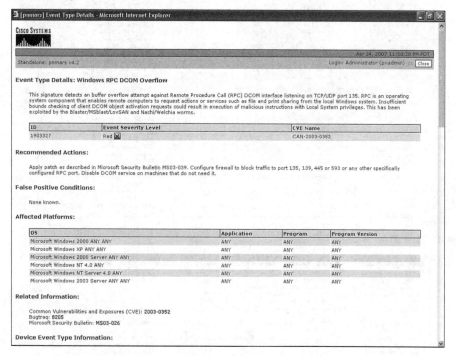

Figure 6-17 *Event Type Details, Continued*

[pnmars] Event Type Details - Microsoft Internet Explorer

Device Event Type Information:

Device Type	Device Event Type	Vendor Info
Cisco IDS 3.1	NR-3327/0	Cisco MySDN IPS Signatures
Cisco IDS 3.1	NR-3327/1	Cisco MySDN IPS Signatures
Cisco IDS 3.1	NR-3327/2	Cisco MySDN IPS Signatures
Cisco IDS 3.1	NR-3327/3	Cisco MySDN IPS Signatures
Cisco IDS 3.1	NR-3327/4	Cisco MySDN IPS Signatures
Cisco IDS 3.1	NR-3327/6	Cisco MySDN IPS Signatures
Cisco IDS 4.0	NR-3327/0	Cisco MySDN IPS Signatures
Cisco IDS 4.0	NR-3327/10	Cisco MySDN IPS Signatures
Cisco IDS 4.0	NR-3327/11	Cisco MySDN IPS Signatures
Cisco IDS 4.0	NR-3327/12	Cisco MySDN IPS Signatures
Cisco IDS 4.0	NR-3327/1	Cisco MySDN IPS Signatures
Cisco IDS 4.0	NR-3327/2	Cisco MySDN IPS Signatures
Cisco IDS 4.0	NR-3327/3	Cisco MySDN IPS Signatures
Cisco IDS 4.0	NR-3327/4	Cisco MySDN IPS Signatures
Cisco IDS 4.0	NR-3327/5	Cisco MySDN IPS Signatures
Cisco IDS 4.0	NR-3327/6	Cisco MySDN IPS Signatures
Cisco IDS 4.0	NR-3327/7	Cisco MySDN IPS Signatures
Cisco IDS 4.0	NR-3327/8	Cisco MySDN IPS Signatures
Cisco IDS 4.0	NR-3327/9	Cisco MySDN IPS Signatures
Cisco IOS 12.2	NR-3327/0	Cisco MySDN IPS Signatures
Cisco IOS 12.2	NR-3327/10	Cisco MySDN IPS Signatures
Cisco IOS 12.2	NR-3327/11	Cisco MySDN IPS Signatures
Cisco IOS 12.2	NR-3327/12	Cisco MySDN IPS Signatures
Cisco IOS 12.2	NR-3327/1	Cisco MySDN IPS Signatures
Cisco IOS 12.2	NR-3327/2	Cisco MySDN IPS Signatures
Cisco IOS 12.2	NR-3327/3	Cisco MySDN IPS Signatures
Cisco IOS 12.2	NR-3327/4	Cisco MySDN IPS Signatures
Cisco IOS 12.2	NR-3327/5	Cisco MySDN IPS Signatures
Cisco IOS 12.2	NR-3327/6	Cisco MySDN IPS Signatures
Cisco IOS 12.2	NR-3327/7	Cisco MySDN IPS Signatures
Cisco IOS 12.2	NR-3327/8	Cisco MySDN IPS Signatures
Cisco IOS 12.2	NR-3327/9	Cisco MySDN IPS Signatures
Cisco IPS 5.x	NR-3327/0	Cisco MySDN IPS Signatures
Cisco IPS 5.x	NR-3327/10	Cisco MySDN IPS Signatures
Cisco IPS 5.x	NR-3327/11	Cisco MySDN IPS Signatures
Cisco IPS 5.x	NR-3327/12	Cisco MySDN IPS Signatures
Cisco IPS 5.x	NR-3327/1	Cisco MySDN IPS Signatures
Cisco IPS 5.x	NR-3327/2	Cisco MySDN IPS Signatures

Figure 6-18 *Event Type Details, Continued*

[pnmars] Event Type Details - Microsoft Internet Explorer

Enterasys Dragon NIDS 6.x	SMB:DCOM-OVERFLOW-445	Dragon NIDS 6.x Signatures
Enterasys Dragon NIDS 6.x	SMB:DCOM-OVERFLOW	Dragon NIDS 6.x Signatures
Entercept Entercept 4.0	RPC DCOM Stack Buffer Overflow (Blaster, Nachi)	
IntruVert IntruShield 1.5	INTRU-DCERPC: Microsoft RPC DCOM Buffer Overflow	
ISS RealSecure 6.5	MSRPC_RemoteActivate_BO	ISS RealSecure 6.5 Signatures
ISS RealSecure 7.0	MSRPC_RemoteActivate_BO	ISS RealSecure 7.0 Signatures
NetScreen IDP 2.1	MS-RPC:DCOM:EXPLOIT	IDP 2.1 Signatures
NetScreen IDP 2.1	NETBIOS:RPC:DCOM-EXPLOIT	IDP 2.1 Signatures
Snort Snort 2.0	SNORT-2351	Snort 2.0 Signatures
Snort Snort 2.0	SNORT-2352	Snort 2.0 Signatures
Snort Snort 2.0	SNORT-3197	Snort 2.0 Signatures
Snort Snort 2.0	SNORT-3198	Snort 2.0 Signatures
Cisco IDS 4.0	NR-5588/0	Cisco MySDN IPS Signatures
Cisco IOS 12.2	NR-5588/0	Cisco MySDN IPS Signatures
Cisco IPS 5.x	NR-5588/0	Cisco MySDN IPS Signatures
IntruVert IntruShield 1.5	INTRU-RPC DCOM Stack Buffer Overflow (Blaster, Nachi)	

Event Type Groups:

Event Type Group	Description	Member Event Types
Penetrate/All	This group includes all events which indicate remote attempts to gain access to host or unauthorized information, or to attack a host, including buffer overflow, remote code execution, escalate to an unauthorized privilege, connect to backdoor, etc.	".386" Email Attachment Via POP3, ".ADE" Email Attachment Via POP3, ".ADP" Email Attachment Via POP3, ".ANI" Email Attachment Via SMTP, ".BAS" or ".wal" Email Attachment Via POP3, (8,098 More...)
Penetrate/BufferOverflow/RPC	This group includes events that indicate buffer overflow attempts on an RPC service such as statd, cmsd, nfs, mountd, automountd, yppaswdd, rwalld etc.	Buffer overflows can lead to arbitrary command execution, Computer Associates BrightStor ARCserve Backup Buffer Overflow, DCERPC: Auth Length Overly Long, DCERPC: Frag Length Overly Long, DCERPC: Microsoft Message Queue Service Heap Overflow, (372 More...)

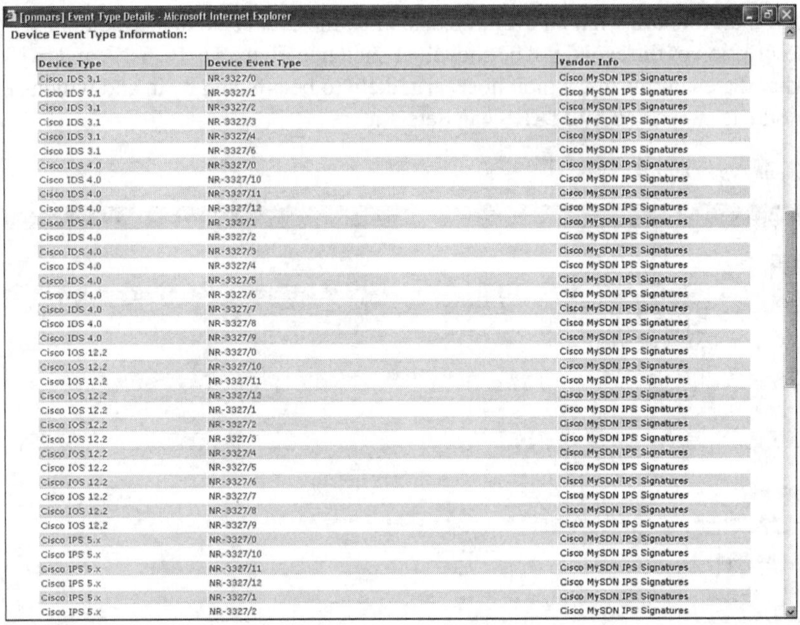

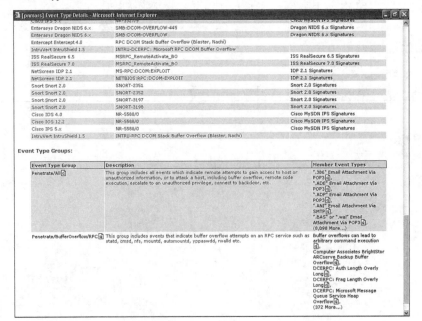

Finishing Your Investigation

Case notes are important to help you maintain your information. Whenever you find more useful information, click the **More** button (at the top of any page) to open a text area for adding notes. Additionally, if you ever lose your place and want to return to the incident, you can always click the case name that appears at the top of every page until the case is deselected.

When you click the case name, you'll see a page that's similar to Figure 6-15, showing all information gathered so far.

A full case history appears at the bottom of the Case History page. At the bottom of the page, you can click the **View Case Document** button. This opens a single printable document that shows all information gathered so far, including the incident, all reports, and the full case history.

If you need to work on a different case, be sure to deselect the current case or close it if it is completed.

False-Positive Tuning

You'll often find that what first appears to be malicious activity is normal traffic. When this happens, you need to tune either a monitored device or MARS itself to remove the unnecessary incidents.

Deciding Where to Tune

You have to decide where it makes the most sense to tune. Tuning typically means one of two things:

- A certain network behavior that looks malicious is actually normal.
- A network behavior isn't bad in certain circumstances.

When you need to tune, is it easier and more effective to configure the security or network device to not send events in a certain condition, or is it easier and more effective to configure MARS to ignore certain events? This decision varies according to your needs and the capabilities of your monitored devices and software, in addition to the way your organization is structured.

As an example, if your organization has only a single network IPS, it might be equally easy to tune the events on the sensor or on the MARS appliance. However, if you have more than one IPS sensor, and maybe even more than one vendor, it quickly becomes unworkable to tune at the sensor.

If separate teams within your organization manage devices or applications such as IPS, antivirus, firewalling, and security monitoring, it also might be unworkable to tune at the network device.

In general, most organizations decide to tune at the network device only if the event is a valid false positive—meaning that the security event is falsely identifying what it is supposed to identify. All other tuning is done on the MARS appliance.

A valid false positive is different from wanting to filter an event that violates your security policy only if it occurs on certain hosts.

Legitimate network traffic that is falsely identified as a network attack is a valid false positive. MARS uses the term *false positive* somewhat loosely. For example, if a legitimate attack is launched at a host on your network that is not vulnerable to the attack because it has been sufficiently patched, MARS considers the attack a false positive. While this intelligence is convenient and saves a lot of work on your part, it is not a false positive by the actual definition of the term.

Tuning False Positives in MARS

Within MARS, you have the following three ways to tune false positives:

- **False Positive Wizard**—When you are looking at the Incident Details page, as shown in Figure 6-19, you can tune events by clicking the **False Positive** link at the far right of each line. This steps you through the process of either ignoring events or not creating incidents on them.

- **Create or edit a drop rule**—This is a more flexible way of accomplishing the same thing that the False Positive Wizard does. However, instead of using a step-by-step wizard, you create it much like any rule.

- **Modify a system rule**—The previous two methods of tuning allow you to create a rule that works like an exception to another rule. By modifying an existing system rule, you exclude some conditions without the need for an additional rule. In general, you are discouraged from tuning with this method, but some rules are best handled this way. For example, the built-in rules called Inactive CS-MARS Reporting Device and Client Exploit—Mass Mailing Worm are both intended to be modified to only include applicable hosts.

Figure 6-19 *False Positive Wizard Link*

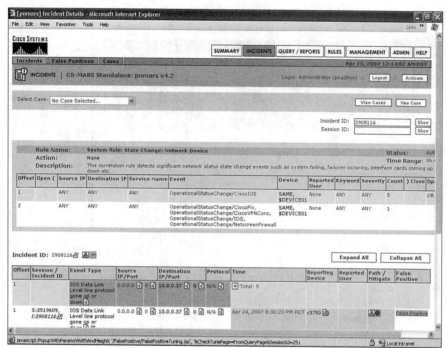

Using the False Positive Wizard

Figure 6-19 showed the incidents created when a host that is connected to a monitored switch is rebooted or unplugged. IOS interface hardware has gone up or down. If you click the **Raw Events** icon next to the reporting device in the incident table, you see Figure 6-20. This incident was triggered because interface FastEthernet1/0/20 on the monitored switch changed state to Down. This occurs regularly anywhere people shut down or restart their computers.

Figure 6-20 *Raw Event Data*

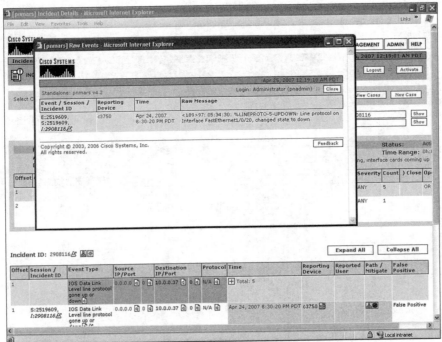

Is this really a false positive? No, it is not. However, it is a log message that you might not care about, and it would be nice to remove the clutter of these incidents from the MARS console.

The False Positive Wizard makes it easy to filter out these messages. Click the **False Positive** link on the Incident Details screen shown in Figure 6-19. The wizard launches, looking much like Figure 6-21. Select the event type at the top of this screen, and select the most appropriate source and destination addresses. You do not have a great deal of flexibility in selecting addresses at this time, but you can edit the drop rule this creates later to make it more granular. Click the **Tune** button.

Figure 6-21 *Launching the False Positive Wizard*

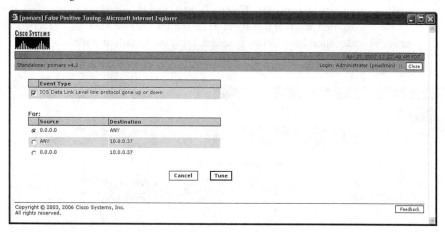

The second step in the wizard is to choose whether to drop events or log them to the database only. If you decide to drop the events, be aware that they are deleted. You cannot run reports on the events that would have been created. If you decide to log the events to the database, they cannot be used in a rule, and therefore do not appear as an incident. However, they will still be accessible if you ever need to run a report on them.

If in doubt, log them to the database and click the **Next** button, as illustrated in Figure 6-22.

Figure 6-22 *Select Tuning Option*

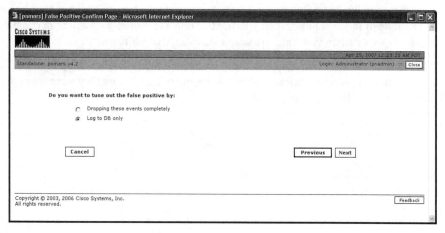

You are nearly finished with the wizard. If you look at Figure 6-23, you can see that the completed drop rule is displayed. If you want to change any of the fields, click the desired field. Recommended practice is that you at least click the rule name and description to make it easier to understand later. When finished, click the **Confirm** button.

Figure 6-23 *Completed Drop Rule from the Wizard*

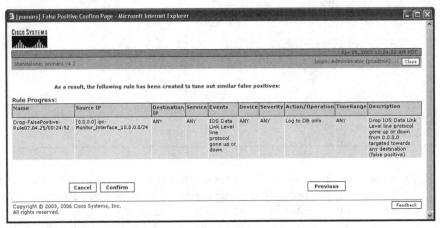

Creating or Editing a Drop Rule Without the False Positive Wizard

Although the False Positive Wizard is user friendly and simple, at times it is quicker and easier, or at least more powerful, to create or change a drop rule without the wizard. An example of this would be when you want to tune for multiple source or destination IP addresses, or when you want to use an entire range of addresses while excluding just a few.

From the main window, click the **Rules** button and then click the **Drop Rules** tab. All drop rules on the appliance appear as shown in Figure 6-24, whether they were created manually or with the False Positive Wizard.

Figure 6-24 *Drop Rules*

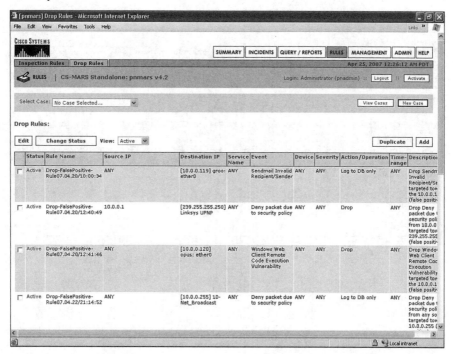

Editing a System Rule

Typically, you should not edit the built-in rules. However, you'll occasionally find it necessary to do this. One example that most companies run into is with the Client Exploit—Mass Mailing Worm rule, as illustrated in Figure 6-25.

Figure 6-25 *Client Exploit—Mass Mailing Worm*

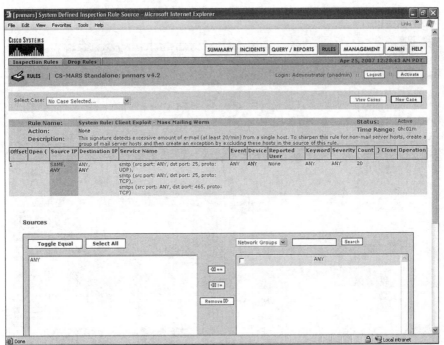

This rule is triggered when a single host sends more than 20 e-mail messages in a single minute. In general, hosts should never send this many e-mails. However, your company's Simple Mail Transfer Protocol (SMTP) relay servers might send out many times more than this each minute, and this does not mean they are infected with a worm.

The best way to tune these incidents is to exclude the SMTP servers within the rule itself. If you have more than one SMTP server in your organization that should be exempt from this rule, it is easiest to first create a group. Creating a group is an optional step, but it can make your life easier in the future. Follow these steps to create a group:

Step 1 From the main window, click the **MANAGEMENT** button, and then click the **IP Management** tab. The resulting page should look like Figure 6-26.

Step 2 Click the **Add Group** button to show the next window, as illustrated in Figure 6-27.

Figure 6-26 *IP Management*

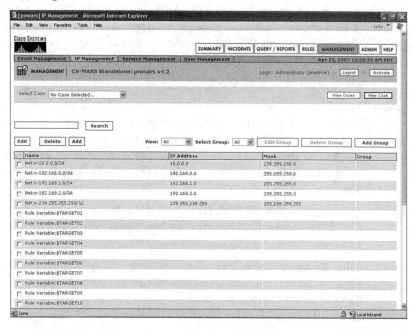

Figure 6-27 *Add Group*

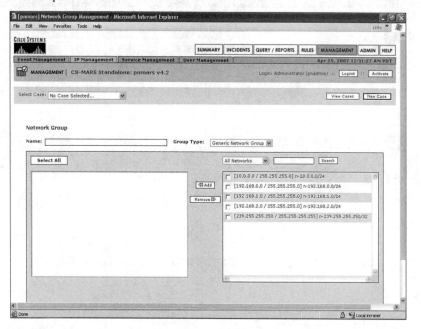

Step 3 Provide a name for the group, such as "SMTP Servers." For the group type, select **Generic Network Group**. In the right panel, select **All IP Addresses**, and then scroll through the list to find the IP addresses of your SMTP servers. Select these servers and click the **Add** button to add them to the left panel. When finished, click the **Submit** button.

This group is now available to all rules, queries, and reports.

Step 4 Modify the system rule, Client Exploit—Mass Mailing Worm. Click the **Rules** button and locate the rule. You might need to broaden the number of rules that appear on a single page and search by pressing **Ctrl-F**. When you find the rule, place a check mark next to it and click the **Edit** button at the top or bottom of the page. Refer to Figure 6-25 to see the resulting page.

Step 5 For sources, select **Network Groups** in the right panel and select the **SMTP Servers** group. Then click the **Not Equal** icon, which looks like !=.

Step 6 Click the **Apply** button. You should see a rule summary that looks like Figure 6-28. In the Source IP column, notice that the SMTP Servers are now excluded from the rule. These hosts will now be ignored by this rule.

Figure 6-28 *Rule Summary*

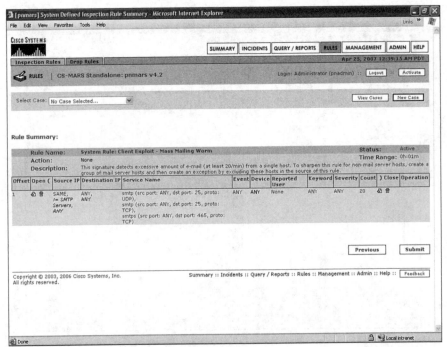

TIP	When you're finished modifying rules or devices, always click the **Activate** button at the upper-right corner of the screen.

Summary

In this chapter, you learned valuable information regarding how to use CS-MARS during the investigation of a security incident. Remember the six steps to properly handle an incident:

Step 1   **Preparation**—This includes a policy that describes how you are to handle the incident, in addition to prior training in using the tools at your disposal, such as CS-MARS.

Step 2   **Identification**—Use CS-MARS and other tools at your disposal to determine what occurred.

Step 3   **Containment**—Isolate the incident.

Step 4   **Eradication**—Repair or replace compromised systems.

Step 5   **Recovery**—Put your systems back online.

Step 6   **Lessons learned**—Learn from the incident. Train others as well.

Additionally, this chapter taught you how to tune MARS for your environment.

## CHAPTER 7

Archiving and Disaster Recovery

Cisco Security Monitoring, Analysis, and Response System (CS-MARS) appliances are built with a fair amount of redundancy, especially if you're deploying one of the larger models, such as the MARS-100/100e or MARS-200, both of which have the following features:

- Dual power supplies
- Redundant Array of Independent Disks (RAID) 1+0 hard-disk arrays
- Multiple processors

Even with this built-in redundancy, you still need to plan for disaster recovery. You need to consider the process of recovering from a hardware failure of the MARS appliance, in addition to how to recover from a larger-scale disaster, such as a fire, earthquake, or flood. All recovery plans should be well documented and tested, and MARS is no different.

Another thing you need to consider is how to access historical data. Logging consumes a lot of storage, and even though MARS appliances have considerable on-box storage, it's a finite amount, and you will eventually run out of space. MARS automatically manages storage by deleting old information and replacing it with new. After this occurs, though, how do you run reports on the older data? How do you investigate security incidents that might have occurred in the past? You must consider these questions early in your deployment.

You might eventually decide that a larger, more powerful MARS appliance is needed because of your increasing logging requirements. The capability to upgrade or move your MARS settings, logs, reports, and rules to another appliance currently doesn't exist. Instead, you need to use the archiving features.

This chapter explains MARS archiving functions, and describes how to configure and test them. You also learn how to plan for disasters, whether this is a simple hardware failure of an appliance or a natural disaster that destroys a facility in which the MARS appliance resides.

Understanding CS-MARS Archiving

CS-MARS uses the Network File System (NFS) for archive and restore functionality. Archiving is critical for any MARS deployment and should be configured as soon as possible. Be aware that archiving is the only backup system available to you in the case of total hardware failure. It's also the only method to migrate your information to a larger appliance. MARS appliances can deal with the loss of a hard drive, because the appliances (MARS-100/100e and MARS-200) use RAID for hard-disk redundancy. However, if the entire system fails or if a disaster destroys the appliance, restoration from the archive is your only option for recovery of the event data and reports.

Begin archiving as soon as possible after installing your appliance. You cannot save information from MARS to the archive server from a time prior to configuring archiving. As an example, assume that you've been using a MARS appliance for several months and then decide to configure archiving. From that moment in time, events, sessions, and incidents are written to the archive server. No information prior to that time is written to archive. If the MARS appliance experiences a hardware failure and needs to be replaced, you will not be able to restore the data from the initial several months of the deployment.

When archives are written, the entire configuration of the MARS appliance, in addition to all reports, incidents, sessions, and events, is saved to the archive server.

At approximately 1:00 a.m. every day, the operating system and all system settings are written to the archive server. Two copies of these files, called the *pnos* files, are stored. One is the most recent copy, and the other is the second most recent copy.

As you can see from the following example, two copies of the pnos files are stored on the archive server:

```
[root@opus pnos]# ls -l
total 933320
-rw-rw-r-- 1 nobody nobody 477319992 Jun 20 01:39 pnos_415.pna
-rw-rw-r-- 1 nobody nobody 477451238 Jun 19 01:39 pnos-old.pna
```

Approximately every ten minutes, the event store and other forensic information are compressed and written to the archive. In case of total system failure, the greatest amount of data that can be lost, then, is just under ten minutes' worth.

Planning and Selecting the Archive Server

Cisco recommends either Solaris or Linux as the operating system for your archive server; however, the decision is yours. If this will be a dedicated system, it is relatively unimportant that the archive server have fast processors or a lot of memory. Instead, you should make sure that plenty of hard-disk space is available to fit your needs.

The pnos files will each be approximately 500 MB in size. You should plan on having at least 1.5 GB of space for these files alone, because two copies are stored, and until the oldest is deleted, you will have three copies on the archive server for a short period of time each day.

The event store and other forensic information are all compressed. The exact compression ratio varies depending on which types of devices generated the logs and on how large the individual event messages are. Additionally, some logs are binary, while others are text. Compression ratios typically range from 12:1 to 36:1.

Refer to Chapter 3, "CS-MARS Deployment Scenarios," for information on how to calculate the number of days your MARS appliance can store events. This same information can help you determine how much storage space your archive server needs to have to store as much data as your policies require.

If you've determined, for example, that on a MARS-200, you can store 180 days of data, if you have 1 TB of archive space available, you should be able to store at least seven years of events on the archive server.

Here is how this is estimated:

> Available storage on a MARS-200 is approximately 800 GB. If you initially determine how long data could be stored with no compression, you would find that by simple ratio, 1 TB of archive storage would store 225 days of data if it would stay for 180 days on 800 GB.
>
> 180 days * 1000 GB / 800 GB = 225 days

At the worst case, the compression ratio for archived events should be 12:1. So, 225 days at 12:1 compression becomes 2700 days, or 7.4 years.

You need to determine how long information needs to reside on the archive server and provide a server with sufficient storage space available. This is a decision that you'll most likely need assistance making. Depending on the type of organization you work for and where it is located, different requirements exist. Compliance or legal reasons why you need to store information for a lengthy period of time might exist. Many states are implementing privacy regulations that place requirements on log storage. If you deal with health-care providers and are required to comply with Health Insurance Portability and Accountability Act (HIPAA) requirements, you'll need a written policy that sets your limits on log data storage.

Work with your company's teams that focus on compliance issues to determine how long security logs need to be stored. This period of time should also be stated in a policy document.

Configuring the Archiving Server

The first step in setting up archiving is to configure the archive server. Most companies choose a Linux server for archiving; however, this is not your only choice. Linux is available both as open source (free) and as a commercially available operating system. It is powerful and flexible, and it runs on a variety of computer hardware. The steps for setting up the archiving server are as follows:

Step 1 Make sure that the NFS service is enabled on the server. You might also need to modify firewall rules to allow UDP port 2049 and portmapper to accept connections. If the NFS service is not enabled, you might need to enlist the assistance of a system administrator for the server you're using to get the service running properly.

Step 2 While logged in as a root user on the server, create a directory for the archive files. The following example creates a base directory for all CS-MARS archives, and also creates a directory (called mars-lc) for the first MARS appliance to write to. If you later install more appliances, you can use other subdirectories of /nfs for their archives. Make sure that you have sufficient storage space on the disk you're using:

```
mkdir -p /nfs/mars-lc
chown -R nobody.nobody /nfs
chmod -R 777 /nfs
```

Step 3 Add a new line to /etc/exports. This file, on a Linux or UNIX host, defines which file systems are made available to other hosts. In the following example, the CS-MARS appliance has 10.0.0.91 as its IP address. It is allowed to write to the /nfs directory:

```
/nfs                          10.0.0.91(rw,sync,nohide)
```

Step 4 Restart the NFS service:

```
/etc/init.d/nfs restart
```

Configuring CS-MARS for Archiving

After the NFS archive server has been configured, the next step is to configure MARS for writing to the archive. This is simple to do.

From the CS-MARS web interface, click the **ADMIN** button, and then click the **System Maintenance** tab. On the form provided (shown in Figure 7-1), enter the following information:

- **Remote Host IP**—Enter the IP address of the NFS server.

- **Remote Path**—Enter the directory that MARS should write to on the archive server.

- **Archiving Protocol**—Select NFS, if it isn't already selected. NFS is currently the only protocol available for archiving.

- **Remote Storage Capacity in Days**—Enter the length of time in days that you want to store archived information. Be aware that MARS will automatically delete any archive information older than this. Also be aware that MARS will not be able to check for available storage space on the archive, because of limitations with NFS.

Figure 7-1   *CS-MARS Archive Configuration*

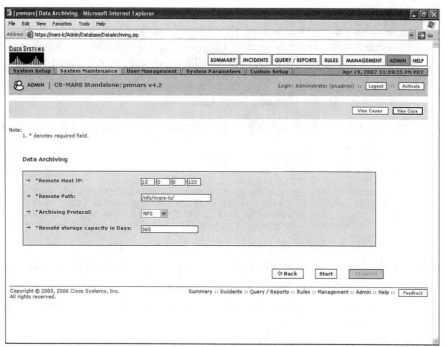

Using the Archives

Several reasons exist for using the archived information:

- To allow you to restore your MARS appliance to a working condition, including historical events and other information, in case of a complete system failure. This same functionality is used if you need to migrate from a smaller MARS appliance to a larger one.

- To provide a mechanism for reporting on information that is no longer stored on the local MARS appliance. This involves using a second appliance, which is dedicated to running the reports, and restoring the necessary information to it.

- To allow a third-party tool or scripting interface into data. When MARS writes information to the archive, it is a compressed clear text format. This information, although raw in nature, is easily readable by third-party tools, such as Perl.

- To allow the easy retrieval of old information through the existing MARS user interface.

Restoring from Archive

No interface to the restore capabilities of a CS-MARS appliance exists from the web user interface. Instead, you must connect to MARS from the command-line interface (CLI). This requires that you either connect a keyboard and monitor to the appliance or Secure Shell (SSH) to the appliance. Only the pnadmin user can log in through SSH.

After you've logged in to CLI, use the **pnrestore** command to configure how information is copied to the MARS appliance from the archive.

Typing **pnrestore –h** displays a brief help screen, as shown in the following example:

```
[pnadmin]$ pnrestore -h
pnrestore: option requires an argument -- h
Usage:  pnrestore options
  -h --help         Display this usage information.
  -m --mode         Restoring mode. Enter 1 (default) to restore config only, 2 to
    restore both config and events, or 5 to restore config from local image.
  -t --time         Restore the data dated from this time (in 'MM/DD/YY:HH' format).
  -p --data_path    Name of the directory where the archived data are stored.
  example:
  pnrestore -m 1 -p nfs_server_ip:/nfs_export/pnarchive -t 06/03/03:0
```

The following three modes are available to you when performing the restore:

* Mode 1 (**-m 1**) restores the operating system (pnos) and system configuration and event and incident information. However, all other dynamic information is not restored.

* Mode 2 (**-m 2**) restores the operating system, configuration of the appliance, and all events, incidents, and other dynamic information, beginning at the starting time you select with the **–t** flag.

* Mode 5 (**-m 5**) does not restore the operating system. Instead, it restores only what is essentially the configuration of the appliance as it existed the previous day. Events, incidents, and other dynamic data are not restored. However, dynamic data related to cases is restored.

TIP   A hidden switch (**-r 1**) is available that might be useful in some circumstances. This switch does not appear in the command reference or on the MARS help screens. The switch instructs the pnrestore utility to leave the IP address as currently configured, rather than changing it to what appears in the archived configuration.

You might find this switch useful if you want to restore from the archive to a different MARS appliance. Some people do this with a separate, development appliance, or if they need to run reports from historical data.

If you need to replace a MARS appliance, whether it's because of a system failure or because you've chosen to upgrade to a larger-capacity appliance, follow these steps:

Step 1 Install the identical MARS software version onto the new appliance that you were running on the old appliance. This step is critical. Mismatched versions can result in a failure to restore to a functional appliance. If you're not sure what version you were running, look in the pnos directory on your archive server. For this example, this would be in /nfs/mars-lc/ pnos. The filename of the latest file shows the version you're running. For the example used throughout the chapter, this is pnos_415.pna, so you would need to use the CS-MARS 4.1.5 recovery DVD to install the correct version. You can find ISO images for the various releases at Cisco.com.

Step 2 Perform a bootstrap installation of the appliance. This means performing the basic setup steps that you would perform to install a new appliance. Use the same IP address as the original appliance was using. Don't add devices or modify any rules.

Step 3 Verify IP connectivity between the archive server and the MARS appliance. The simplest way to do this is to ping the archive server from MARS or vice versa.

Step 4 From the MARS CLI, use the **pnrestore** command to begin the restoration process. The following example restores the configuration of the MARS appliance and all events since January 1, 2006:

```
pnrestore -m 1 -p 10.0.0.120:/nfs/mars-lc -t 01/01/06:0
```

CAUTION You cannot use the **pnrestore** command to migrate to a lower-capacity MARS appliance. At the current time, you cannot restore to anything but the same-capacity appliance or larger. Also, you should calculate the date from which to begin the restoration. The **pnrestore** command doesn't currently allow for calculating whether the new appliance can store all the events being restored to it.

Restoring from archive is a time-intensive process. Depending on how large the appliance is, how much data is being restored, and how fast the network infrastructure is, this entire process could take several hours.

Restoring to a Reporting Appliance

You can choose to keep a separate CS-MARS appliance for reporting on old, archived data. Although obvious benefits to this exist, you should also be aware of some pretty rigid limitations.

The first limitation to address was discussed in the previous section. When using the pnrestore utility to restore the configuration and events to a different MARS appliance, the new appliance *must* be the same model or bigger. For example, you cannot restore data that was archived from a MARS-200 to a MARS-50. However, you can restore data that was archived from a MARS-50 to a MARS-200, MARS-100, MARS-100e, or a MARS-50. This means that you might spend more money on a reporting appliance than you might like. On the other hand, a reporting appliance can always be pressed into duty as a primary MARS appliance in case of hardware or other catastrophic failure.

The second limitation exists in MARS 4.2 software and earlier releases. In these releases, the pnrestore utility does not allow for specifying an ending date and time when selecting the time range of events to restore. This means that importing a specific range of events requires additional work on the archive server before data can be restored.

As long as you keep these two limitations in mind, a second MARS appliance can be useful for running reports on data that no longer resides on your primary appliance.

For example, assume that you're saving one year of events on your archive server. Because of the rate of events that your primary MARS appliance receives, however, you're able to store only eight months of event data on your MARS-100.

An auditor has asked you to provide a report showing all configuration changes that were performed on your perimeter firewall during a 30-day period one year ago. Your perimeter firewall is a Cisco ASA-5540, and it's already configured to send logs through syslog to MARS. This report is simple to define, because a report is already defined that can be used as a template. However, on the production MARS appliance, it reports only on the data it has available on its local hard drives.

Figure 7-2 shows a built-in report that can be modified to suit your needs. This report displays network device configuration changes over a short period of time. This can easily be modified to report over a longer period of time and can be filtered to display only changes from a single device.

You have a second MARS-100 that's dedicated for reporting and other development tasks. Using the pnrestore utility with MARS 4.2.1, you can specify the starting date and time, but not the ending date and time.

Figure 7-2 *CS-MARS Firewall Configuration Changes Report*

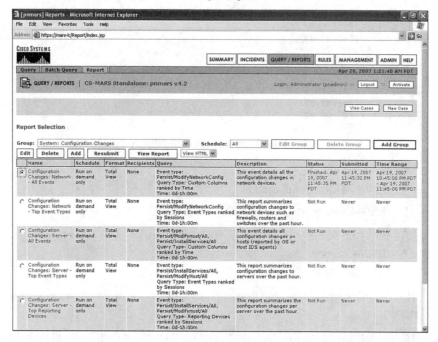

To restore the necessary data to the reporting appliance, follow these steps:

Step 1 Calculate whether your reporting appliance can store the number of events you expect to restore. In this case, because your production MARS can maintain about eight months of events, you should experience no problems when restoring a single month or so to your reporting appliance.

Step 2 Log in to your archive server and copy only the files you'll need to a separate directory.

Step 3 Bootstrap the reporting MARS appliance to the correct version of software and appropriate network configuration. This is the same process you follow when initially configuring a MARS appliance. This process consists of logging in with your web browser and entering the initial IP address, passwords, and so on.

Step 4 Use the pnrestore utility to restore these events to the reporting appliance. The following example is similar to what you would use if your NFS archive server is 10.0.0.120 and you want data restored from June 4, 2006, and later:

```
pnrestore -m 1 -r 1 -p 10.0.0.120/nfs/report -t 06/04/06:0
```

If you look at the archive server, you'll see that the directory structure is something like this:

```
/nfs/
    /mars-lc/
        /2006-06-04/
        /2006-06-05/
        /2006-06-06/
        /.../
        /.../
        /.../
        /2006-08-07/
        /2006-08-08/
        /pnos/
```

Within each of the dates, you'll see the following directory structure:

- **/AL/**—Audit Logs
- **/CF/**—MARS Configuration
- **/ES/**—Event Store
- **/IN/**—Incidents
- **/RR/**—Reports
- **/ST/**—Statistics

This directory structure within the date directories is the event information you need to import.

The easiest way to copy all necessary files from an entire month would be to first create a target directory for the files. In this case, a good choice might be **/nfs/report**, as follows:

```
mkdir /nfs/report
```

The following command, in Linux, would copy the necessary files from the month of June 2006:

```
cp -r 2006-06* /nfs/report
```

Next, copy the pnos files to /nfs/report/pnos:

```
cp pnos/* /nfs/report/pnos
```

When this is finished, you're ready to use the **pnrestore** command just as if you were recovering from a disaster, but rather than restoring /nfs/mars-lc, you'll recover /nfs/report instead.

Direct Access of Archived Events

If you are proficient at using tools such as Python or Perl, or if someone on your staff is, you might want to write a short script that parses the event store on the archive server. A sample script using Python is shown in Appendix A, "Querying the Archive."

TIP	A good resource for scripting with Python is *Programming Python, Third Edition*, by Mark Lutz (published by O'Reilly Media, Inc.).

As shown in the preceding section, the ES directories on the archive server contain the event store information. This information is compressed using gzip.

You'll see filenames similar to these:

```
es-4150-415_2006-06-13-18-05-29_2006-06-13-18-15-41.gz
rm-4150-415_2006-06-13-16-44-57_2006-06-13-16-55-12.gz
```

The files that begin with *es* contain human-readable event information and look exactly like what you see when you use the MARS interface to retrieve raw messages.

The files that begin with *rm* are raw messages, in Base64, and are not easily read.

Retrieving Raw Events from Archive

A time might come when you need to provide an auditor, law enforcement officer, or a court with copies of raw logs rather than the summarized and correlated view that MARS provides. In this case, it is usually easiest to retrieve the logs using the MARS user interface.

To retrieve the raw logs, follow these steps:

Step 1   Click the **Admin** button, click the **System Maintenance** tab, and then click the **Retrieve Raw Messages** link (see Figure 7-3) .

Figure 7-3 *CS-MARS System Maintenance Page*

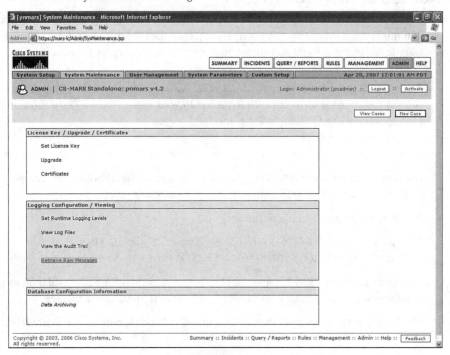

Step 2 Select the events to retrieve (see Figure 7-4).

You have several options for retrieving raw messages. First, you can select a time range for the events to fall within. If you do not select a time range, the default time period is only ten minutes.

You can choose between retrieving raw messages from either the local database on the appliance or from the archive server (if the archive server has been configured). Retrieving messages from the archive server is significantly faster, but this method should be used only when you either want to retrieve messages that are less than one hour old or want to retrieve messages that are so old that they no longer exist on the local database. Additionally, if you have just configured archiving for the first time, you need to wait until the initial archive functions occur at 1:00 a.m. before you can retrieve messages from the archive.

Figure 7-4   *CS-MARS Retrieve Raw Messages Screen*

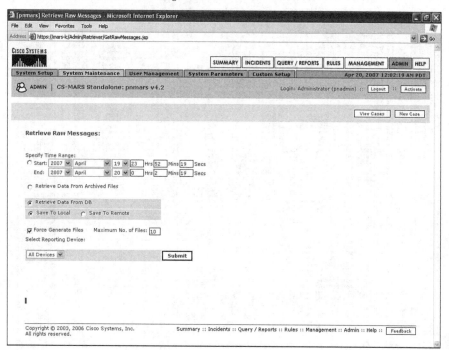

If you choose to retrieve raw messages from the local database (see Figure 7-5), you also gain the ability to select from which devices to retrieve messages. If you do not select a device, messages from all devices are retrieved. Otherwise, you can select a single device's logs.

Additionally, if you retrieve messages from the local database, you can select where to write the files. You always have the option to download the files from the web interface, but the files are also written to a directory on either the local appliance, to be used as a cache, or to the archive server.

The **Force Generate Files** option tells the MARS appliance to overwrite previously retrieved raw messages with the new messages.

Figure 7-5 *Sample Cisco Firewall Raw Messages*

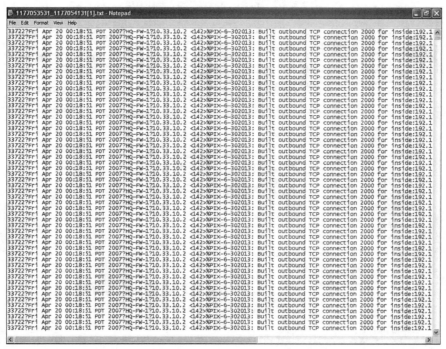

Summary

In this chapter, you learned the importance of setting up and maintaining an archive server. Archiving should be considered a necessary part of installing your MARS appliance and should be done immediately.

Remember, you cannot perform an on-demand backup of the data on a MARS appliance. Regular backups through archiving are the only method of backing up your configuration and data.

P A R T III

CS-MARS Advanced Topics

CHAPTER 8

Integration with Cisco Security Manager

Cisco Security Manager (CS-Manager) is a Cisco enterprise security management suite. CS-Manager provides the capability to manage various Cisco security devices and routers, including intrusion prevention systems (IPS), firewalls, and Virtual Private Networks (VPN). CS-Manager is easy to use and allows both small and large companies to manage their security devices from a central console. By integrating CS-Manager into the Cisco Security Monitoring, Analysis, and Response System (CS-MARS), you can correlate the security incidents you see in MARS with the rules that relate to them within CS-Manager.

CS-Manager provides the following three different views for managing your security products:

- **Device view**—Allows you to individually manage the various Cisco security devices (see Figure 8-1).

- **Policy view**—Allows you to manage all or some aspects of security using a policy you've defined. The policies are assigned to groups of devices and let you provide both default and mandatory rules (see Figure 8-2) .

- **Map view**—Allows you to logically manage your security devices by placing them on a map (see Figure 8-3). Security settings and rules can be changed by clicking the device and selecting a category from a submenu. The map view also shows VPNs that are defined throughout your network.

Figure 8-1 *Cisco Security Manager Device View*

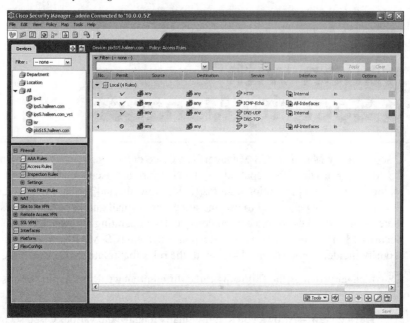

Figure 8-2 *Cisco Security Manager Policy View*

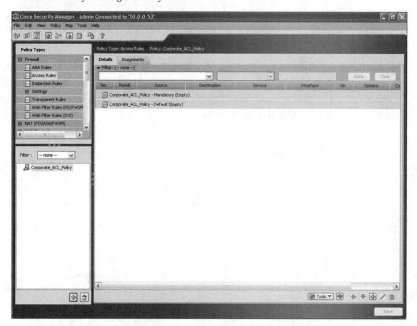

Figure 8-3 *Cisco Security Manager Map View*

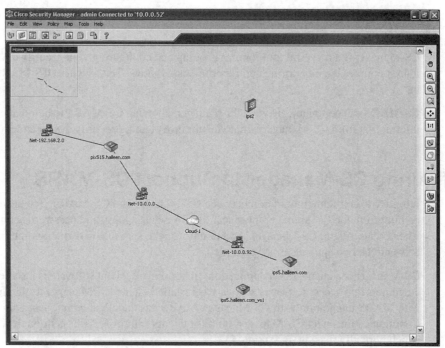

With version 3.1 software, CS-Manager supports the following Cisco devices:

- Cisco ASA security appliances
- Cisco PIX firewalls
- Cisco Firewall Services Module
- Cisco IPS Sensors
- Cisco IDSM-2
- Cisco Integrated Services Router (ISR)
- Cisco 7600 series routers
- Cisco 7500 series routers
- Cisco 7300 series routers
- Cisco 7200 series routers
- Cisco 7100 series routers
- Cisco 6500 series switches
- Cisco 6500 series VPN Services Module

- Cisco 6500 series VPN Shared Port Adapter
- Cisco IOS Routers
- Cisco IOS Router IDS Module

CS-Manager is a powerful tool for provisioning and configuring your security devices, but it does not provide monitoring and reporting capabilities. This is where CS-MARS comes in.

CS-MARS can communicate with CS-Manager, allowing CS-MARS to automatically pull information from CS-Manager while you are investigating security events and incidents.

Configuring CS-Manager to Support CS-MARS

It is easy to configure integration between CS-Manager and CS-MARS. You need to do nothing from the CS-Manager interface. MARS needs a login and password set up to use when connecting to CS-Manager. Additionally, make sure that network communications between the two appliances are permitted.

CS-Manager is a client-server application. In normal use, client software is installed on the computers that access it. Server software is installed on the CS-Manager itself. However, with MARS integration with CS-Manager, MARS has the client component built in. Communications with CS-Manager, both for clients and for MARS, is through HTTPS, which normally runs on TCP port 443.

For CS-MARS to communicate with CS-Manager, you have to make sure that TCP port 443 is permitted. You can configure an alternate port if you prefer.

CS-Manager has granular user permissions, if you choose to use them. However, it also has the following set of predefined default roles:

- **Help desk**—Help desk users can view, but not modify, devices, policies, maps, and objects.
- **Network operator**—A network operator has the same rights as help desk and can also view command-line interface (CLI) and administrative settings. Network operators can issue certain commands (such as **ping**) to devices and can modify the configuration archive.
- **Approver**—An approver has the same rights as a network operator and can also approve or reject deployment jobs. Not all installations use approvers. This role is used when a feature called Workflow is enabled.
- **Network administrator**—A network administrator has complete view and modify permissions, except for modifying administrative settings. Network administrators cannot approve or reject jobs, but they can deploy jobs that have already been approved.

- **System administrator**—System administrators have full access to all CS-Manager permissions. They can perform all actions, without restrictions.

CS-MARS needs to have view rights to the CS-Manager system. Make sure that you create a user with at least help desk or equivalent rights with which MARS can log in to CS-Manager.

Configuring CS-MARS to Integrate with CS-Manager

CS-Manager is added to CS-MARS in much the same way as any other security or network device is added. You treat CS-Manager as security software running on a host. This means, from within CS-MARS, you first add the server that it is running on, and then you add CS-Manager as software running on that server.

From any screen in MARS, click the **ADMIN** tab, and then click on **Security and Monitor Devices**. Click the **Add** button, and select **Add SW security apps on new host** or **Add SW security apps on existing host** if that server is already defined in MARS.

As shown in Figure 8-4, enter the device name and IP addresses, including the interface IP address and network mask. Then click the **Next** button.

Figure 8-4   *Add CS-Manager Server to MARS*

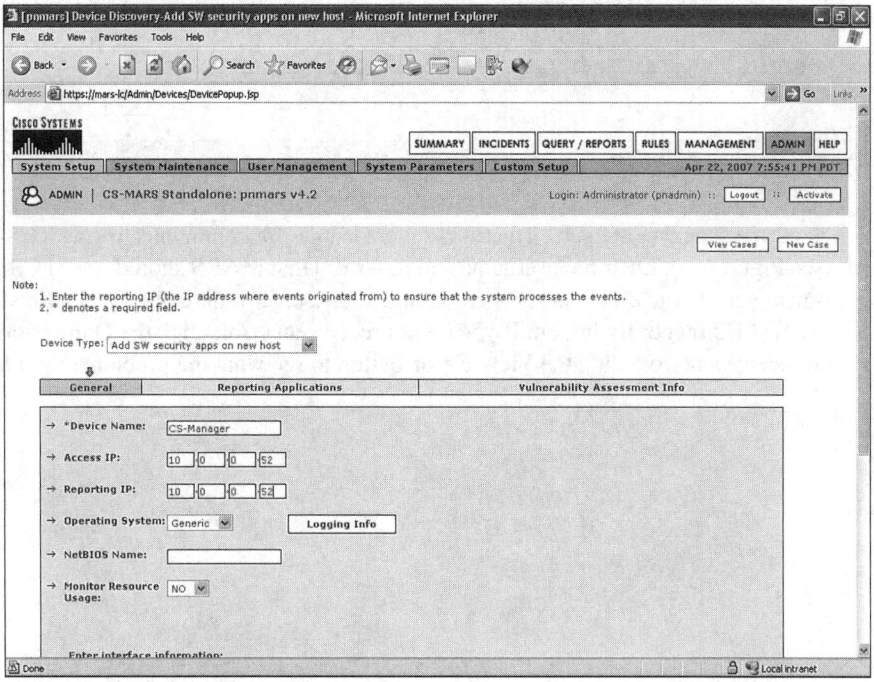

You should now be on the screen shown in Figure 8-5, where you can select the applications running on the server. From the **Select application** drop-down list, select **Cisco Security Manager ANY**; then click the **Add** button and click the **Done** button.

Figure 8-5 *Add CS-Manager Software to CS-Manager*

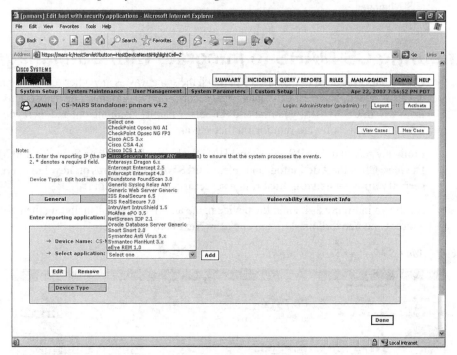

Next, you should be at a screen that asks for credentials for communicating with CS-Manager (see Figure 8-6). Enter the username and password that MARS should use. If CS-Manager is using an alternate TCP port for communications, enter it here also. When finished, click the **Test Connectivity** button. If you do not receive an error, click the **Done** button. If you do receive an error, click the **View Error** button to see what the problem might be.

Figure 8-6   *Enter CS-Manager Credentials*

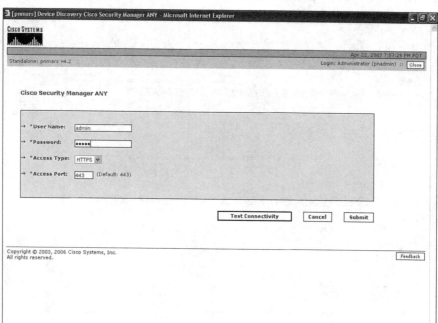

The most common errors you're likely to see are incorrectly entered usernames and passwords. Remember that the login name and password are case sensitive. In addition, remember that CS-MARS communicates with CS-Manager using HTTPS over TCP port 443, by default. You might need to verify that a firewall or router access control list (ACL) isn't blocking communications between the two systems.

You should next be back at the Reporting Applications screen, as shown in Figure 8-7. Click the **Done** button and then the **Activate** button. CS-MARS is now configured to communicate with Cisco Security Manager.

Figure 8-7 *Finish Adding CS-Manager to MARS*

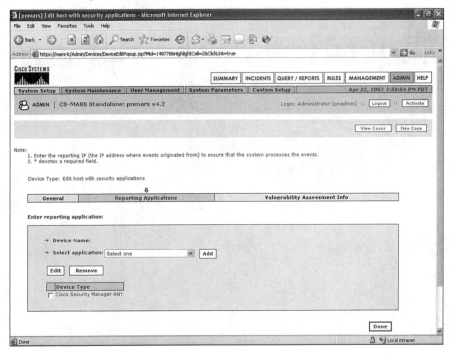

Using CS-Manager Within CS-MARS

Integration of CS-Manager is useful when investigating security incidents. CS-Manager does not send events to MARS. Instead, it allows MARS to pull information from CS-Manager, on demand.

Consider the example that follows.

In Figure 8-8, the MARS console is showing traffic being denied by the pix515 firewall. It appears that a host with address 10.0.0.61 is attempting to communicate with 192.168.2.25 using TCP port 5.

Figure 8-8   *PIX Firewall Denied Traffic*

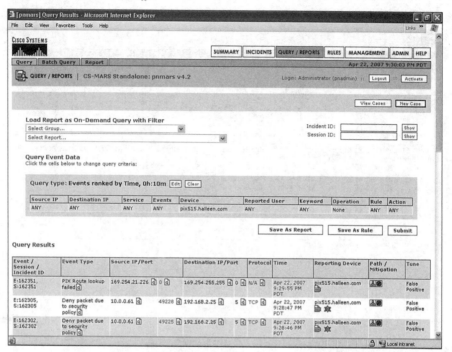

If you click the event number that appears in Figure 8-8 (162305), you'll see more details about the event. You've seen screens like this in other chapters. What is new, though, is the policy lookup icon (the new icon is blue and looks like an atom) in the Reporting Device column.

Clicking the policy lookup icon opens a new window, as you can see in Figure 8-9, and displays the exact policy that appears for the firewall you're querying. As you can see from this figure, the firewall was dropping traffic because it was matching on the deny rule at the end of the access control list. This line is highlighted to make it easy to find. If you have very long ACLs, this can make it much easier to locate the rules that are an issue.

Figure 8-9 *CS-Manager Policy Lookup*

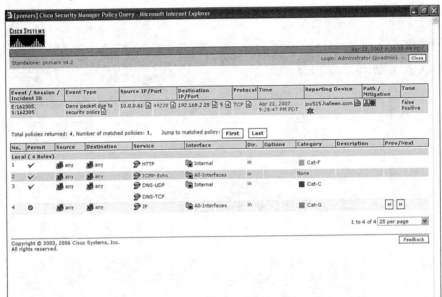

Summary

The capability to display the firewall rule that generates an event, from within CS-MARS, is a useful feature. This capability reduces the time and effort that are required to investigate a potential security issue.

At this time, the capability to perform the policy lookup is restricted to Cisco firewalls that are managed with Cisco Security Manager. However, it does not matter what type of Cisco firewall they are. This policy lookup works equally well with PIX, ASA, Firewall Services Module (FWSM), or IOS Firewall (firewall software running on a Cisco router).

## CHAPTER 9

Troubleshooting CS-MARS

The Cisco Security Monitoring, Analysis, and Response System (CS-MARS) is a complex product, and it contains information that is critical to your organization. You must understand what to do when a problem occurs with the system, or when something doesn't seem to work like it should.

This chapter provides you with the steps you need to efficiently troubleshoot MARS. Don't forget, however, that the Cisco Technical Assistance Center (TAC) is always available to assist. In the United States, you can call the TAC at 1-800-553-2447. Outside the United States, refer to the TAC directory at http://www.cisco.com/warp/public/687/Directory/DirTAC.shtml.

Be Prepared

When you install CS-MARS, make sure that configuring archiving is one of your top priorities. Too often, archiving is set aside as a task that will happen later, when you have more time. This is a mistake! Archiving is your safety net in case of disaster. Many things can happen that might require you to restore data or configurations. This might be a catastrophic hardware failure, for example, requiring replacement of the appliance. It could also be something as simple as a power outage. Hopefully, you connect all your systems to uninterruptible power supplies (UPS), but sometimes the batteries fail in a UPS. Data can be scrambled when power is suddenly interrupted while MARS is writing to disk.

For more information on archiving, refer to Chapter 7, "Archiving and Disaster Recovery."

In addition to archiving, you should also document your installation. Some tasks, such as custom parsing, are time intensive. It would be unfortunate and costly to have to rewrite these rules from scratch. Document any customizations you've made to the MARS system to allow you to re-create them quickly in case of disaster. Additionally, this documentation can be useful when dealing with the Cisco TAC.

Troubleshooting MARS Hardware

If MARS is experiencing a hardware problem, you should contact the Cisco TAC immediately for assistance. The topics discussed throughout the rest of this chapter are intended to aid you in your discussions with TAC, and to help you understand potential problems you might encounter.

Beeping Noises

Beeping noises coming from MARS are usually related to a power issue. The MARS-100E and larger appliances each have redundant power supplies. If one of the power supplies is not plugged in, or has lost power, the MARS appliance will begin beeping continuously or emit a high-pitched whine.

Degraded RAID Array

MARS-100E and larger appliances feature Redundant Array of Independent Disks (RAID) to provide protection against data loss. RAID allows MARS to lose a hard drive without losing data, or even requiring a reboot.

A degraded RAID array can occur when the data on a hard disk is damaged. This usually occurs when an appliance is not cleanly shut down or rebooted, such as when power is lost. Power surges and drops (also known as *brownouts*) can also cause damage to your hard disks. You can help prevent these unpleasant problems by using a high-quality UPS.

When you have a degraded RAID array, MARS sends an e-mail notification to the pnadmin user, if that user has an e-mail address defined. MARS also changes the LED for the degraded drive from green to yellow. If you reboot MARS, the RAID status will display on-screen if you have a monitor connected.

If you do not have the pnadmin e-mail address configured within MARS, you should take the time to do that right away. Figure 9-1 shows the field to complete within User Manager, which you can reach by clicking the **MANAGEMENT** button, and then clicking the **User Management** tab.

From the command-line interface (CLI), you can use the **raidstatus** command to see whether all disks are operating properly. This command shows you the current status of each of the hard disks installed in the MARS-100E and larger appliances. The MARS-50 and below do not use RAID.

Figure 9-2 shows the output of the **raidstatus** command with degraded status.

Figure 9-1   *Enter E-Mail Address for pnadmin User*

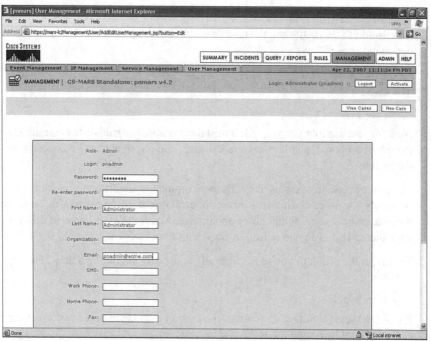

Figure 9-2   *RAID Array in Degraded Status*

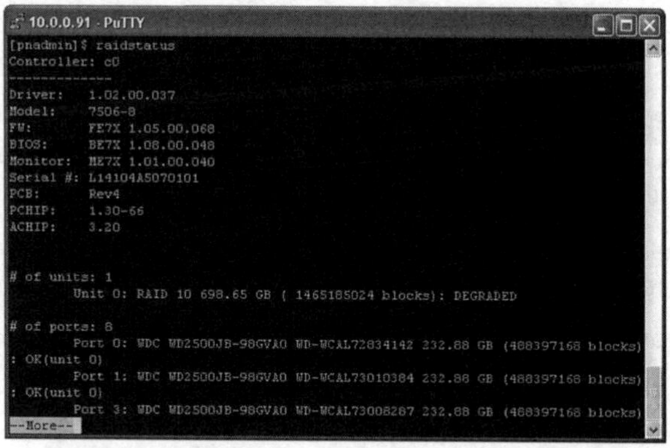

When a hard disk is in a degraded state, you can attempt to correct this state by using the
hotswap command. Be careful when using this command. In fact, this is one time when
you should have the Cisco TAC on the phone. The basic idea of correcting this problem is
pretty simple. However, the syntax for doing it is not intuitive.

Consider the following example.

On a MARS-200, the **raidstatus** command shows that physical port 1 is in a degraded state. You decide to try rebuilding the drive with the **hotswap** command. The syntax for this command is as follows:

```
hotswap <add¦remove> disk
```

You enter:

```
hotswap remove 1
```

Now, you realize that you've made a mistake, because the **raidstatus** command now shows that physical port 1 is still in a degraded state, and physical port 7 has been removed from the system.

The port or disk numbers used by the two commands are different from each other. Normally, the order in which the drives are displayed with the **raidstatus** command defines the disk number used by the **hotswap** command, although this can also differ with some appliances. This is a good reason to work with the Cisco TAC when fixing a degraded disk.

To correct the problem you've accidentally caused by degrading a new disk, type the following:

```
hotswap add 1
```

It will take several minutes to correct the problem, and then you can correct the original degraded disk by typing the following:

```
hotswap remove 7
hotswap add 7
```

Troubleshooting Software and Devices

This section can help you determine why MARS might not behave like you expect sometimes, and how you can fix various problems. Some questions and situations you might encounter are as follows:

- I've added a new router as a monitored device, and events are being received from "Unknown Reporting Device IP." Why is this?

- Why are the logs from my Check Point firewall not being understood by MARS?

- How can I determine how long the events and incidents I've already collected will remain accessible on my MARS appliance?

- Why don't e-mail notifications sent to the Admin Group arrive?

- Why isn't MARS receiving events from some devices?

These questions are answered in the following sections.

Unknown Reporting Device IP

When your event logs contain entries from unknown reporting devices, this usually means that a device is configured to send logs to MARS, but MARS isn't configured to receive them. You might have also simply forgotten to click the **Activate** button at the upper-right corner of the MARS screen. If you're sure that you've correctly configured MARS to receive logs from a device, but they are still showing up from an unknown reporting device, try activating your changes.

Figure 9-3 shows an example of what your logs look like with an unknown reporting device. Note that these types of logs show up only when you look at raw events. Figure 9-4 shows how to select **All Matching Event Raw Messages** from the Query page.

Figure 9-3 *Unknown Reporting Device IP*

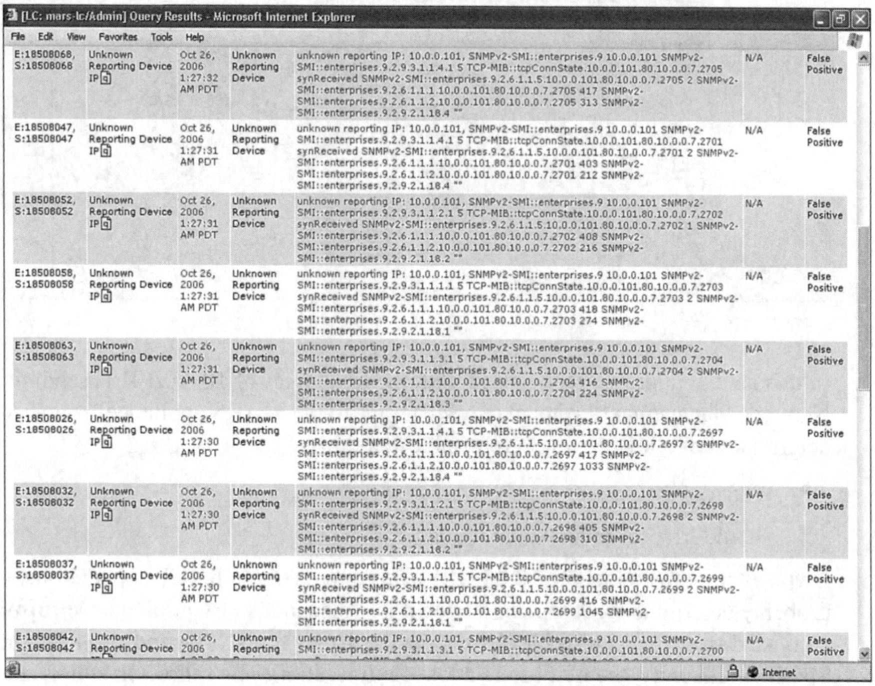

Figure 9-4 *All Matching Event Raw Messages*

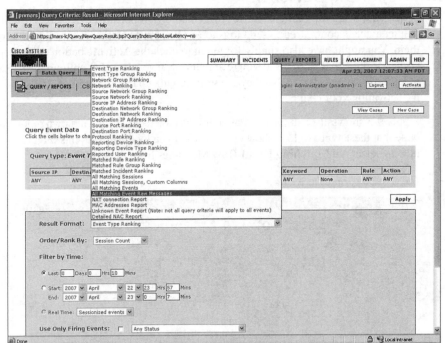

In this case, it appears that a device with the IP address of 10.0.0.101 is sending Simple Network Management Protocol (SNMP) traps to the MARS appliance. You need to determine the following things to troubleshoot this:

- What device is this?
- Should MARS understand the logs?

If you attempt to connect to 10.0.0.101 using some common TCP applications, you can probably determine what type of device it is. You can also try issuing an **snmpwalk** command from the MARS CLI. If the device listens for SNMP, and you have the correct SNMP community, the CLI offers a lot of information. The following command can help:

```
snmpwalk -c community_name 10.0.0.101
```

The **snmpwalk** command has several available options. To see them all, just enter the command by itself at the CLI.

In this instance, you determine that the host is a Cisco wireless access point. MARS does not know how to understand logs from this device, and you need to create custom parsing rules to handle logs from these types of devices. This is covered in Chapter 11, "CS-MARS Custom Parser."

You might see these logs at other times, though, when you already think the device should be properly configured. Consider an example Cisco IOS Router. This router might have a handful of interfaces, each with its own IP address:

- Loopback 0: 192.168.254.1
- Ethernet0/1: 10.1.1.1
- Ethernet0/2: 10.2.1.1
- Ethernet0/3: 10.3.1.1

When this device is added to CS-MARS as a monitored device, you probably needed to specify the following two IP addresses:

- **One for the access IP**—The access IP address is used for MARS to connect to the router for discovery purposes, such as learning the directly connected networks.

- **One for the reporting IP**—The reporting IP address associates logs with the proper device.

The access IP address should be the IP address that MARS can reach to perform discoveries, and to pull data if that's the reporting method. For simplicity, many organizations use the loopback address. In this case, you might have configured the access IP address to be 192.168.254.1.

Unless otherwise configured, Cisco routers send syslog messages stamped with the IP address of the interface that sends the message. So, unless you've configured it to do differently, the syslog messages are being sent to MARS from one of the other addresses— 10.1.1.1, 10.2.1.1, or 10.3.1.1. If you configured MARS to use 192.168.254.1 as the reporting IP address, syslog messages will appear as "Unknown Reporting Device IP." Even if you entered a different address, if a network issue causes messages to leave the router from a different interface, the messages will still be from an unknown reporting device IP.

On the IOS Router, you need to always specify what IP address to use for syslog messages. If you want continuity, and you've configured the loopback interface for access IP, use the same interface for reporting IP. On the router, enter the following commands in configuration mode:

```
logging source-interface loopback 0
```

Obviously, you can substitute the exact interface you want to use. When this router is configured within MARS, make sure that the IP address associated with this *source-interface* is entered as the reporting address.

NOTE   If MARS is receiving NetFlow data from this router or switch, be sure that it is also configured to send from the same source interface. If it is not, all NetFlow data will show up as "Unknown Reporting Device IP" as well.

Check Point or Other Logs Are Incorrectly Parsed

It is common for at least some log entries to appear as "Unknown Device Event Type." This often occurs when a rarely used log message is seen, or when a new feature is introduced for a device, but MARS does not yet understand the log messages. However, when you've configured a supported device to send logs to MARS, and you've configured MARS to receive the logs, but all events show up as Unknowns, something has been improperly configured.

This problem is most often seen when security software, such as Check Point's firewall software, is running on a general-purpose operating system. Check Point is used here as an example, but this issue can occur on any reporting application.

A common mistake made by MARS administrators is to specify the underlying operating system of these security applications when adding the firewall as a monitored application. Figure 9-5 shows the process of adding a Check Point firewall to MARS. Be sure to select **Generic** from the Operating System drop-down list. Even though this particular firewall is running in Linux or Windows, you do not want to specify that. If you do, MARS will attempt to parse all logs from the firewall in the format that that particular operating system sends OS logs.

Figure 9-5 *When Adding a Software-Based Monitored Application, Such as Check Point, Leave the Operating System Set to Generic*

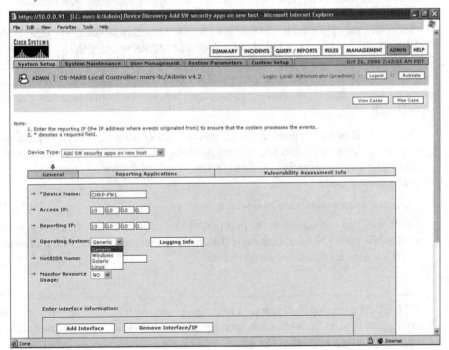

New Monitored Device Logs Still Not Parsed

Anytime you've added a new device, application, custom parser, or similar thing to MARS, make sure to click the **Activate** button at the upper-right corner of the MARS screen. This button appears on every screen. This is one of the most common resolutions seen by the Cisco TAC. Try to make a point of activating your changes frequently.

You can try the following solutions when you appear to have communications problems between MARS and monitored devices:

- Issue the **tcpdump** command from the MARS command line. This shows you an entry on the command line each time traffic arrives at MARS. You can filter the results to only show traffic arriving from the device in question. If you do not see traffic arriving, and you think you should, a device misconfiguration or network issue is probably to blame. Figure 9-6 shows an example.

- Try connecting from the MARS command line to the monitored device using the connection method you're expecting the devices to use. For example, if MARS should be trying to telnet to the device, manually try to telnet from the MARS CLI. Figure 9-7 shows an example.

- Run a query from the MARS Query page, and select **Raw events** from the Real Time drop-down list. You should select **All Matching Event Raw Messages** also. This creates a scrolling page that continually updates as events you're interested in arrive at MARS. Figure 9-8 shows an example. Note that you should further filter this query to look only at a single device or type of device.

Figure 9-6 *Use the **tcpdump** Command to Troubleshoot Device Communications*

Figure 9-7 *Command-Line Telnet*

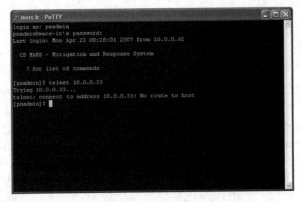

Figure 9-8 *Real-Time Event Viewer for Troubleshooting Devices*

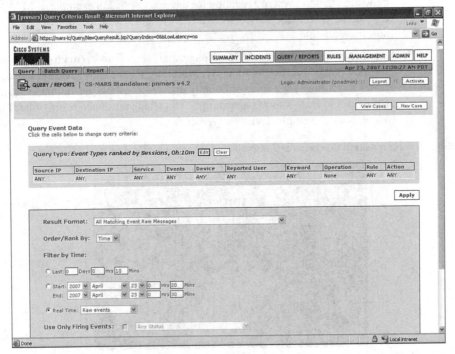

How Much Storage Is Being Used, and How Long Will It Last?

These are common questions. How easily can you determine how much storage is currently in use on your MARS appliance? Also, how long will your events, sessions, and incidents remain on your appliance before they are overwritten?

As of the MARS 4.2 software releases, you cannot answer these questions from the web interface. Instead, you need to log in from the command line. Remember that only the pnadmin user can Secure Shell (SSH) to a MARS appliance.

The **diskusage** command can answer the first question. If you are familiar with Linux or other UNIX variants, the **diskusage** command is identical to the **df** command. It shows the size of each of the file systems and how much space is available on them. Additionally, if archiving is enabled, it shows how much space exists on the archive server:

```
[pnadmin]$ diskusage
Filesystem          Size  Used Avail Use% Mounted on
/dev/sda3            20G  1.4G   17G   8% /
/dev/sda1           129M   14M  108M  12% /boot
/dev/sda6            20G   49M   18G   1% /log
/dev/sda5            20G  1.1G   17G   6% /opt
/dev/sda7            29G   36M   27G   1% /pnarchive
none                1.9G     0  1.9G   0% /dev/shm
/dev/sda8            20G  2.5G   16G  13% /u01
/dev/sda10          795G   22G  765G   3% /u02
/dev/sda9           9.8G  8.1G  1.3G  87% /u03
10.0.0.120:/nfs/mars-lc
                    130G   87G   37G  70% /mnt/pnarchive
```

The preceding example shows the **diskusage** command on a MARS-200. Notice that the archive location is shown. The /dev/sda10 file system, which is mounted on /u02, is the file system used for storing event, session, and incident information. You can determine this because it is a much larger file system than the others on the appliance. Out of 795 GB available storage, you've only used 22 GB.

The **pndbusage** command calculates how long data will remain on your appliance, based on the events-per-second (eps) rate you've seen to date. The following example shows output from this command:

```
[pnadmin]$ pndbusage
Current partition started on Fri Oct  6 00:39:25 PDT 2006 and uses 2.76% of its
available capacity.
   Switching to next partition is estimated for Thu Oct  2 11:53:22 PDT 2008.
9 empty partitions are available for storage
```

At the current eps rate, this MARS appliance will maintain data for more than two years.

E-Mail Notifications Sent to Admin Group Never Arrive

Several things can cause e-mail notifications to fail to arrive. First, try sending a report or notification to a single user.

If all e-mail notifications are failing, your problem is related to the Simple Mail Transfer Protocol (SMTP) configuration within MARS, or with your SMTP server that accepts e-mail from MARS. Verify the settings by clicking the **ADMIN** button, and then clicking the **System Setup** tab to reach the screen shown in Figure 9-9.

Figure 9-9 *SMTP Settings*

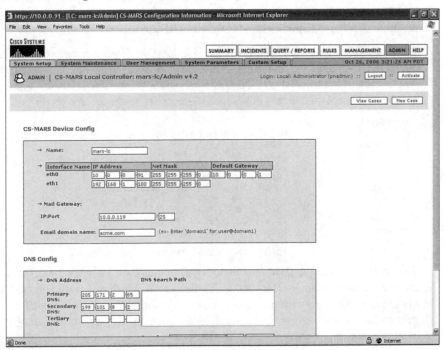

If all e-mail notifications appear to work fine, except e-mail to the Admin Group (as a group), the problem is most likely a missing e-mail address for the pnadmin user. Click the **MANAGEMENT** button, and then click the **User Management** tab. Select the check box for the pnadmin user and click the **Edit** button. From the screen shown in Figure 9-10, ensure that a valid e-mail address is shown.

Figure 9-10 *Verify Valid E-Mail Address for pnadmin User*

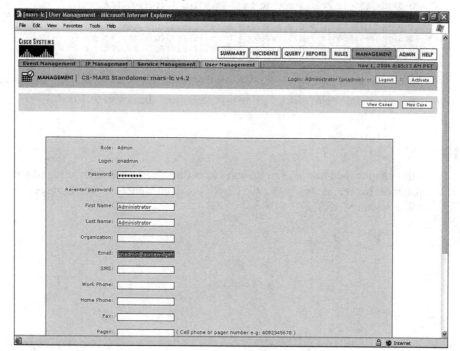

MARS Is Not Receiving Events from Devices

If MARS does not appear to be receiving events from monitored devices, this is typically caused by a network problem, or by having both Ethernet interfaces connected at the same time. If you need to use both interfaces, make sure that you only need a single default gateway. MARS cannot use a default gateway per interface.

You need to verify that the Ethernet interface is connected, and then see whether any traffic is reaching MARS.

From the CLI, use the **ifconfig** command to verify basic connectivity to the network infrastructure. This command shows you whether the interfaces are up and whether they are transmitting and receiving packets.

You can use the **tcpdump** command to see what traffic is reaching the MARS appliance. This command is a standard open source application, and it uses all common **tcpdump** filters and expressions.

If you are using SSH to access the CLI, you must filter out your own IP address from **tcpdump**. Otherwise, you'll simply see your own traffic, and you won't see event data. Try issuing the following command (for this example, assume that your IP address is 10.0.0.7):

```
[pnadmin]$ tcpdump host not 10.0.0.7
03:37:54.555460 802.1d config 8000.00:07:eb:1a:be:00.8012 root
  8000.00:07:eb:1a:be:00 pathcost 0 age 0 max 20 hello 2 fdelay 15
03:37:54.648459 10.0.0.1.syslog > mars-lc.syslog:   udp 129
03:37:54.648460 10.0.0.1.syslog > mars-lc.syslog:   udp 78
03:37:54.661457 10.0.0.1.syslog > mars-lc.syslog:   udp 60
03:37:54.661458 10.0.0.1.syslog > mars-lc.syslog:   udp 106
03:37:54.661459 10.0.0.1.syslog > mars-lc.syslog:   udp 155
03:37:54.721956 802.1Q vlan#101 P7 1:0:c:cc:cc:cd > 0:7:eb:1a:be:6 sap aa ui/C
```

In this example, you're seeing syslog messages from the device at 10.0.0.1.

Summary

In this chapter, you learned several ways to perform basic troubleshooting of your MARS appliance. Remember to contact the Cisco TAC immediately if something appears to be broken within MARS.

## CHAPTER 10

Network Admission Control

Network Admission Control (NAC) is a technology that allows the network to check endpoints for compliance with your network security policy. NAC is an industrywide effort and is led by Cisco.

Your security policy might require that all Windows computers adhere to a base level of security and patching. For example, you might require that your computers do the following:

- Run antivirus (AV) software, which must be updated to the latest version and scanning capabilities
- Run a personal firewall, such as Cisco Security Agent
- Be patched to the latest Microsoft service pack and hot fix
- Be owned by the company, rather than by the employee
- Not have certain undesirable applications installed or running
- Run only an approved version of Windows or other operating system
- Run only an approved image of the operating system

Each of these requirements can be enforced with Network Admission Control. NAC is powerful, and it puts teeth into a written security policy. Each of these requirements can be enforced, if you desire, before the user can access your company's network.

NAC is flexible to meet your requirements. By gaining the ability to posture-check hosts before they access your network, you are better able to protect against a wide range of threats and to provide the following additional benefits:

- Prevention of network access from untrusted endpoints
- Prevention of "contagious" endpoints from infecting other hosts on the network with known and unknown worms and viruses
- Increased network availability, resilience, and productivity by improving the network's capability to adapt to threats
- Providing guests (vendors and visitors) with Internet access without threat to your network and hosts

With NAC, your wired, wireless, or remote-access network gains significant protections against various threats. When a host is out of compliance with the policies, you have the flexibility to either permit certain or all traffic, deny the traffic, quarantine the host, or provide restricted access for a period of time required to bring the host back into compliance. This could mean allowing the host to access the Windows Update website. It could also mean providing a remediation server that contains a minimum level of software.

Types of Cisco NAC

Cisco NAC currently comes in the following flavors:

- NAC Framework
- NAC Appliance

NAC Framework uses Cisco routers, switches, and firewalls as network access devices (NAD), which communicate with a Cisco Trust Agent (CTA). The CTA is installed on each endpoint and is the agent that queries the operating system and installed software on the computer. Cisco Secure Access Control Server (CS-ACS) functions as the policy control point and is the point of origin where the security policy is defined.

NAC Appliance is a simplified, appliance-based NAC. With NAC Appliance, an appliance is used as the NAD. The appliance can be placed in-line or out-of-band, depending on the needs of the customer. When a NAC Appliance is installed in-line, it functions much as a policy enforcement firewall. Only hosts that meet your security policy requirements are allowed to communicate through the appliance. Others are quarantined or otherwise restricted. When the NAC Appliance is running in out-of-band mode, it is temporarily inserted into the path of a host's communications when that host attempts to connect to the network. After the host is successfully posture-checked, the NAC Appliance is taken out of the communications path.

With NAC Appliance, the central policy is defined on a separate appliance called the *NAC Manager*. The NAC Manager periodically connects to Cisco to pull the latest information regarding patches, antivirus appliances, and more.

Both NAC Framework and NAC Appliance accomplish the same thing. They both posture-check hosts that attempt to use your network and enforce your security policy. You should study both to determine which method of NAC best fits your needs.

The Cisco Security Monitoring, Analysis, and Response System (CS-MARS) currently can report on NAC activities that are reported by NAC Framework. However, it is expected that NAC Appliance will soon be supported also.

NAC Framework Host Conditions

Both NAC Framework and NAC Appliance assign tokens to describe the posture of each host that is checked by NAC. With NAC Framework, these tokens are passed to the NAD, which is preconfigured with network access policies for each token.

The tokens in the list that follows are supported with NAC Framework. Remember that NAC doesn't mandate a particular action or permission based on the posture token. The descriptions that follow are simply recommendations. NAC is a flexible technology, and it allows you to determine the proper action or permission based on reported posture tokens:

- **Healthy**—The endpoint device complies with the security policy, and no restrictions are needed for this device.

- **Checkup**—The endpoint device is within policy, but does not have the latest software. NAC recommends that the host be updated. The Checkup token is useful for triggering an automatic remediation, such as instructing the antivirus software to auto-update itself.

- **Transition**—The endpoint device is in the process of being postured. This token is seen when the host is booting, and not all services might be running. Posture results are not yet available.

- **Quarantine**—The endpoint device is severely out of compliance and needs to be quarantined from the rest of the network for remediation. The device does not appear to be infecting or attacking other hosts, but is vulnerable to infection or attack from others.

- **Infected**—The endpoint device is an active threat to other systems. Network access should be severely restricted or prevented.

- **Unknown**—NAC cannot posture-check this endpoint.

Understanding NAC Framework Communications

Although this chapter isn't meant to be a tutorial on NAC, it is helpful to have a basic understanding of how NAC Framework functions. Be aware that the descriptions provided are applicable to NAC Framework only. NAC Appliance functions similarly, but also contains significant differences in how the various components communicate, as described in the sections that follow.

Endpoint, or Personal Computer

You must install an agent, known as the Cisco Trust Agent (CTA), on each computer that is going to be posture-checked. This agent is responsible for communicating with the operating system, antivirus applications, personal firewalls, and other software that NAC will be checking. The CTA also communicates with an 802.1x supplicant, if one is installed on the computer.

CTA is included in several other software applications, including Cisco Security Agent (CSA) and some antivirus applications.

NOTE   The 802.1x protocol is a standard, port-based, network access control protocol. This means that it performs authentications of the computer and user before the host receives an IP address through Dynamic Host Configuration Protocol (DHCP). This contrasts with NAC, which relies on IP for authentication and posture checking.

To support 802.1x in your network, you must have a network infrastructure that supports it, and you must also have operating system support, or a supplicant installed on each computer.

The 802.1x protocol is commonly used to secure enterprise wireless networks.

Supplicants securely authenticate to the network, whether wired or wireless, before being granted access to the network. Authentication (through the supplicant) and posture checking (through the CTA) are natural components to combine. In fact, some supplicant vendors, as well as antivirus vendors, include the CTA as part of their individual products. Cisco offers CTA at no charge to anyone wanting to use it.

The CTA communicates with the NAD securely, using either Extensible Authentication Protocol (EAP) over 802.1x or over User Datagram Protocol (UDP).

Network Access Devices (NAD)

NADs are Cisco access routers, Virtual Private Network (VPN) gateways (VPN 3000 series), PIX and ASA firewalls, Catalyst switches, and wireless access points that are configured to watch for endpoints that are required to be posture-checked.

Posture checking is triggered when a host becomes active on the network or when a host begins communicating through a Layer 3 device. For example, posture checking would be triggered when a host is connected to a switch or when a VPN tunnel is established to a VPN device or firewall.

The NAD communicates to the CTA on the endpoint using EAP over either UDP or 802.1x. The NAD communicates also to the authentication, authorization, and accounting (AAA) server.

AAA Server

Cisco Secure ACS is the Cisco AAA server with support for NAC. The AAA server functions as the policy decision point. This is where individual checks are defined that determine the posture tokens assigned to endpoints.

Communication between the NAD and the AAA server is through Remote Authentication Dial-In User Service (RADIUS). The AAA server can optionally communicate with a posture validation server.

Posture Validation Server

In a large environment, it would be tedious to regularly update the checks and policies defined in the AAA server. Rather than manually define antivirus scan engine versions, .dat file versions, and dates, it is much more scalable to simply delegate this function to a third-party posture validation server. This is a server, such as McAfee's or Trend Micro's antivirus management station, that already keeps track of the most recent information regarding the antivirus versions and dates. The AAA server can gain access to this information by configuring Host Credentials Authorization Protocol (HCAP).

Putting It All Together

The following steps describe a sample posture check, using NAC Framework:

1 A payroll clerk logs in to her computer at ACME Gadgets and Gizmos. Because the network doesn't yet know and trust this host, it is temporarily placed in an isolated VLAN.

2 The EAP supplicant verifies that the computer is owned by ACME Gadgets and Gizmos and passes the user's Windows authentication seamlessly to Cisco Secure ACS.

3 Upon successful authentication, the Cisco switch, functioning as a NAD, challenges the CTA on the computer for posture information, using EAP over 802.1x. It requests Windows operating system versions and information, as well as hot fixes and antivirus information.

4 The CTA on the computer verifies the authenticity of the NAD and passes the requested information back to the NAD using EAP over 802.1x.

5 The switch passes the information directly to Cisco Secure ACS, using the RADIUS protocol.

6 Cisco Secure ACS receives the information and consults the defined posture rules.

7 The policy is configured to require Trend Micro antivirus, with all files current to within two days. Using HCAP, ACS queries Trend Micro's AV server for valid versions.

8 If the host is compliant with the requirements, ACS uses RADIUS to assign a Healthy token and provide it to the Cisco switch.

9 The switch returns Healthy to the CTA on the PC, using EAP over 802.1x, and also changes the switch port to the Payroll VLAN, which is where the end user works.

The entire process takes just 1–2 seconds.

Configuration of CS-MARS for NAC Framework Reporting

CS-MARS has built-in capabilities for monitoring 802.1x and Network Admission Control log messages; however, this is not a core reason for deploying MARS.

MARS can parse, normalize, correlate, and report on NAC and 802.1x events from Cisco IOS and CatOS switches and from Cisco Secure ACS. This allows you to troubleshoot and report on authentication, host posture, and communications between ACS and external databases, such as Windows Active Directory.

To provide these reporting capabilities, you must perform the following steps:

Step 1 Add the switches and any routers to MARS as reporting devices.

Step 2 Enable DHCP snooping on the switches.

Step 3 Add the CS-ACS as a reporting device. Depending on the version of ACS, this might require installation of a free agent on the ACS server. You can download the agent from Cisco.com.

Information Available on CS-MARS

After the devices and MARS are configured for NAC and 802.1x monitoring, the reports MARS has for NAC become useful. Remember that you might need to schedule them to run on a regular basis.

Figure 10-1 shows a report showing all healthy hosts, sorted by authenticated usernames.

Figure 10-1 *Report: Healthy Secure Posture*

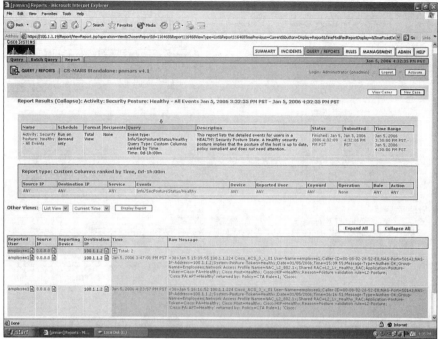

Figure 10-2, on the other hand, shows a report for hosts that are not in a healthy posture. In this example, the host used by username employee1 has failed the posture check for Cisco Security Agent. The Cisco:HIP check places the computer in a quarantine posture. HIP stands for host intrusion prevention.

Figure 10-2 *Report: Not Healthy Security Posture*

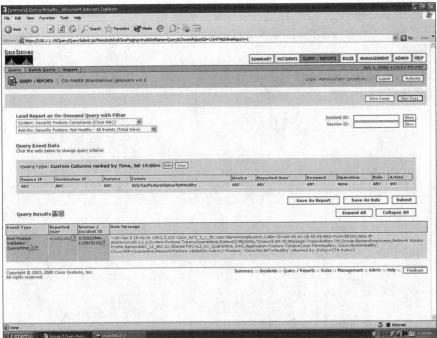

Summary

Network Admission Control is a powerful feature to enable on your network. NAC provides key protections to help prevent your computers from being infected or attacked. Additionally, it can provide guest access, and it allows the network to enforce your written security policies.

CS-MARS natively supports the Cisco NAC Framework and provides valuable troubleshooting capabilities.

## CHAPTER 11

CS-MARS Custom Parser

What do you do when you want to collect logs from an unsupported device? Consider the following examples:

- A firewall that isn't natively supported
- Antispam software on your mail server
- Application logs on a Windows server

The custom parser allows you to define new devices and applications for reporting to the Cisco Security Monitoring, Analysis, and Response System (CS-MARS). This process takes three or four steps, depending on what you're hoping to accomplish:

Step 1 **Define the device or application**—This is a simple name, model, and version that tie the parser together.

Step 2 **Create parser templates**—The parser templates are instructions to MARS about how to interpret the individual log messages.

Step 3 **Define rules**—This step is optional. It depends on whether you simply want the ability to run reports or whether you want to create incidents based on the log messages you've interpreted from Step 2.

Step 4 **Create or modify reports**—Depending on your needs, you might need to create new reports. You might also need to modify existing reports.

After you have defined the custom parser, MARS can understand the log messages. You can either use existing reports and queries with the messages, or you can create your own. Use what fits your needs.

Using the custom parser to create your own device support is not difficult. In fact, after you've done it a few times, it gets pretty easy. However, you need to think about the goal you want to accomplish:

- Are you looking for new rules that can trigger incidents?
- Are you simply looking for a way to periodically run reports?
- Are you looking for a way to easily match certain keywords in log messages?

Each of these goals might change the way you parse messages, or at the very least, determine what types of rules and reports you'll use.

This chapter uses sendmail logs as an example. The sendmail server that we're using is also running Clam Antivirus. Both sendmail and ClamAV are open source applications. Sendmail is one of the most popular Simple Mail Transfer Protocol (SMTP) mail servers, and ClamAV is a popular antivirus application that prevents viruses, worms, and phishing e-mails.

Why would you send sendmail logs to MARS? Maybe your company wants to track the percentage of clean e-mails versus those with viruses. Maybe it's to help locate machines within the network that are sending viruses. In this example, the mail server runs ClamAV, which is a commonly used open source antivirus application. The goal is to determine the ratio of clean to infected e-mails, as well as to see whether e-mail tends to come from specific source machines or networks.

The goal in monitoring sendmail and ClamAV is to track the number of clean e-mails compared to those with viruses, worms, and phishing.

Getting Messages to CS-MARS

The first step in creating your custom parser is to send log messages to MARS. MARS supports the following two protocols for this:

- Syslog
- SNMP Trap

Syslog is probably the easiest to use, primarily because the log messages tend to be easier to understand. Simple Network Management Protocol (SNMP) traps tend to be more cryptic and rely on codes to explain a message. These are general statements, however, and might not be the case with the device or software you're using.

Most UNIX and Linux hosts have built-in syslog support, extending to individual applications running on the host. Windows hosts don't have the robust logging support that UNIX and Linux hosts have. For this reason, many people turn to open source tools, such as Snare, which allows flexible syslogging of both operating system event logs and text file application logs.

When you begin sending logs to MARS from an unsupported application or device, MARS cannot understand the messages. They show up in the event log as Unknown Device Event Type messages. Figure 11-1 shows the entry required in Linux to send mail logs to MARS. This file is /etc/syslog.conf. The @mars text assumes that the server can resolve mars to an IP address. In the sample network, the MARS appliance has an IP address of 10.0.0.91. The line in the file could also have @10.0.0.91.

Figure 11-1 *Configuring /etc/syslog.conf to Send Mail Logs to MARS*

Figure 11-2 shows a query for All Matching Events, Raw Messages, when syslog is enabled for sendmail logs from a Linux host named groo. As discussed in earlier chapters, to get here, click the **QUERY/REPORTS** button, and then click the **Edit** button.

Figure 11-2 *Unknown Device Event Types for Sendmail Messages*

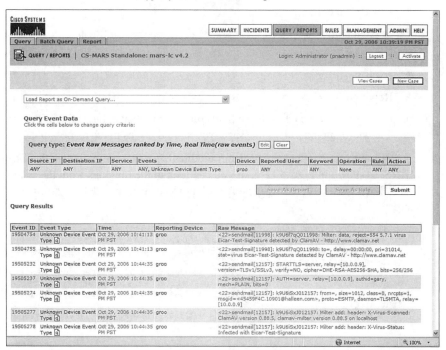

Determining What to Parse

After you have the events being sent to MARS, the next thing you want to do is determine what types of messages you need to parse, and what information you need from each message. As you look through these messages, you need to understand what fields are available within MARS to store the information.

The following fields are available within MARS:

- Source Address
- Destination Address
- Source Port
- Destination Port
- Protocol
- NAT Source Address
- NAT Destination Address
- NAT Source Port
- NAT Destination Port
- Device Time Stamp
- Session Duration
- Received Time Stamp
- Exchanged Bytes
- Reported User

You don't need to use each of these fields on every message, but if the information is available within an individual message, you should use as much as possible.

Look at some of the raw messages from sendmail. You can either look at them from within MARS, as shown in Figure 11-2, or you can look at the raw logs from the sendmail host. The following is a series of log messages of a successful e-mail delivery from a remote mail server:

```
Oct 30 00:40:37 groo sendmail[13757]: k9U8eax9013757:
  from=<someone@acmegadgets.com>, size=1965, class=0, nrcpts=1,
  msgid=<8C8CA163230D91E-228-950A@WEBMAIL.acme.com>, proto=ESMTP, daemon=MTA,
  relay=m.mx.acme.com [10.12.138.207]
Oct 30 00:40:37 groo sendmail[13757]: k9U8eax9013757: Milter add: header: X-Virus-
  Scanned: ClamAV version 0.88.5, clamav-milter version 0.88.5 on localhost
Oct 30 00:40:37 groo sendmail[13757]: k9U8eax9013757: Milter add: header: X-Virus-
  Status: Clean
Oct 30 00:40:43 groo sendmail[13760]: k9U8eax9013757: to=<gary@acmewidgets.net>,
  delay=00:00:06, xdelay=00:00:06, mailer=local, pri=32262, dsn=2.0.0, stat=Sent
```

The first message shows who the message is from, a unique identifying text, the protocol used, how many are bytes in the message, and the IP address of the sending server.

The second message uses the same identifying text and shows you that the message has been scanned with ClamAV.

The third message shows that the message does not contain a virus. Notice that it still has the same identifying text.

The last message shows you that the e-mail was delivered successfully.

If you look at other messages, you can see what a message that is not clean from viruses or malicious code looks like:

```
Oct 29 20:50:40 groo sendmail[9949]: k9U4obqJ009949: Milter add: header: X-Virus-
     Status: Infected with HTML.Phishing.Bank-626
Oct 29 20:50:40 groo sendmail[9949]: k9U4obqJ009949: Milter: data, reject=554 5.7.1
     virus HTML.Phishing.Bank-626 detected by ClamAV - http://www.clamav.net
Oct 29 22:41:07 groo sendmail[11998]: k9U6f7qQ011998: Milter add: header: X-Virus-
     Status: Infected with Eicar-Test-Signature
Oct 29 22:41:07 groo sendmail[11998]: k9U6f7qQ011998: Milter: data, reject=554 5.7.1
     virus Eicar-Test-Signature detected by ClamAV - http://www.clamav.net
```

Now, you see that when a virus or malicious code, such as a phishing e-mail, is detected, ClamAV does a couple things in the logs. First, as shown in the first and third lines, the log contains a Virus-Status of Infected. Next, it provides a rejection code (554). You can use this information when creating rules and reports.

You might find additional messages that you'll need to parse, but this provides a good start.

Adding the Device or Application Type

You're ready to begin configuring MARS to parse events from sendmail. The first step is to define the application or device you're using. Because you're logging from an application called sendmail on a Linux host, you add it as an application instead of a device.

Click the **ADMIN** button, and then click the **Custom Setup** tab to open the window shown in Figure 11-3.

Click **User Defined Log Parser Templates**, and then click the **Add** button to open the window shown in Figure 11-4.

Figure 11-3 *MARS Custom Setup*

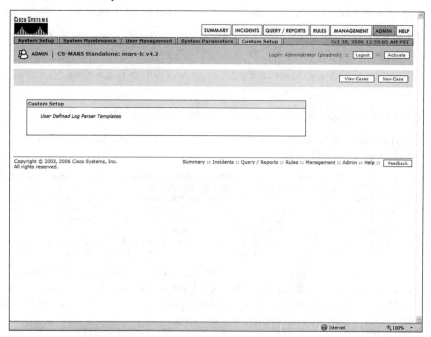

Figure 11-4 *Add Software Type Definition*

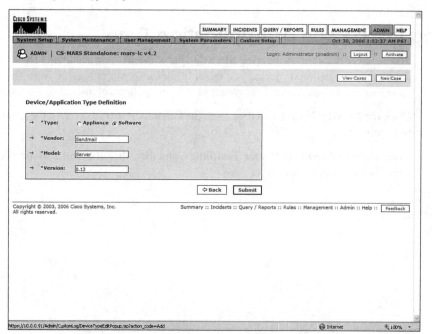

Fill in a type, vendor, model, and version in the available text boxes, and then click the **Submit** button. You're now ready to begin adding in the individual log templates, as Figure 11-5 shows.

Figure 11-5 *Ready to Add Log Templates*

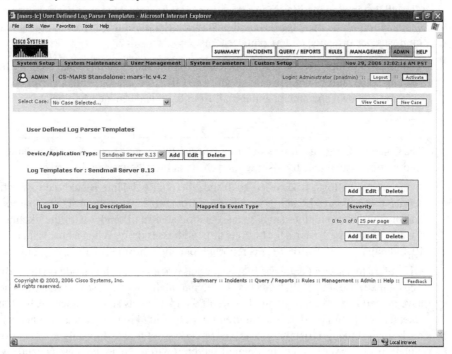

Adding Log Templates

As you read through your sample log messages, try to determine what fields you need in your rules, queries, and reports. Where are the IP addresses? Where are the port numbers? Do you need certain fields but can't find a good place to put them?

Also, as you're studying the sample log messages, determine what text exists within each message that makes it different from other messages. Each position in the log template is used to either find and store a value, or to find some text to make the message unique. Usually it's pretty easy to find the differences, but occasionally it's more difficult. MARS uses regular expressions to perform the string matches. Look at the following example. These logs are from the Cisco Content Security and Control (CSC) Module for the ASA firewalls:

```
<158>Nov 30 22:43:58 CSC-SSM is-nrs: 2006/11/30 22:53:58¦10.97.245.59¦RBL-Pass¦QIL-
Fail¦RejectWithErrorCode-450¦
```

```
<158>Nov 30 22:46:35 CSC-SSM is-nrs: 2006/11/30 22:46:35¦10.3.16.47¦RBL-Fail¦QIL-
NA¦RejectWithErrorCode-550¦
```

These logs are similar, but some of the text is a bit different. The Cisco CSC Module supports a feature called Network Reputation Services, which compares IP addresses from which e-mail messages are sent with a constantly updated database of known spammers. This allows immediate filtering of spam e-mail messages prior to performing any content examination of the message. Using the Network Reputation Services feature greatly improves performance of antispam systems.

The first log, which uses an error code of 450, is for sites that have just recently begun sending spam and are not permanently blocked. The second log, with an error code of 550, is for well-known spammers, and e-mail from them is permanently blocked.

NOTE   The Cisco CSC Module uses software provided by Trend Micro. A large amount of information is available by visiting its website at http://www.trendmicro.com.

In the preceding logs, **RBL** refers to Trend Micro's Real-Time Blackhole List, which is a service that validates IP addresses against a Domain Name System (DNS)–based comprehensive reputation database, associating an e-mail sender with the likelihood that the e-mail is spam. RBL tracks billions of IP addresses daily. When a host is matched in the RBL database, a 550 error code is returned, placing a host permanently in a blocked state.

QIL refers to a second database that is queried when no match is made on the RBL query. The Quick IP Lookup (QIL) database is a dynamic threat database that identifies hosts that have recently been sending spam but aren't well known as spam senders. A host that was recently compromised or misconfigured might be found in this database. When a match is made against the QIL database, a 450 error code is returned, resulting in a rejection of the e-mail. If the server is a legitimate mail server, it will requeue the message and try again later.

It would make sense to use the RBL and QIL fields to differentiate the two messages from each other. For simplicity of running reports later, it might make sense to store the 450 and 550 values in either a source or destination port or protocol number.

First Log Template

Make sure that the new application is selected and click the **Add** button within the Log Templates box. This lets you begin defining the individual log messages.

Because you're not going to use an existing event definition, you need to create your own. At the bottom of the page, click the **Add** button and create a new definition, similar to what Figure 11-6 shows.

Figure 11-6 *Create New Event Definition*

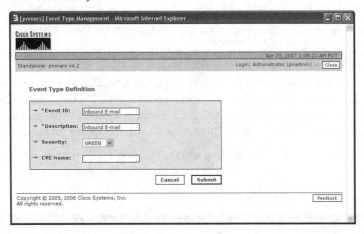

Select the new event type in the right panel and move it to the left (see Figure 11-7). The selector button, which moves the event type to the left, looks like two arrows and is placed in the center of the screen. Click the **Apply** button, and then click the **Patterns** button.

Figure 11-7 *Choose Event Definition*

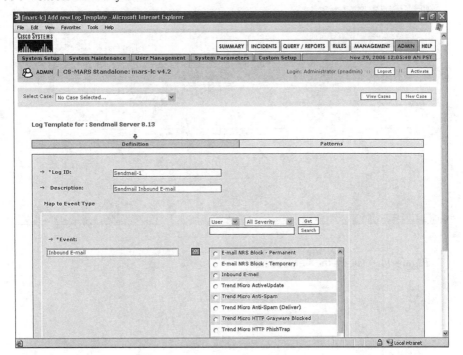

You're now ready to define the various fields to use in the log message. Look at the log message, as it is arriving on MARS:

```
parsing error: <22>sendmail[7566]: kAT88q0M007566: from=<fred@acmegadgets.com>,
size=1849, class=-60, nrcpts=1,
msgid=<076879756C476F6873736C6C75356A767474589560@acmegadgets.com>, proto=SMTP,
daemon=MTA, relay=smtp.acme.com [10.216.88.43]
```

The first field you'll parse is the number that appears after **sendmail[**. You need to parse this because it is a common number that appears in all log messages related to the same e-mail message. Because MARS doesn't have a generic field you can use for this, you need to reuse one of the other fields. In this case, use the Source Port field.

Click the **Add** button. You need to add the Position 1 information in the screen shown in Figure 11-8.

Figure 11-8 *Add Position 1 (Message Number)*

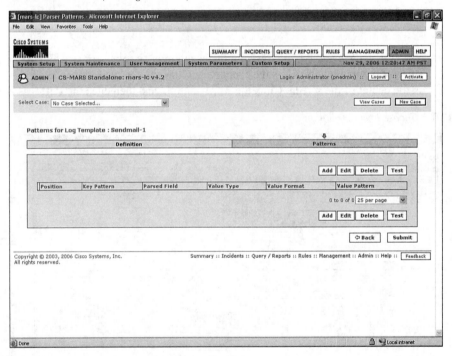

Figure 11-9 shows the fields to add.

Figure 11-9 *Parsed Fields*

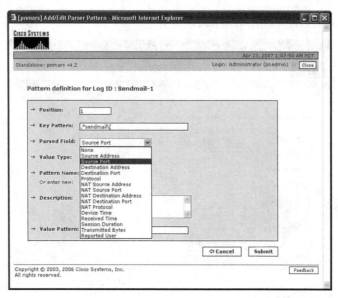

- **Position—1** means that this is the first field you're looking for in the log message.
- **Key Pattern**—This is the text you're looking for. In regular expressions (regex), the period (.) is a wildcard that can replace any single character or white space. The asterisk (*) is the counter of how many characters you're looking for. By combining these into **.***, you're saying to match on any number of any character, followed by **sendmail**, all in lowercase characters and followed by a left bracket ([). A backslash (\) is added prior to the left bracket to ensure that the left bracket is interpreted literally. Good documentation of the Perl Compatible Regular Expressions (PCRE) library and regular expressions can be found at http://www.pcre.org.
- **Parsed Field**—Click the drop-down list and select the type of field this is. **Source Port** is selected in Figure 11-9.
- **Value Type**—Value type means to describe what the value looks like in the raw log message. The choices are **Port (Number)** and **Port (String)**. Because the log message for this example shows a number after the word **sendmail**, select **Port (Number)**.
- **Pattern Name**—This allows you to select how you want the parsed value to appear in MARS. Your choices here are **None** and **PORT_NUMBER**. Select **PORT_NUMBER** to auto-fill the remaining fields on the form.

Figure 11-10 shows the completed pattern definition.

Figure 11-10 *Completed Pattern Definition for Position 1*

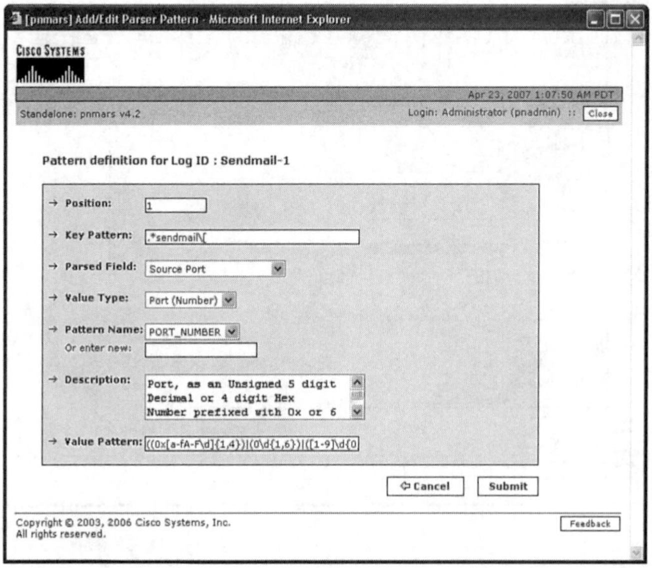

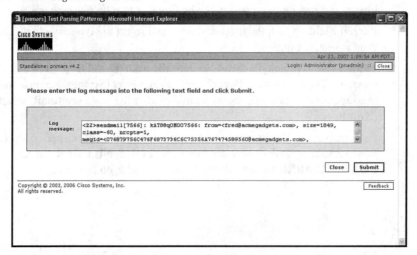

Now, it's a good idea to test the initial parse of the message. Click the **Test** button, as shown previously in Figure 11-8. Each time you complete a pattern definition, you'll see the option for a test.

Paste the first log message into the text box, as shown in Figure 11-11, and click the **Submit** button.

Figure 11-11 *Paste Log Message to Test*

If all has gone well, you should see a screen like Figure 11-12, showing that the source port was successfully parsed. If you do not correctly parse the value, and if you don't see a status of **Ok** for each line, rework this parsing template until it is correct.

Figure 11-12   *Source Port (SMTP Message Number) Successfully Parsed*

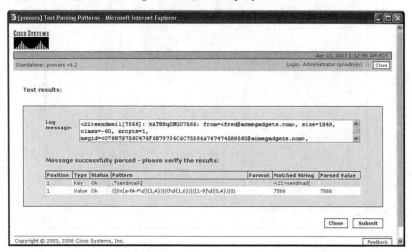

Now, you need to repeat this process for all the other fields you are going to use. The next field to parse is the value that appears after **size=**. Here's the log message again:

```
parsing error: <22>sendmail[7566]: kAT88q0M007566: from=<fred@acmegadgets.com>,
  size=1849, class=-60, nrcpts=1,
  msgid=<076879756C476F6873736C6C75356A767474589560@acmegadgets.com>, proto=SMTP,
  daemon=MTA, relay=smtp.acme.com [10.216.88.43]
```

This doesn't need to be stored as a value, but it's good to parse it because it is a unique text string that differentiates this type of message from another. Figure 11-13 shows that this pattern is similar to the one finalized previously in Figure 11-10.

Figure 11-13 *Parsing for size=*

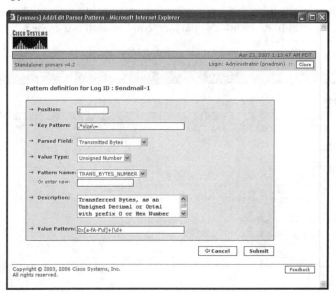

NOTE
If this isn't clear, consider the following example. Assume that you want to look for:

```
foo*ball
```

If you used **foo*ball** as a regex expression, you would match on these strings:

```
fooball
foooooooooooooooooball
```

But, you would not match on this:

```
foo*ball
```

That's because the asterisk is being interpreted as a special character, which is saying to look for any number of **o** characters, followed by the word **ball**.

If you wanted to match on just that word, you would use **foo*ball** for your regex expression instead.

Your string is looking for any number of characters, followed by the case-sensitive word **size**, followed by an equal sign. Notice that the pattern match begins from the end of the previous pattern, rather than from the beginning of the raw message. MARS does not parse the entire message again; instead, it continues to parse from where it left off on the last expression.

If you test the parser created so far, you can see (in Figure 11-14) that it's still properly parsing the message.

Figure 11-14   *Testing the Second Position*

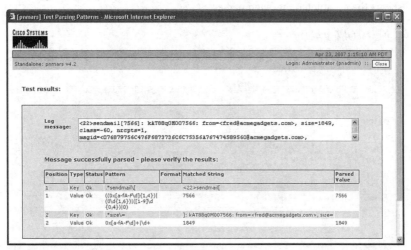

The final pattern you're going to look for in this message is the source IP address of the server that is sending the e-mail message. From the log message, this is the address that follows **relay=**:

```
parsing error: <22>sendmail[7566]: kAT88q0M007566: from=<fred@acmegadgets.com>,
size=1849, class=-60, nrcpts=1,
msgid=<076879756C476F6873736C6C75356A767474589560@acmegadgets.com>, proto=SMTP,
daemon=MTA, relay=smtp.acme.com [10.216.88.43]
```

As Figure 11-15 shows, this is just like the last pattern.

Figure 11-15   *Parsing for relay=*

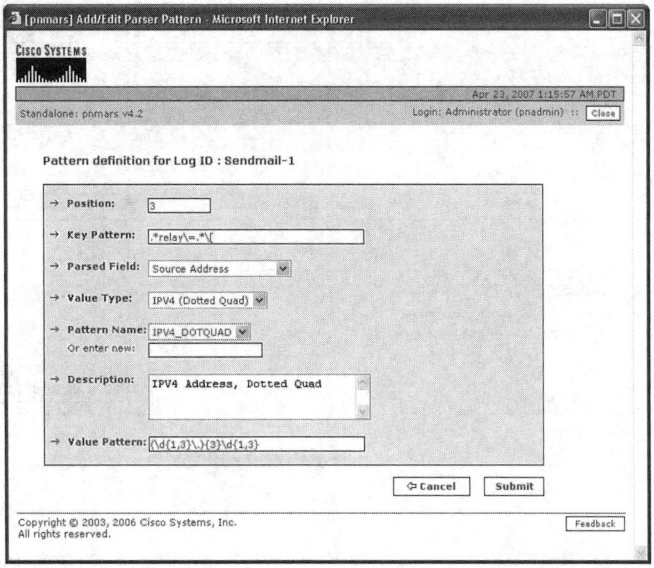

Figure 11-16 shows the test of the message parser after all fields are parsed. Figure 11-17 shows the completed message parser.

Figure 11-16 *Successful Test of Parser*

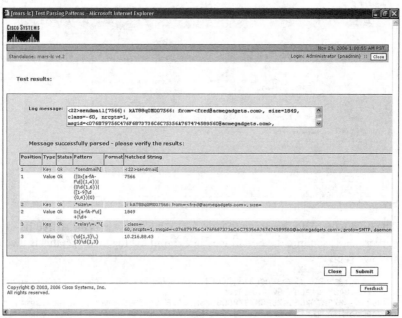

Figure 11-17 *Completed Message Parser*

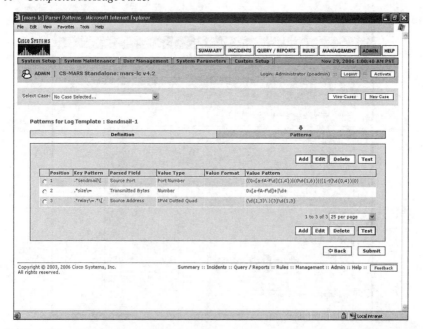

Click the **Submit** button when you're finished with this message parser. As Figure 11-18 shows, you now have a green Severity message for when sendmail reports on an inbound message arriving on the server.

Figure 11-18   *First Log Template Complete*

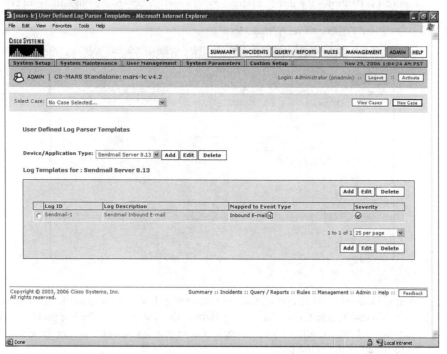

Second and Third Log Templates

Now that the first log template is completed, it's time to move to the next log message and write a new template for it. The first message you parsed was the log message showing an inbound e-mail message, but it doesn't necessarily show whether the message was successfully delivered.

The next log to parse will be messages showing whether the inbound e-mail was infected with malware. Here are a few samples of what the messages might look like:

```
Oct 29 20:50:40 groo sendmail[9949]: k9U4obqJ009949: Milter add: header: X-Virus-
    Status: Infected with HTML.Phishing.Bank-626
Oct 29 22:41:07 groo sendmail[11998]: k9U6f7qQ011998: Milter add: header: X-Virus-
    Status: Infected with Eicar-Test-Signature
Oct 30 00:40:37 groo sendmail[13757]: k9U8eax9013757: Milter add: header: X-Virus-
    Status: Clean
```

Use these messages for the two log templates that follow:

- Look for messages with Virus-Status: Clean
- Look for messages with Virus-Status: Infected

Figure 11-19 shows the newly created event type (rather than a built-in event type).

Figure 11-19 *New Event Type for Clean E-Mail Messages*

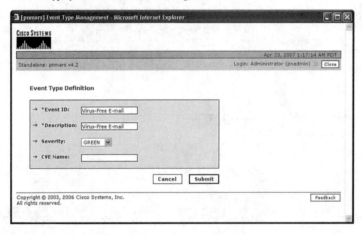

Figure 11-20 shows the completed log parser template. Notice that the last line is looking for **X-Virus-Status: Clea**. The word **Clean** is the last word in the log message. However, each key pattern must have a value pattern to return. By searching only for **Clea**, the **n** can be returned as the value pattern.

Figure 11-20 *Completed Log Template for Clean E-Mail Messages*

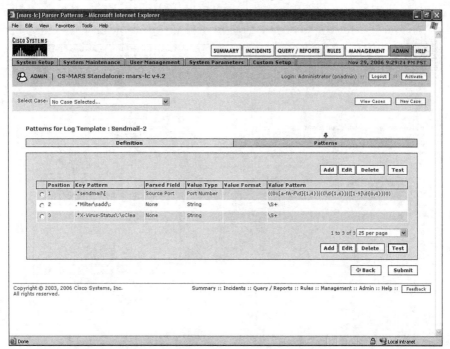

Figure 11-21 shows the log parser template for e-mails that are infected.

With the infected messages, rather than writing a parser for every virus that might be reported, write a single parser that stores the virus or worm name in the Reported User field. This might not make much sense, but if you look at the list of available fields, Reported User is the only one that supports a user-defined text value.

Figure 11-22 shows the details of Position 3 of this parser. With the default text values, you cannot have any type of nonalphabetical characters as part of the string. It's been modified to allow for other characters. You might need to use the same modification.

Figure 11-21 *Completed Log Template for Infected E-Mail Messages*

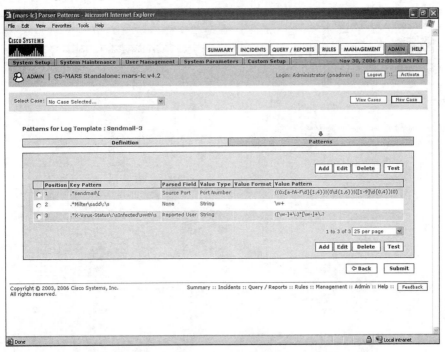

Figure 11-22 *Position 3 of Infected E-Mail Message Parser*

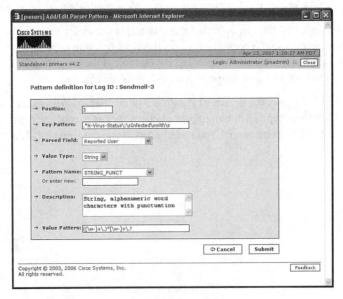

Fourth and Fifth Log Templates

The fourth log message is the one that tells you whether the e-mail message was delivered. You should see messages like the these:

```
Nov 30 00:01:43 groo sendmail[13760]: k9U8eax9013757: to=<gary@acmewidgets.net>,
   delay=00:00:06, xdelay=00:00:06, mailer=local, pri=32262, dsn=2.0.0, stat=Sent
Nov 30 00:09:29 groo sendmail[25917]: kAU89Pwq027915: to="¦/usr/bin/procmail",
   ctladdr=<arne@acme-gadgets.com> (508/508), delay=00:00:03, xdelay=00:00:03,
   mailer=prog, pri=139763, dsn=2.0.0, stat=Sent
Nov 30 22:42:37 groo sendmail[26707]: kAU6gbHF026707: Milter: data, reject=554 5.7.1
   virus Eicar-Test-Signature detected by ClamAV - http://www.clamav.net
```

The first message shows an e-mail successfully delivered locally on the server.

The second message shows an e-mail successfully delivered through a program.

The third message shows an e-mail that was not delivered because it was infected.

A single log template can work for the first two. A separate log template will be created for the rejected message.

Figure 11-23 shows the completed log parser template for the two successfully delivered messages.

Figure 11-23 *Completed Log Template for Successfully Delivered E-Mails*

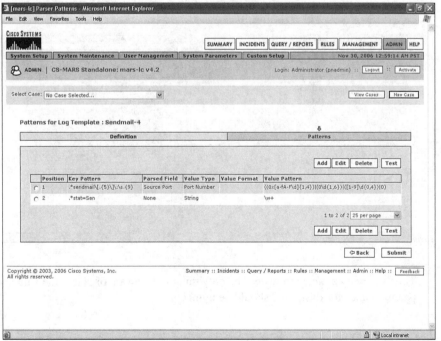

You need to do two things differently on this template:

- The sendmail process number changes in the sent messages. However, the original number is the last five characters of the long string after the sendmail process number. The regular expression for finding this is different, because now you're looking in a different place. A regular expression such as **.{5}** means that you're looking for any five characters. A regular expression such as **.{4,6}** means that you're looking for 4, 5, or 6 of any character.

- As with the Clean message (refer to Figure 11-20), the word **Sent** is at the end of the log message. Because MARS requires a value, you're looking only for **stat=Sen** instead of **stat=Sent**.

Figure 11-24 shows the completed log parser template for the rejected e-mail messages.

Figure 11-24 *Completed Log Template for Rejected, Infected E-Mails*

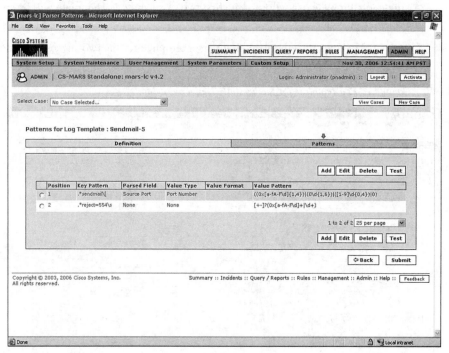

This is a pretty simple template. The only thing to be aware of is that the value type and pattern names for Position 2 should be numbers.

Additional Messages

You will likely see some additional messages that show up as Unknown Device Event Type. These additional messages might not cause an adverse effect, but defining the log message can clean up the event viewer.

Here's one that you might see:

```
Nov 30 03:00:40 groo sendmail[28280]: kAU8gDV4028280: Milter add: header: X-Virus-
    Scanned: ClamAV version 0.88.6, clamav-milter version 0.88.6 on localhost
```

This message is simply telling you that the virus scanner scanned the e-mail, but it doesn't give you the results. However, you might want to parse this anyway.

Figure 11-25 shows a completed log parser template for this message.

Figure 11-25 *Completed Log Template for Antivirus Status Message*

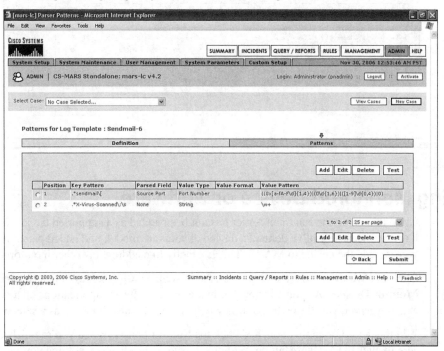

Figure 11-26 shows a summary of all parser templates for Sendmail, so far.

Figure 11-26 *Summary of All Log Parser Templates for Sendmail*

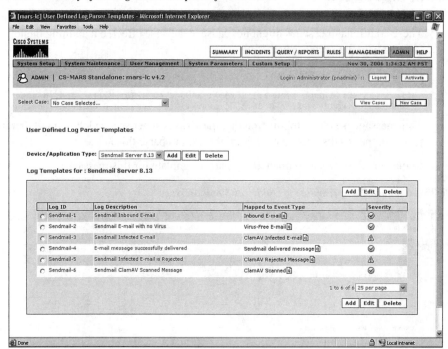

Adding Monitored Device or Software

Up to this point, the sendmail server has not been added as a supported device. Now, however, because you've defined a device or software model, and added parser templates, you can add the device to MARS. This is exactly like adding any other monitored device.

Click the **Admin** button, and then click the **System Setup** tab. Now, click **Security and Monitor Devices**. As you add new hardware or add software applications on a new or existing server, you'll see that your newly defined software shows up as a selection.

Add the device or application, and click the **Submit** button. When you're finished, make sure to click the **Activate** button. Without activating the changes, nothing you've done will take effect.

Queries, Reports, and Rules

After you have created the custom parser templates and added the monitored device, you can start using the new data just like any other type of device. If you have used existing event types with your new templates, you will have little left to do, because logs from the new device will already work with existing rules and reports. If you created new event types, though, you will need to define the conditions you are looking for.

Queries

Experiment with different queries to see how the new information is presented to you. Figure 11-27 shows a sample query that looks for the event type you created, called ClamAV Infected E-mail. For some types of events, you might need to generate an event on purpose, or you can let MARS run for several hours to wait for a type of activity to occur. In this case, we waited for about one day to let an e-mail virus attempt delivery. In addition, we sent a European Institute for Computer Antivirus Research (EICAR) test virus several times from one of the other Linux servers to generate some events.

Figure 11-27 *Query for ClamAV Infected E-Mail*

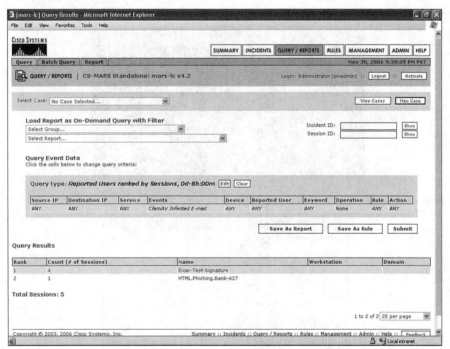

NOTE EICAR test viruses are widely used to test antivirus systems. These harmless files can be safely opened or sent on systems to generate events without accidentally infecting hosts.

Several variants of the EICAR test file can be downloaded at http://www.eicar.org. Additionally, the file can be created simply on any host by writing this string of text to any file:

```
X50!P%@AP[4\PZX54(P^)7CC)7}$EICAR-STANDARD-ANTIVIRUS-TEST-FILE!$H+H*
```

The entire file should be 68 bytes in length. If you want, it can have white space appended for a total length of up to 128 characters.

Figure 11-28 shows how to create the file from a Windows command prompt using the **copy con** command. Type **copy con** and the filename you want to create. Paste the EICAR text on the screen and press **Ctrl-Z** to write the file. In Figure 11-29, notice how Norton AntiVirus has detected and prevented the write. If you have desktop antivirus software on the host on which you're creating this file, you need to temporarily disable it.

Figure 11-28   *Creating an EICAR Virus Test File*

Figure 11-29   *Norton AntiVirus Detecting and Deleting the EICAR File*

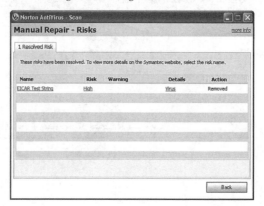

If you give the EICAR test file an executable extension and run it, it will simply write "EICAR-STANDARD-ANTIVIRUS-TEST-FILE" to the screen.

Figure 11-30 shows another query to verify that the created parser templates are functioning properly. This is looking for the event type Inbound E-mail.

Figure 11-30 *Query for Inbound E-Mail Messages*

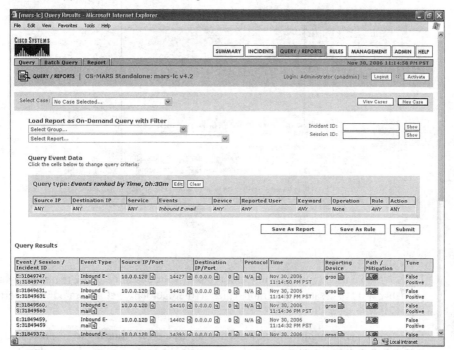

Reports

You can create numerous reports within MARS to present information in useful formats. These reports can be created using the information from your custom parsers without the need to first create a rule. Or, if you prefer, you can create a rule and use it to generate a report. The primary difference in this choice is whether you want incidents to be created when event data is received by MARS that matches the rule you've defined.

If you want to be able to quickly view a report on a regular basis, consider placing it in **My Reports**, which is a subtab on the Dashboard page.

Figure 11-31 shows what a report looks like on the My Reports page. You can click the **View Report** button to see the entire report. This is showing e-mail viruses that were prevented by the antivirus software on the sendmail server.

Figure 11-31 *E-Mail Viruses Rejected Report on the My Reports Page*

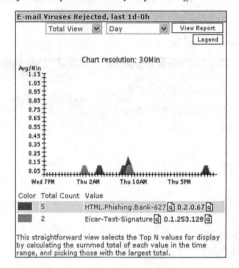

Rules

Unless you've used only built-in event types in your custom parsing templates, you'll probably want to create one or more rules so that incidents get generated when certain bad behaviors are seen.

For example, you might want an incident to be created anytime a virus is prevented. We use that to demonstrate creating a rule to work with the custom parser for sendmail.

You can create a rule in the following ways:

- Create a query. After it's been tested, click the **Save as Rule** button.
- Click the **Rules** button, and then click the **Add** button.

Use whichever method you feel comfortable with. The following example uses the second method:

Step 1 Click the **Rules** button at the top of the page.

Step 2 Click the **Add** button.

Step 3 Use the wizard to step through creating a single-line or multiline rule.

Step 4 Click the **Submit** button, and then click the **Activate** button.

Figure 11-32 shows the completed rule. This is a three-line rule that is looking for all three event types (Inbound E-mail, ClamAV Infected E-mail, and ClamAV Rejected Message), all using the same source port. Remember that you used the source port field to identify log messages that refer to the same sendmail message ID. By using the same source port, you specify that these three event types have to all occur with the same e-mail message.

Figure 11-32 *User Rule: E-Mail Virus Rejected*

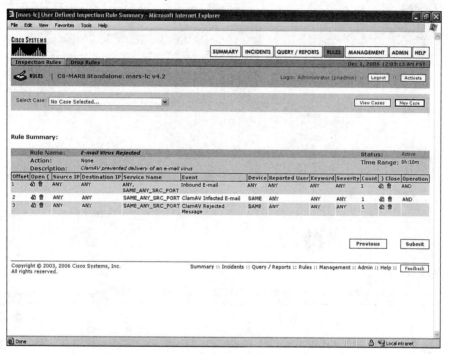

Figure 11-33 shows an incident that fired on this rule when an e-mail virus was rejected on the sendmail server.

Figure 11-33 *Incident Created by E-Mail Virus Rejected Rule*

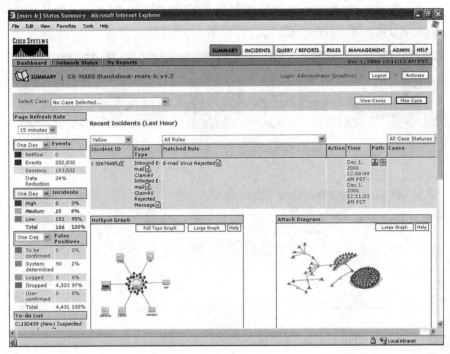

When you click the incident ID on the Dashboard, the incident details open, and you can see that this rejected virus was another EICAR test virus, as Figure 11-34 shows.

Figure 11-34 *Incident Details*

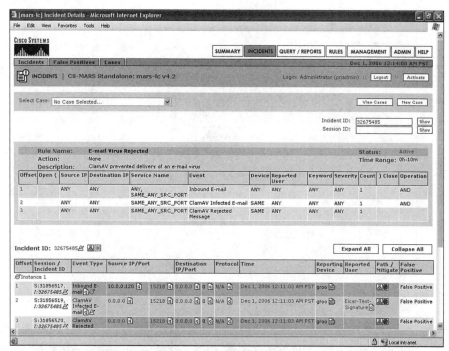

Custom Parser for Cisco CSC Module

The Cisco CSC Module is a popular product. Figures 11-35 through 11-50 show a summary of 13 of the logs produced by this module, as well as the log parser templates needed to report on these logs.

The CSC Module has its own management user interface and its own IP address, even though it is physically inserted into an ASA security appliance. Enable logging, through syslog, with it much as you would with any other application.

The following figures are not a complete list, but they cover a large number of the possible log messages you are likely to see from the Cisco CSC Module with version 6.1 software.

Figure 11-35 *Log Templates for Cisco CSC 6.1*

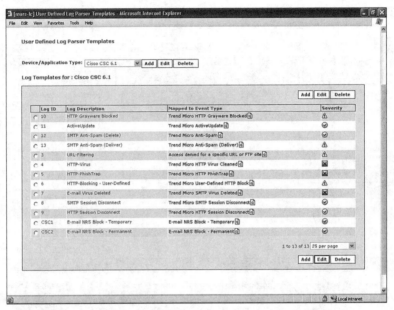

Figure 11-36 *Cisco CSC Patterns for E-Mail NRS Block—Temporary*

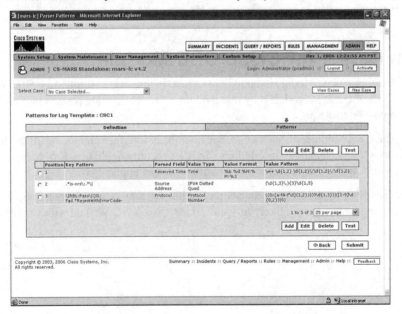

Figure 11-37 *Cisco CSC Patterns for E-Mail NRS Block—Permanent*

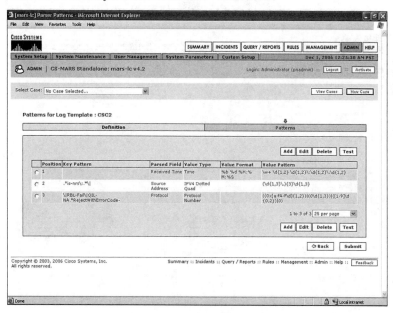

Figure 11-38 *Cisco CSC Patterns for URL Filtering*

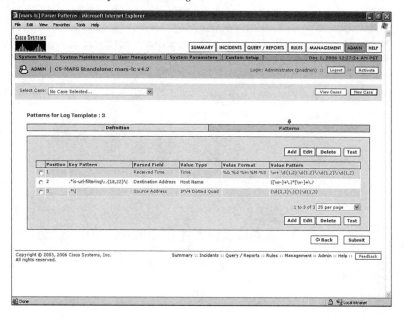

Figure 11-39 *Cisco CSC Patterns for HTTP Virus*

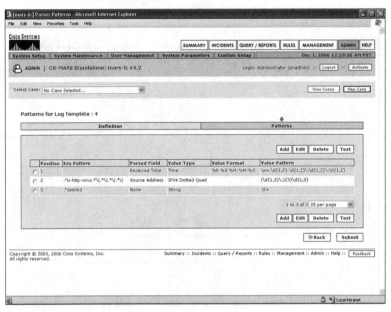

Figure 11-40 *Cisco CSC Patterns for HTTP PhishTrap*

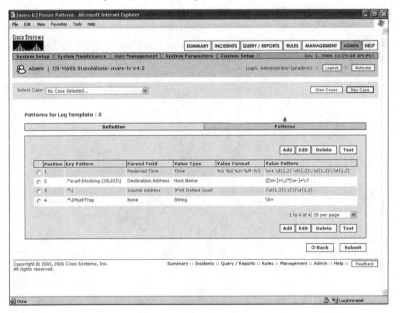

Figure 11-41 *Cisco CSC Patterns for HTTP Blocking—User-Defined*

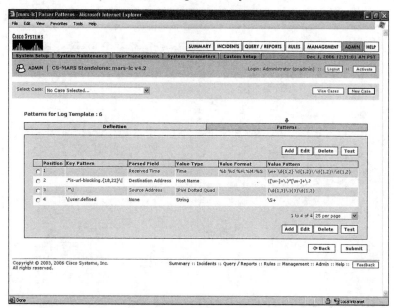

Figure 11-42 *Cisco CSC Patterns for E-Mail Virus Deleted*

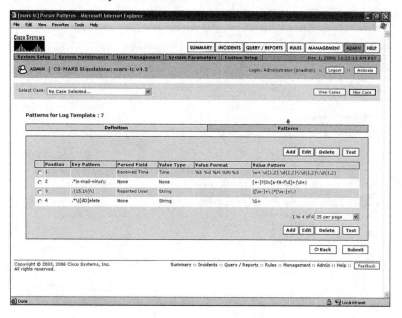

Figure 11-43 *Cisco CSC Patterns for SMTP Session Disconnect*

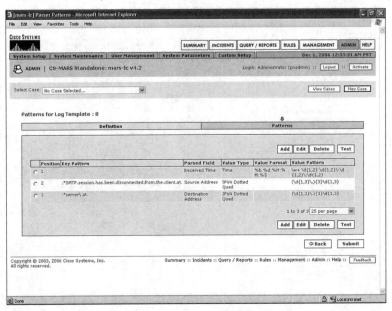

Figure 11-44 *Cisco CSC Patterns for HTTP Session Disconnect*

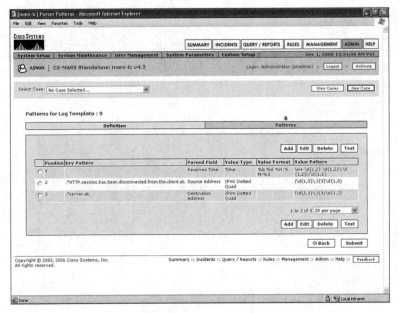

Figure 11-45 *Cisco CSC Patterns for HTTP Grayware Blocked*

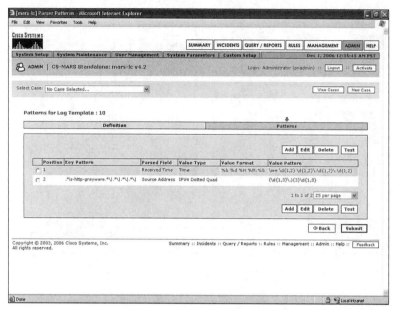

Figure 11-46 *Cisco CSC Patterns for ActiveUpdate*

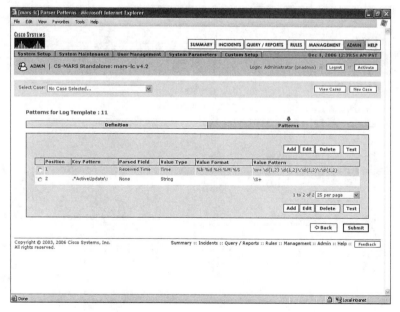

Figure 11-47 *Cisco CSC Patterns for SMTP Anti-Spam (Delete)*

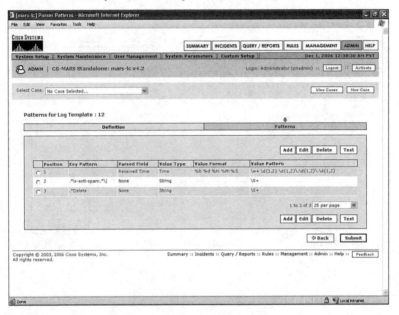

Figure 11-48 *Cisco CSC Patterns for SMTP Anti-Spam (Deliver)*

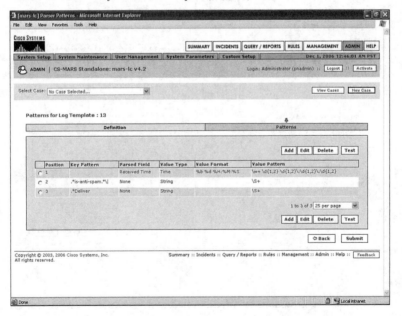

Figure 11-49 *My Reports Graph for Cisco CSC Module*

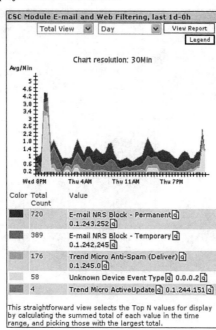

Figure 11-50 *Full Report*

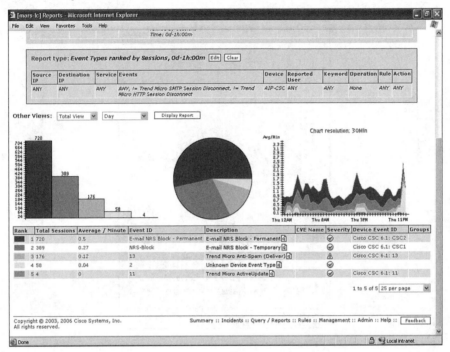

Summary

This chapter contains a lot of information. The MARS custom parser is a powerful tool, providing you with the means to integrate appliances and software that don't normally work with MARS.

Although working with the custom parser might seem complicated at first, you'll find that it quickly becomes easy and intuitive.

Don't forget that queries, reports, and rules might need to be modified or created to make the best use of the parsers you've created here.

## CHAPTER 12

CS-MARS Global Controller

A global controller (GC) provides several key capabilities that are important in a larger Cisco Security Monitoring, Analysis, and Response System (CS-MARS) deployment. As you've learned in previous chapters, many organizations can be successful with a single CS-MARS appliance. However, for various reasons, it is often desirable to have a distributed deployment instead, with a centralized console that controls the various local controllers (LC).

The following is a list of some of the reasons why you might want to deploy a GC:

- **Large amount of event data**—If your reporting devices send more events per second than a single MARS local controller can process, this load can be distributed across more local controllers. Additionally, if you need to store data, on-box, for a longer period of time, more LCs can help.

- **Organization spans slower WAN links**—When your organization has several regional operations, and these are connected with slower WAN links, you can reduce the amount of event data that traverses the WAN by localizing the reporting to local controllers. Each LC sends summarized information to the GC instead of all information.

- **Organization has different business units**—You might want to provide separation of the security reporting by business units.

- **Geographic locations**—Your organization might be geographically dispersed, where it makes sense to have local controllers in different countries or states.

Understanding the Global Controller

The following two models of global controllers are currently available:

- **CS-MARS-GC**—This is the main model. This GC is unrestricted and can manage all the CS-MARS local controllers.

- **CS-MARS-GCm**—This is a restricted model. It runs on the same hardware platform, but it can manage only CS-MARS-20R, -20, and -50 local controllers. It also has a limit of five local controllers.

Communications between the MARS-GC and each of the MARS-LCs is through Secure Socket Layer (SSL)–encrypted HTTP using TCP port 8444. If a firewall or other filtering device sits between the GC and LC, make sure that this port is open.

As events are received and processed by the local controller (LC), it performs several functions. First, the events are sessionized. This means that events from multiple reporting devices (firewalls, routers, IDS, IPS, web servers, for example) are compared and correlated. Events that are reporting on the same traffic are grouped into a *session*.

Sessionized information is then processed through the rules engine. This means that the sessions are analyzed to see whether a predefined behavior is apparent in the sessions. When a match is found in this analysis, an *incident* is created.

When an incident is created by the local controller, the incident is delivered to the GC, where it can be displayed on the GC's dashboard, and used in reports or any other MARS function. The GC receives these incidents from all LCs, but does not automatically receive the sessions or events associated with the incidents. Because the GC receives only a small amount of data, it can scale a deployment to large amounts of information, as the first reason for deploying a GC indicated. Also, because the information delivered to the GC is relatively small, it is friendly to deployments that use slower-speed WAN links, as the second reason indicated.

Correlation and consolidation of information across a large deployment is one of the primary benefits of deploying a global controller. Other reasons include the following:

- Ability to create custom rules and reports that are automatically pushed to individual local controllers

- Centralized user database

- Automatic deployment of custom parsing rules to multiple local controllers without having to enter them separately

- Simplified software and rule upgrades

The remainder of the chapter examines each of these in greater detail.

Zones

When an LC is added to a global controller, it takes on the name of a *zone*. A zone gives a description to an LC. It also allows you to select zone names from the global controller interface when investigating security incidents, running reports, or doing other tasks.

Consider the following example. If ACME Networking has a GC at its data center, and also has a MARS-20 deployed at each of its five regional offices, you can define the zone names by the region it services. You might have zones called Northwest, Southwest, Midwest, Northeast, and South. This is much easier to work with than Domain Name System (DNS) names, such as MLC-1.acme.net.

Some organizations choose to use business functions instead of regional names. ACME Technology Corporation might have zone names called Manufacturing, Datacenter, and Sales.

With current MARS software, each local controller belongs to its own zone. Each zone contains only a single local controller.

Installing the Global Controller

The GC is installed in the same manner as an LC. The user interface is similar, and most screens look the same as the interface on the LC. The biggest difference many users will notice is the lack of Topology Discovery and Vulnerability Scanning sections in the System Setup page. This is because the GC does not communicate directly with monitored devices. The GC is the reporting Dashboard for multiple local controllers, but the LCs still need to be configured for the devices they communicate with.

Deploying a GC is a two-step process:

Step 1   **Configuring the GC itself**—This is the same process as configuring an LC. After mounting the new appliance in a rack, you need to enter basic network settings, change the default password, and enter an activation key. Step-by-step installation instructions are not provided in this book, but can be found in the official CS-MARS documentation.

Step 2   **Exchanging certificates between the GC and LCs**—Each of the LCs needs to have the GC's certificate entered, and the GC needs to have each of the LC's certificates. Without entering these certificates, no communications can occur between the LC and the GC.

NOTE   Before a GC can communicate with an LC, the appliances' time must be similar, and the controllers need to be running the same software version.

The best way to synchronize time is to use Network Time Protocol (NTP). NTP must be configured from the command-line interface (CLI). Use Secure Shell (SSH) to connect to each of the controllers, and log in as pnadmin.

The **ntp** command defines the NTP servers, forces a time synchronization, and disables time synchronization. The syntax for configuring NTP is as follows:

```
[pnadmin]$ ntp ?
Usage : ntp server [ntp server1] [ntp server2]
        ntp sync
        ntp disable
```

If you have your own NTP servers, use them. If you do not, a number of public NTP servers are available at http://ntp.isc.org/bin/view/Servers/WebHome.

The following example defines both a primary and secondary NTP server, using public servers:

```
[pnadmin]$ ntp server 0.north-america.pool.ntp.org 1.north-
  america.pool.ntp.org
Thu Oct  5 22:49:19 PDT 2006
```

Enabling Communications Between Controllers

When you've verified that the GCs and LCs are all running the same version of software, and time is synchronized between them, you then enable communications between them. This process also changes the mode the LCs are running in. Prior to this, they have been operating as standalone controllers.

Begin by logging in to the GC as a system administrator (or pnadmin). Click the **ADMIN** button, and then click **Local Controller Management**.

Figure 12-1 shows the page that appears. This page, called Zone Controller Information, is where information for all local controllers needs to be entered.

Figure 12-1 *Zone Controller Information*

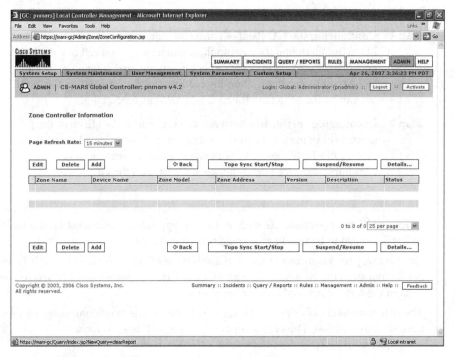

Click the **Add** button, and then enter information about the zone name, description, and LC IP address. Refer to Figure 12-2 for an example.

You are then returned to the Zone Controller Information page and should see something similar to Figure 12-3. Notice the status of the controller you've added. You have not yet added a certificate on the GC for the LC. You also haven't added a certificate for the LC on the GC. Until this happens, only partial communications can occur.

Figure 12-2 *Local Controller Information Added*

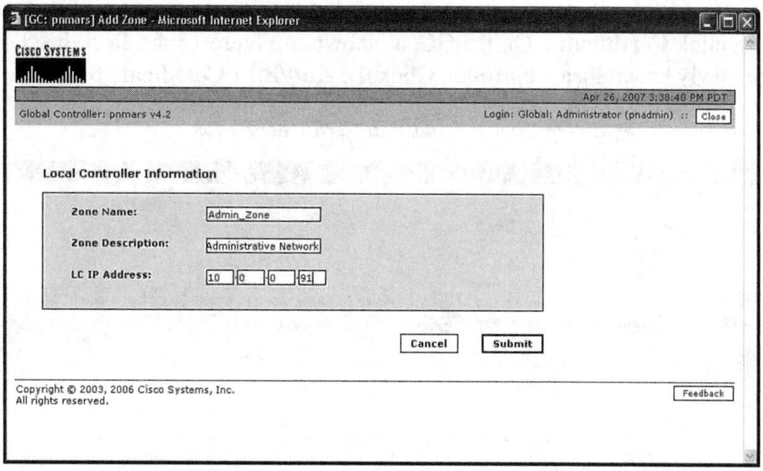

Figure 12-3 *Controller Status on the Zone Controller Information Page*

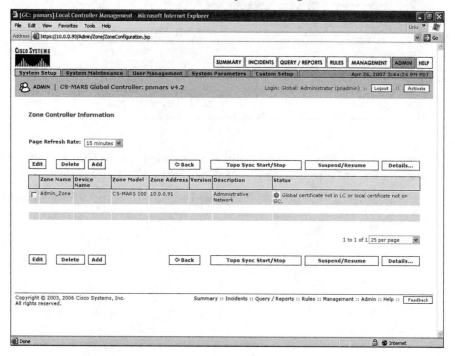

With two web browser windows open, make sure that you're logged in to both the GC and LC. Go to the same page on both systems by clicking the **System Maintenance** tab, and then click **Certificates**. On the GC, as shown in Figure 12-4, select the check box next to the newly added local controller. Click the **Add/Edit Certificate** button.

Figure 12-4   *From Global Controller, Click the **Add/Edit Certificate** Button*

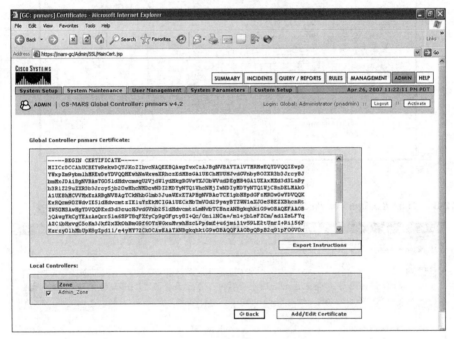

Now, on the LC, select the entire certificate. It's easiest to press **Ctrl-A** to select all. Right-click the text and copy it to the clipboard. See Figure 12-5 for an example.

Go back to the GC, and paste this certificate into the text area, as shown in Figure 12-6.

Figure 12-5 *Copy LC Certificate to the Clipboard*

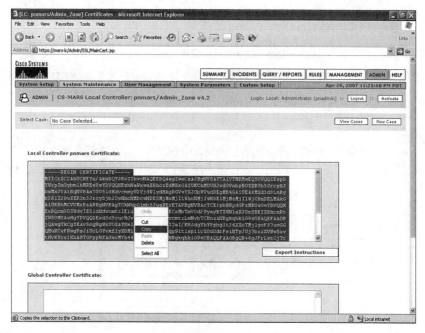

Figure 12-6 *Paste LC's Certificate to the GC*

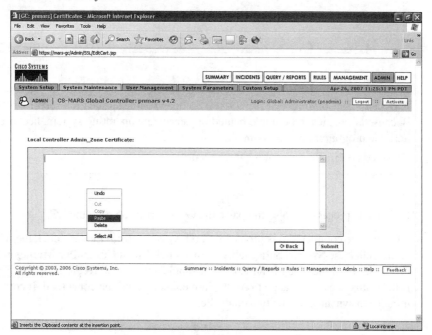

If the certificate is successfully added, you'll see a message that the JBoss will restart, as shown in Figure 12-7. Wait for a few minutes and click any tab. You'll be forced to log in to the MARS-GC again.

Figure 12-7 *Imported LC's Certificate into GC; JBoss Will Restart*

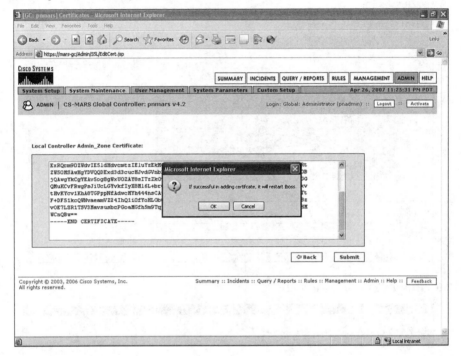

NOTE   JBoss (which is pronounced *Jay Boss*) is an open source application server written in Java. Because of this, it can be implemented on nearly any operating system, because Java is a portable programming environment.

JBoss was originally written by Marc Fleury.

Repeat this process to copy and paste the GC's certificate onto the LC.

After you've completed this process on both systems, from the GC, click the **ADMIN** button, click the **System Setup** tab, and then click **Local Controller Management**. Look for the status of the recently added LC. It should show as Active, as shown in Figure 12-8. If the status does not change to Active immediately, don't be concerned. It could take 3–4 minutes to synchronize the two controllers.

Figure 12-8 *Local Controller Status*

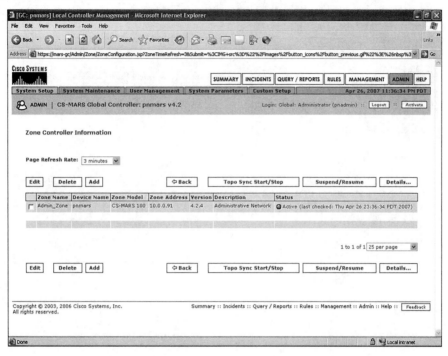

Troubleshooting

If you did not make sure that both controllers were running the same software version prior to adding the LC to the GC, and adding certificates, you'll see a status on the Local Controller Management screen in the Status column that says "Zone version is different," as shown in Figure 12-9. If you see this message, you need to simply upgrade one or both of the controllers to the same version. After you do this, the error message should go away.

Figure 12-9 *Zone Version Is Different*

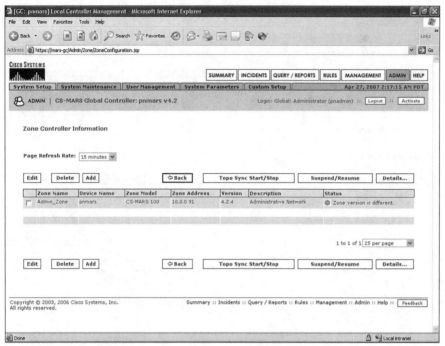

Using the Global Controller Interface

Although the user interface of the GC and LC is similar, several key differences exist. The following sections discuss the differences and show you how to accomplish various tasks.

Logging In to the Controller

The login page for the MARS-GC shows text boxes for a login name and password only. On the LCs, you see login, password, and type fields. If you define users on the GC, these users can also use those login names and passwords to log in to any of the LCs, without having to define local accounts on each controller.

To log in to an LC using the central user database, select **Global** in the Type field, as shown in Figure 12-10.

Figure 12-10 *Log In to Local Controller with Centralized Users*

Dashboard

The Dashboard page of the MARS-GC is similar to the LC's Dashboard, as Figure 12-11 shows. Notice that the Recent Incidents table at the top of the page provides a selector to view a single zone or all zones together. The incidents that show up in the table show you which zone the incident occurred in.

A new tab at the top of the page allows you to view HotSpot diagrams from all LCs at the same time.

Figure 12-11 *Global Controller's Dashboard Page*

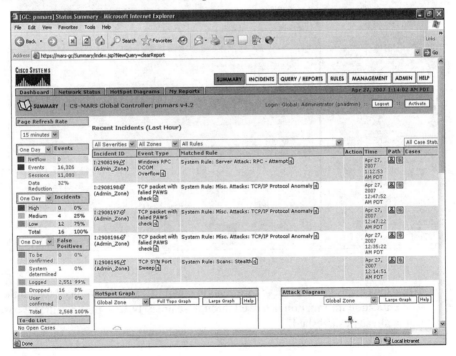

Drilling Down into an Incident

When you click an incident number or one of the path icons, your web browser opens a new window and connects to the specific LC. This is because the GC does not contain event data. However, the GCs and LCs use the same unique numbering system for incidents, sessions, and events. This allows quick and easy linking to the requested data from a local controller.

Figure 12-12 shows two browser windows open. The window in the foreground opened when the incident ID was clicked. Notice how the background window says Global Controller, while the foreground window says Local Controller.

Figure 12-12 *Clicking an Incident ID Opens a Second Window That Accesses a Local Controller*

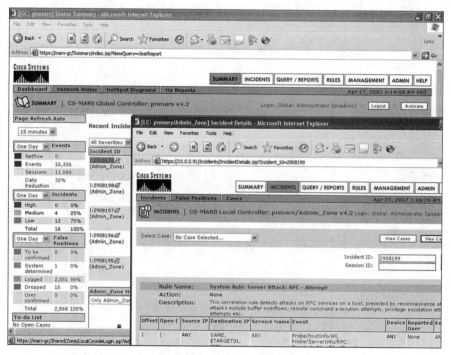

When the GC provides a link to information on an LC, you do not need to reauthenticate. Authentication information is passed through seamlessly, using the certificate-based trust that is already established.

Query/Reports

On the Query/Reports page, there are a number of differences from what you see on the local controller.

First, you can select a zone, as you can see in Figure 12-13. The default value is ANY. Clicking **ANY** allows you to select one or more available zones to use in your query or report.

Figure 12-13   *Global Controller Query Page Has New Options*

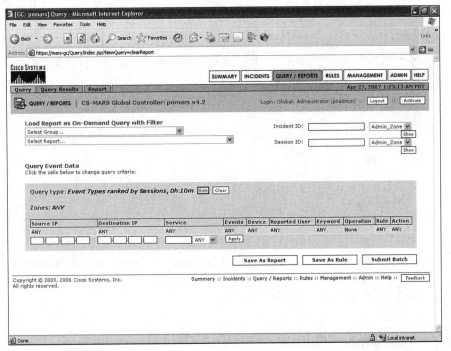

Second, when you click **Query type**, you'll notice from Figure 12-14 that many options you're used to seeing don't show up anymore. This is because of the restriction of seeing only incident data on the GC. You cannot see options for query type that require seeing session or event information. For that reason, you don't see query types such as All Matching Sessions, All Matching Events, or All Matching Event Raw Messages. You can still run these types of queries, though. You simply have to run them from the LC instead of the GC.

Figure 12-14 *Global Controller's Available Query Types*

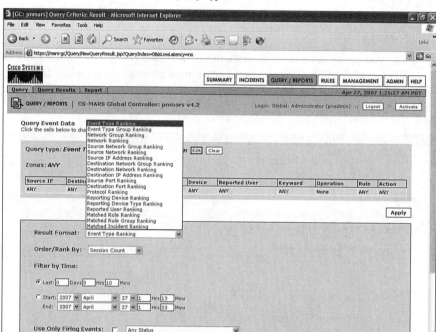

Other things you'll notice on the Query/Reports page are the lack of an option for viewing Realtime events, as well as the Submit Inline options for viewing the results. This is because the GC does not see sessions or events.

Local Versus Global Rules

When you are using a GC, you need to consider where to create any rules you need. In general, you should create all new rules from the GC. By doing this, the rules are pushed automatically to the individual LCs. When an incident is created because of one of these rules, the incident gets pushed automatically to the GC.

However, if you create a rule on an LC instead of the GC, that rule stays local to the LC. The rule does not get pushed to the GC. Also, any incidents that are created when a local rule is matched are *not* pushed to the GC. This could potentially cause confusion if you and your staff are not aware of this behavior.

Security and Monitor Devices

On the Security and Monitoring Information page, you see a list of all devices and software your controllers are currently configured to report on. As you might expect, the biggest new thing you'll notice on this page is the option to search for devices from a specific zone. Additionally, you see the zone name for a device in the table of devices and software. Figure 12-15 shows an example.

Figure 12-15   *GC's Security and Monitoring Information Page*

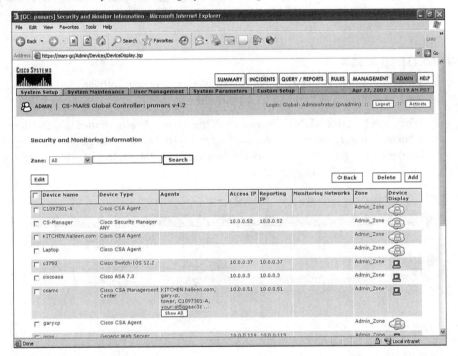

You must understand the relationship between devices and software defined here with those defined directly on a local controller's interface. When you edit an existing device or add a new device from the GC's interface, a new window opens from the specific zone's LC. You can make your changes or add the new information here and submit it. The changes you make automatically appear in the GC's interface.

You can add new devices by directly logging in to an LC. This shortens the process somewhat and causes no problems on the GC.

If you need to edit an existing device, though, you *must* log in to the GC and edit the device through it. If, instead, you log in directly to the LC and edit the device there, the change shows up properly on the LC, but not on the GC. If you or one of your staff inadvertently edits a device through the LC, you can easily correct the problem by clicking the **Edit** button from the GC, and then clicking the **Submit** button without making any changes. This forces the GC's device database to synchronize the information with the LC.

Custom Parser

Custom parsers and the rules associated with them should be created only on the GC. Much as the local rules discussed earlier, if you create custom parsers on an LC, they will stay on the LC. However, if you create them on the GC, they are pushed automatically to all LCs you have. Chapter 11, "CS-MARS Custom Parser," covers custom parsers in greater detail.

Software Upgrades

A useful feature of the GC is the capability to deploy new software and rules updates automatically across multiple local controllers.

When you click the **ADMIN** button, click the **System Maintenance** tab, and then click the **Upgrade** button, you see a page like Figure 12-16. On this page, if you're using the web interface for upgrading your software, you can optionally select LCs to be upgraded at the same time as the GC is upgraded.

Figure 12-16   *Simultaneously Upgrading Global and Local Controllers*

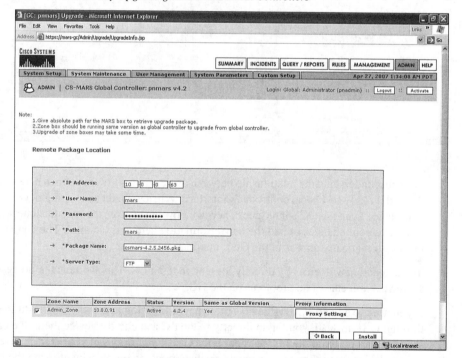

Status messages during the upgrade are not very informative. In fact, all you see is the message "Installation in progress." When you see this message, such as that shown in Figure 12-17, close your browser and wait for 30 minutes or so. The upgrade can take some time for the global controller. Also, depending on connectivity to the local controllers, it could take anywhere from about the same time as the GC to a few hours. It's a good idea to perform upgrades during defined maintenance hours. Your GC and LC will continue to process data during the time period that the upgrade file is transferring, but it will stop processing for a period of time to perform the upgrade.

Figure 12-17 *Status Message During Upgrade*

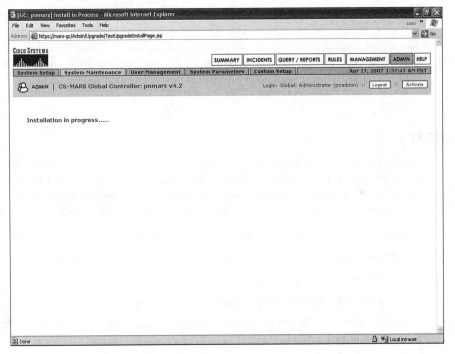

The upgrade occurs on the GC first and then on the LC. During the time period that the GC is unavailable, data continues to be processed on the LC. When the GC becomes available again, any data is transferred to the GC.

When you select one or more LCs to upgrade while the GC is upgrading, the GC downloads software from the designated network location, using either FTP or HTTPS. The software is then downloaded automatically by the LCs from the GC. If network connectivity is slow across these links, the upgrade could take a significant amount of time.

Global Controller Recovery

At some time, you might need to remove the association between a GC and its LCs. Typically, this occurs when a hardware replacement of the GC is necessary, and you need to reassociate the LCs with a new GC.

To remove the GC's information from the LCs, run the following command from the command line of each of the local controllers:

```
pnreset -g
```

This begins a process that can take up to about 30 minutes to complete. At the end, you can reinstall the LC with an association to a new GC.

CAUTION   Make sure that you type the command properly. If you remove the **-g** from the command, the LC will instead revert to factory default status, with an empty database!

Summary

Deploying CS-MARS hierarchically, with a GC, is an effective way to linearly increase the number of events per second that MARS can process. Additionally, it is effective in scenarios where separation of monitoring consoles is desired, either because of a need to separate business units or because of limited bandwidth across a WAN.

While great benefits to deploying a GC exist, you should also consider the following items:

- Placement of rules
- Placement of custom parsers
- Location of incidents versus session and event data

These considerations should in no way prevent a GC deployment but are simply behaviors that need to be understood.

Appendixes

Querying the Archive

Chapter 7, "Archiving and Disaster Recovery," describes the Cisco Security Monitoring, Analysis, and Response System (CS-MARS) archiving capabilities. The archives provide critical backup and recovery functionality, as well as the capability to run queries against the archives from within the CS-MARS user interface. Although this functionality is handy, sometimes you might find the need to use other tools to query the data.

If you have properly configured archiving, MARS will regularly write all event data to the Network File System (NFS) archive within minutes of being processed by MARS. This data is easily accessible through the command line from the host on which the data sits.

You might need to manipulate user rights on that host, which is often running Linux, to view the event data, but Linux contains utilities that make the event data easily accessible.

CAUTION   Take care to limit user rights so that they are read-only. This allows authorized users to run queries, but it prevents them from making changes to the event data. This is especially important in case you ever need to submit this information as evidence in a criminal investigation. If you are unable to tell law enforcement that this information was protected with read-only privileges, this information might not be allowed as evidence.

If you look at the archive server, you'll see that the directory structure is something like the following, as described in Chapter 7:

```
/nfs/
    /mars-lc/
        /2006-06-04/
        /2006-06-05/
        /2006-06-06/
        /.../
        /.../
        /.../
        /2006-08-07/
        /2006-08-08/
            /AL/
            /CF/
            /ES/
            /IN/
            /RR/
            /ST/
        /pnos/
```

Each of the dates contains the same subdirectory structure, as follows:

- **/AL/**—Audit logs
- **/CF/**—MARS configuration
- **/ES/**—Event store
- **/IN/**—Incidents
- **/RR/**—Reports
- **/ST/**—Statistics

Of these directories, the only ones you need to access for command-line queries are the ES directories. Within those directories are two different file types, which look like this:

```
es-4220-422-0_2007-01-02-10-23-01_2007-01-02-10-33-07.gz
rm-4220-422-0_2007-01-02-00-04-53_2007-01-02-00-15-56.gz
```

The files that contain human-readable event information all begin with "rm." You can ignore the others.

To understand what you're looking at, you need to understand how to read the filenames. The following list breaks one down:

- **rm-** — This indicates that the file contains raw messages.
- **4220-422-0**—This indicates the CS-MARS version.
- **2007-01-02**—This indicates the start date of the messages within the file.
- **00-04-53**—This indicates the start time of the messages within the file. This example means that the file contains messages beginning at 12:04:53 a.m. on January 2, 2007.
- **2007-01-02**—This indicates the end date of the messages within the file.
- **00-15-56**—This indicates the ending time of the messages within the file. In this case, the last message in the file has a timestamp of 12:15:56 a.m. on January 2, 2007.

The files are each compressed using the gzip method, as the .gz file extension indicates.

Command-Line Query

The simplest way to access the archive data is with the **zgrep** command. This command is identical to the commonly used **grep** command, except it is used for searching within gzipped files.

A simple query example is as follows:

"Show me all raw events from my Cisco 3750 switch where an interface was unplugged or plugged."

You can change directories to the date you're interested in, and then change to the ES directory and run the following command:

```
zgrep "LINK-3-UPDOWN" rm*
```

This command results in the following output:

```
rm-4220-422-0_2007-01-03-00-33-47_2007-01-03-00-44-01.gz:39967070»01/03/2007
   00:38:13»3750»<187>26: 3d12h: %LINK-3-UPDOWN: Interface FastEthernet1/0/4, changed
   state to down»»

rm-4220-422-0_2007-01-03-00-33-47_2007-01-03-00-44-01.gz:39967073»01/03/2007
   00:38:17»3750»<187>27: 3d12h: %LINK-3-UPDOWN: Interface FastEthernet1/0/4, changed
   state to up»»
```

Now, **zgrep** (and **grep**) are case-sensitive unless you specify otherwise, so the following would make an easier search and not be case-sensitive:

```
zgrep -i "link-3-updown" rm*
```

However, the most power is achieved when you use the regular expression capabilities, as demonstrated here:

```
zgrep -i -P "link-3-updown" /nfs/mars-lc/2007-01-0[1-7]/ES/rm*
```

This command allows you to use a case-insensitive search and specify a date range. In this example, you're looking for the message in the first seven days of January 2007. You can also use regular expressions for the string you're searching for.

You can find documentation on the use of regular expressions at the Perl Compatible Regular Expressions (PCRE) website: http://www.pcre.org/pcre.txt.

Advanced Capabilities

If you are skilled at writing Common Gateway Interface (CGI) or other web applications, you can easily make use of the examples in the preceding section to write web-based applications that allow archive queries. For example, perhaps you would like technicians to search for predefined string matches on dates and times in which they are interested.

You can use languages such as Perl, PHP: Hypertext Preprocessor (PHP), Python, and more to write your web applications. We have included a sample Python application that you can run on your archive server's web server. Feel free to use this application, marchive.py, which you can access through the Downloads section of this book's product page at http://www.ciscopress.com/title/1587052709. Although it has a simple interface, as Figure A-1 illustrates, it is a nice query tool, and you can use your imagination to customize it nicely!

Figure A-1 *Authors' marchive.py Query Tool*

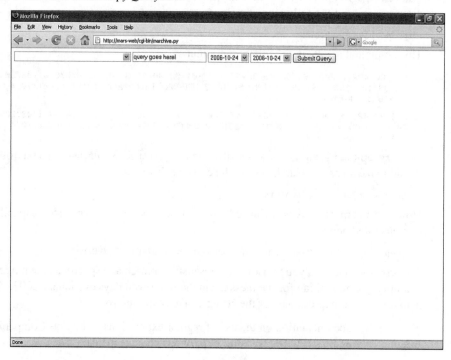

Figure A-2 shows a simple query that is looking for events MARS logs when a traffic anomaly is detected.

Figure A-2   *Enter a Query to Search Archive's Event Store*

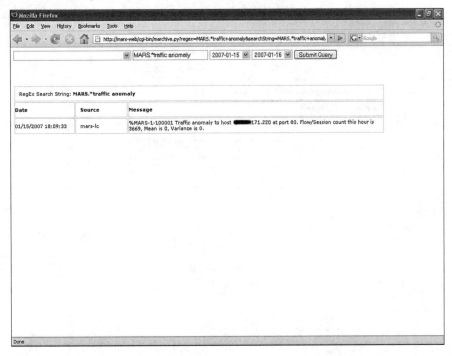

A more advanced query example is when you look for failed or successful logins to one of your Linux servers, using the following regular expression:

```
groo.*(accepted | failed) (password | publickey).*gary
```

This query is looking for the following:

- Host name, **groo**, followed by any number of characters
- **accepted** or **failed**, followed by a space
- **password** or **publickey**, followed by any number of characters and then **gary**

Figure A-3 shows the results of this query.

Figure A-3   *Advanced Regex Query*

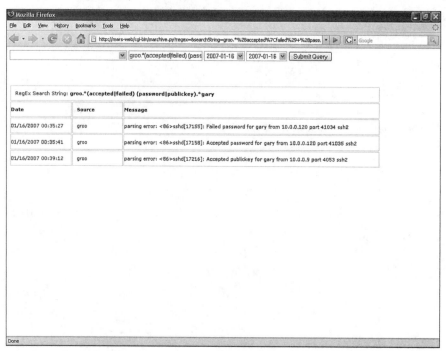

To make commonly run queries easier, you can create a text file that defines the common queries. This file is called marchive.queries and looks like this:

```
ASA Failed User Authentication;'ASA\-.*aaa user authentication rejected'
ASA Commands Executed;'asa-.*user.*executed.*(cmd¦command)'
ASA 'config t' executed;'asa-.*configure terminal'
ASA CSC Module E-mail Viruses;'csc-ssm is-mail-virus'
ClamAV E-mail Viruses;'infected with'
All E-mail Viruses;'(csc-ssm is-mail-virus¦infected with)'
Display WebVPN Connections to ASA  7.x;'asa\-[56]\-[0-9]{6}\:.*Group.*WebVPN'
Display all VPN Connections to ASA 7.x;'asa\-[56]\-[0-9]{6}\:.*Group'
Linux Authentication Failure;'(groo¦opus).*authentication failure'
Linux failed and successful logins;'(groo¦opus).*(accepted¦failed) password'
Linux failed and successful su to  root;'(opus¦groo).*user[= ]root'
MARS-determined Traffic Anomaly;'MARS.*traffic anomaly'
Samba Master Browser Messages;'nmbd.*master.*workgroup'
```

Create as many stored queries as you'd like, but make sure that you don't place an empty line at the end of the file.

This populates the first drop-down menu, as shown in Figure A-4.

Figure A-4 *Stored Queries*

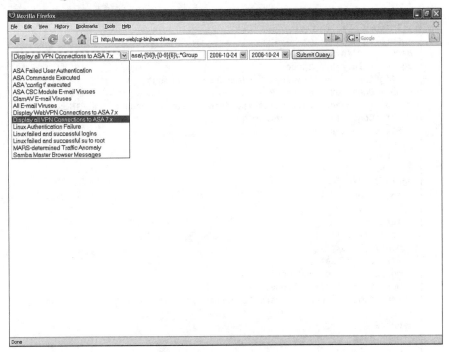

Python Source Code for marchive.py

Many different programming languages are available for creating an application like the one shown in Example A-1. Perl is a common language, and someone who is experienced writing in Perl should have no problem converting our source code.

Python is another commonly used programming language, and it is available for several operating systems. Like Perl, it is an interpreted language, meaning that applications do not need to be compiled before they can be run.

Example A-1 *marchive.py Utility Source Code*

```
#!/usr/bin/env python
# encoding: utf-8
"""

marchive.py
Created by Greg Kellogg on 2007-01-01.
Tool to run zgrep through a CS-MARS archive
"""

__author__ = "Greg Kellogg (greg@dunechaser.org) with help from Gary Halleen
    (gary@halleen.com)"
__version__ = "$Revision: 0.2 $"
__date__ = "$Date: 1/16/07 01:01:34 $"
```

continues

Example A-1 *marchive.py Utility Source Code (Continued)*

```
__copyright__ = "Copyright  2007 Greg Kellogg"
__license__ = "BSD"
import cgi, os, time, sys
marsDir = "/nfs/mars-lc/"
zgrep = '/usr/bin/zgrep -iP'
configFile = "/var/www/cgi-bin/marchive.queries"
# OS X Does not support -P in zgrep
# Required header that tells the browser how to render the HTML.
print "Content-Type: text/html\n\n"
# Style sheet stuff
print """
<HTML>\n
<STYLE>\n
#date {
  top: 60px;
  width: 140px;
  left: 60px;
  font-size: 11px;
  padding: 0px;
  text-align: left;
  border: 1px solid #cccccc;
  border-collapse:collapse;
  font-family: "Lucida Grande", Verdana, Arial, Helvetica, sans-serif;
}
#source {
  top: 60px;
  width: 100px;
  font-size: 11px;
  padding: 10px;
  text-align: left;
  border: 1px solid #cccccc;
  font-family: "Lucida Grande", Verdana, Arial, Helvetica, sans-serif;
}
#message {
  top: 60px;
  width: 600px;
  font-size: 11px;
  padding: 0px;
  text-align: left;
  font-family: "Lucida Grande", Verdana, Arial, Helvetica, sans-serif;
  border: 1px solid #cccccc;
}
#query {
  top: 60px;
  width: 100px;
  font-size: 11px;
  padding: 10px;
  text-align: left;
  border: 1px solid #cccccc;
  font-family: "Lucida Grande", Verdana, Arial, Helvetica, sans-serif;
}
</STYLE>"""
```

Example A-1 *marchive.py Utility Source Code (Continued)*

```python
#Bootstrap application when called, load up the variables with directory information
  def bootstrap():
    try:
        dateDirectories = os.listdir(marsDir)
        return dateDirectories
    except os.error, value:
        print value[0], value[1]
# Here is the form that dynamically builds from the directory structure
def buildForm(fileName,searchString='',startDate='',endDate=''):
    print '<form name="searchForm" method=get action="/cgi-bin/marchive.py">'
    print '<div id="quicksearchbar"><select id="regexbox" name="regex"
      onClick="searchString.value = this.value"><option selected>'

    try:
        f = open(configFile)
    except os.error, value:
        print "File not found"
        print value[0], value[1]

    for i in f.readlines():
        i = i.split(';')
        print '<option value='+i[1]+'>'+i[0]

    print '</select>'
    print '<input type="search" name="searchString" id="quicksearchbox" size="25"
      value="'+searchString+'">'
    print '<select id="startbox" name="startDate" onClick="endDate.value =
      this.value">'
    for x in fileName:
        if not x.startswith('.'):
            if not x == "pnos":
                if x == startDate:
                    print '<option selected>'+x
                else:
                    print '<option>'+x
    print '</select>'
    print '<select id="endbox" name="endDate">'
    for x in fileName:
        if not x.startswith('.'):
            if not x == "pnos":
                if x == endDate:
                    print '<option selected>'+x
                else:
                    print '<option>'+x
    print '</select>'
    print "\t<INPUT TYPE=hidden NAME=\"action\" VALUE =\"display\">\n"
    print '<input id="submit" type="submit"></form></div><br><p><p>'

# This is for the actual searching
def searchRecords(dates, searchString, startDate, endDate):
    start = dates.index(startDate)
    end = dates.index(endDate)
```

continues

Example A-1 *marchive.py Utility Source Code (Continued)*

```
            print '<br><table border="0"><thead>'
            print '<tr><td colspan=3 id="query">RegEx Search String:
              <b>'+searchString+'</b></td></tr>'
            print '<tr>'
            print '<th id="date">Date</th>'
            print '<th id="source">Source</th>'
            print '<th id="message">Message</th></tr></thead>'
            print '<tbody>'
            if start > end:
                print 'Start date must be less than end date...'
            else:
                x = start
                while x <= end:
                    tail = marsDir+dates[x]+'/ES/rm*'

                    get = '%s %s %s' % (zgrep, '"'+searchString+'"', tail)
                    results = os.popen(get, "r")
                    x = x+1
                    y=0
                    for ret in results.xreadlines():
                        splret = ret.split('\xbb')
                        print '<tr><td id="date">'+splret[1]+'</td>'
                        print '<td id="source">'+splret[2]+'</td>'
                        newSpl = splret[3].replace('>','&gt;')
                        newSpl = newSpl.replace('<','&lt;')
                        print '<td id="message">'+newSpl+'</td></tr>'
                        y = y+1
            print "</tbody></table></html></body>"


# Define main function.
def main():
    form = cgi.FieldStorage()
    dates = bootstrap()
    dates.sort()
    if (form.has_key("action") and form.has_key("endDate") and
      form.has_key("startDate") and form.has_key("searchString")):
        if (form["action"].value == "display"):
            buildForm(dates,form["searchString"].value, form["startDate"].value,
              form["endDate"].value)
            searchRecords(dates, form["searchString"].value,
              form["startDate"].value, form["endDate"].value)
    else:
        buildForm(dates)
        print "</html></body>"
# Call main function.
if __name__ == '__main__':
    main()
```

CS-MARS Command Reference

The Cisco Security Monitoring, Analysis, and Response System (CS-MARS) command-line interface (CLI) is currently only available to the "pnadmin" user. The descriptions provided in this command reference are not intended to be a replacement for those in the official Cisco MARS command reference. Please refer to it for detailed information about each of these commands. This reference is intended only as a quick guide to the commands.

? Provides a list of available commands.

arp. Same as the Linux **arp** command. Use the **-help** switch to see the full help screen.

date. Used to display or set the current date. To view the current date, type the following:

```
date
```

To set the date to January 20, 2007, type the following:

```
date 01/20/07
```

or

```
date 01/20/2007
```

diskusage. Used to display the size of each partition within the MARS appliance, as well as how much space is in use within each. This command is exactly the same as the following Linux command:

```
df -H
```

dns. Used to display or set the Domain Name System (DNS) servers that MARS will use for name resolution. Typing **dns** by itself displays the servers. Typing **dns** followed by up to three IP addresses sets the DNS servers and order in which they are queried. Use the following format:

```
dns [primary] [secondary] [tertiary]
```

For example:

```
dns 10.1.1.2 10.1.2.2 10.1.4.2
```

dnssuffix. Used to display the domain name attached to hosts if one isn't specified. Like the **dns** command, this command displays the domain name if used by itself, or it can be used to add or remove a DNS domain name. Use the following format:

```
dnssuffix [add¦del domainname]
```

exit. Logs you out of the CLI.

expert. Used exclusively by the Cisco Technical Assistance Center (TAC) to assist you in correcting problems with solutions that are unavailable through the traditional CLI or web interface. The **expert** command is protected by a password that is known only to the Cisco TAC.

This command is available only after first logging in to the console via the CLI with the pnadmin account. You can provide additional restrictions on the **expert** command through the **passwd expert** command.

gateway. Used to display or set the default gateway.

help. Identical to using the question mark (?).

hostname. Used to either set or display the host name of the MARS appliance.

hotswap. Used to ready the MARS appliance for a hard drive removal and replacement. Chapter 9, "Troubleshooting CS-MARS," has good information on the usage of this command, as well as some warnings. You can get into trouble with this command if you are not careful!

ifconfig. Similar to the same Linux command, and the output looks the same. However, **ifconfig** is limited to setting IP addresses and subnet masks on eth0 and eth1 interfaces.

This command allows you to display or set IP address and network mask parameters. Typing **ifconfig** by itself displays information for troubleshooting communications problems, as Figure B-1 demonstrates.

Figure B-1 **ifconfig** *Command*

model. Displays information about the type of appliance, or model number, as well as whether the appliance is configured to work with a global controller.

netstat. The same as the **netstat** command in Linux, including all switches. For example, **netstat –rn** displays the routing table, as Figure B-2 demonstrates.

Figure B-2 *Using **netstat** Command to Display the Routing Table*

```
demo2.cisco.com - PuTTY
help           - Print list of available commands
hostname       - Set/show host name
hotswap        - hot add or remove disk
ifconfig       - Configure/store network interface
model          - Display the model info of CS-MARS
netstat        - Show network statistics
nslookup       - Look up the IP address or domain name
ntp            - Synchronize system clock with ntp servers
passwd         - Change password
ping           - Ping a host
pnlog          - Show system log/ set log level
pndbusage      - Show database usage info
[pnadmin]$ help netstat
Commands are:
netstat        - Show network statistics

[pnadmin]$ netstat -rn
Kernel IP routing table
Destination     Gateway         Genmask         Flags   MSS Window  irtt Iface
192.168.1.0     0.0.0.0         255.255.255.0   U        40 0          0 eth1
10.4.10.0       0.0.0.0         255.255.255.0   U        40 0          0 eth0
127.0.0.0       0.0.0.0         255.0.0.0       U        40 0          0 lo
0.0.0.0         10.4.10.10      0.0.0.0         UG       40 0          0 eth0
[pnadmin]$
```

nslookup. Used to perform IP address–to–host name resolution and vice versa. Typing **nslookup** by itself places you into interactive mode, and you then type the host name or IP address. Examples of commands available from the interactive prompt are as follows:

- **set type**—Used to set the type of information you want to look up. Example: **set type=MX**.

- **server**—Used to identify the DNS server you want to resolve from.

ntp. Used to configure Network Time Protocol (NTP), which uses User Datagram Protocol (UDP) port 123 to automatically adjust the time on MARS, as Figure B-3 demonstrates. All MARS devices need to have NTP configured to properly synchronize time on all devices.

Figure B-3 *Network Time Protocol*

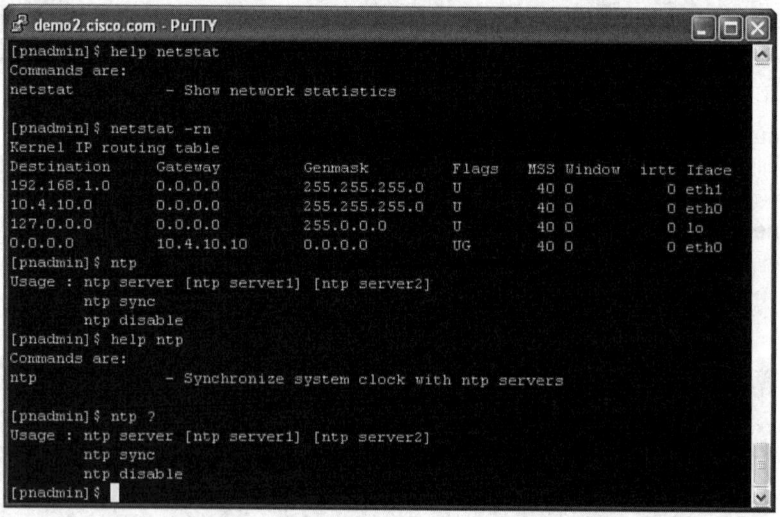

passwd. Used to change the administrative (pnadmin) password used by both the CLI and web interfaces.

passwd expert. Changes the expert password so that two separate passwords must be entered prior to accessing the expert shell on the MARS appliance. One of these passwords is known only to Cisco, and the other is known only to you. As with the regular **expert** command, it also requires access to the MARS appliance, through Secure Shell (SSH) or the console with the regular pnadmin password.

ping. Used to send Internet Control Message Protocol (ICMP) echo packets to a destination host as a test of network connectivity.

pndbusage. Used to display the database usage statistics, as Figure B-4 demonstrates. The output from this command displays what percentage of the current database partition is used, and provides an estimate of when the next partition will be used. If no empty partitions exist, it displays the estimated date that a full partition will be purged for use.

Figure B-4   **pndbusage** *Command*

```
demo2.cisco.com - PuTTY
dns                - Add/remove/show domain name resolving servers
dnssuffix          - Add/remove/show domain name suffixes search path
domainname         - Set/show domain name
exit               - Switch to standard mode/Logout
gateway            - Show/set default gateway
help               - Print list of available commands
hostname           - Set/show host name
hotswap            - hot add or remove disk
ifconfig           - Configure/store network interface
model              - Display the model info of CS-MARS
netstat            - Show network statistics
nslookup           - Look up the IP address or domain name
ntp                - Synchronize system clock with ntp servers
passwd             - Change password
ping               - Ping a host
pnlog              - Show system log/ set log level
pndbusage          - Show database usage info
[pnadmin]$ pndbusage
Current partition started on Thu Apr  5 19:53:13 PDT 2007 and uses 44.9% of its
available capacity.
   Switching to next partition is estimated for Fri Apr  6 08:07:56 PDT 2007.
   1.2e+07 events, received between Tue Apr  3 05:17:52 PDT 2007 and Tue Apr  3
11:58:05 PDT 2007 will be purged.
[pnadmin]$
```

pnlog. Used to perform several functions:

- Displays the running output of the GUI, backend, and Check Point debug logs with the **pnlog show** command.

- Mails the GUI, backend, and Check Point debug logs to a specified e-mail address with the **pnlog mailto** command.

- Sets logging levels for the GUI, backend, and Check Point debug log files with the **pnlog setlevel** command.

pnreset. Used primarily to take a MARS appliance back to its original condition with the current software release. When you do this, it wipes clean the database, all devices, and all other configuration information, leaving the appliance just as it would be after installing the MARS software on a new appliance. The license key is erased, but the pnadmin password might need it, though, if you choose to redeploy a MARS appliance to a different location and want to start from scratch with the configuration. Be aware that the **pnreset** command takes a long time to run. On some models, it could take more than two hours to complete.

A number of switches can be used with the **pnreset** command:

- **-h**—Displays help.
- **-g**—Removes Global Controller data from the local controller.
- **-j**—Resets the web server scheduler.
- **-o**—Removes Oracle client information from the MARS appliance. This is used only when correcting some problems when MARS is monitoring an Oracle server.
- **-s**—Changes a local controller back to standalone mode. This performs all tasks as **–g**, plus it removes Global Controller connectivity information.

pnrestore. Used to restore configuration and/or events from an archive server to a MARS appliance.

pnstart. Used to manually start MARS processes after they have been manually stopped with the **pnstop** command.

pnstatus. Displays a list of all running MARS processes, as well as how long they each have been running.

pnstop. Used to manually halt all MARS processes. They can be restarted with the **pnstart** command.

pnupgrade. Used to instruct the MARS appliance to install a software upgrade.

The syntax for this command is as follows:

```
pnupgrade [location] [user] [password]
```

Acceptable locations include

- CD-ROM (DVD)
- FTP
- HTTP
- HTTPS

The log file created with the appliance upgrade can be displayed by typing the following:

```
pnupgrade log
```

raidstatus. Displays the status of RAID hard drives in MARS appliances that support RAID.

reboot. Instructs the MARS appliance to cleanly shut down all processes and restart.

route. Used to manipulate the MARS IP routing table.

shutdown. Used to cleanly stop all processes and power off the MARS appliance.

snmpwalk. Uses SNMP GETNEXT requests to query a network device for a tree of information.

ssh. Used to log in to another host using Secure Shell.

sslcert. Used to generate a new self-signed Secure Socket Layer (SSL) certificate for the MARS appliance.

sysstatus. Runs similarly to the Linux **top** command. The syntax for **sysstatus** is identical to **top**, as Figure B-5 illustrates. This command shows which processes are currently running on the appliance and how many system resources the processes are using.

Figure B-5 **sysstatus** *Command, Which Is Identical to the Linux* **top** *Command*

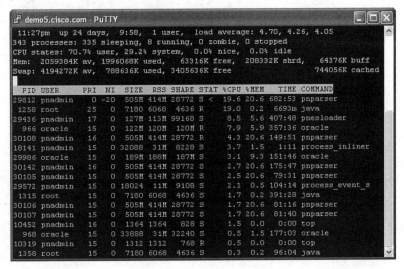

tcpdump. A utility that captures network traffic and displays it. This command is identical to **tcpdump** on a Linux server. If you don't know whether traffic from a specified host is reaching MARS, **tcpdump** can be useful in displaying the traffic.

telnet. Used to establish an insecure, cleartext connection to another host on TCP port 23.

time. Used to set or display the time on the MARS appliance. It is used in the same manner as the **date** command.

timezone. Used to display or set the time zone.

traceroute. Identical to the Linux **traceroute** command, this command is useful for tracing the path that TCP/IP packets take when communicating with a specified host.

version. Used to display the version of MARS software currently running.

Useful Websites

The list of websites in this appendix might be useful to you in your daily administration of the Cisco Security Monitoring, Analysis, and Response System (CS-MARS).

Topic Area	Website
Regular expressions	Several references, both open source and commercial, are available for Perl Compatible Regular Expressions (PCRE). The best starting point is probably the author's man pages, which can be retrieved from http://www.pcre.org/pcre.txt.
CS-MARS data sheets and more	Data sheets: http://www.cisco.com/en/US/products/ps6241/products_data_sheets_list.html.
	Product information: http://www.cisco.com/en/US/products/ps6241/index.html.
	MARS software updates (requires CCO login): http://www.cisco.com/cgi-bin/tablebuild.pl/cs-mars.
	MARS recovery images (requires CCO login): http://www.cisco.com/cgi-bin/tablebuild.pl/cs-mars-recovery.
	MARS supplementary files (requires CCO login): http://www.cisco.com/cgi-bin/tablebuild.pl/cs-mars-misc.
MARS Blog	The MARS Blog is not operated by Cisco Systems. However, it is full of useful information, and should be visited regularly by all MARS users: http://ciscomars.blogspot.com.
Python	Official website for the Python programming language: http://www.python.org.
Regulatory and other compliance sites	Payment Card Industry PCI Data Security Standard: http://usa.visa.com/business/accepting_visa/ops_risk_management/cisp.html.
	Sarbanes-Oxley: http://www.sarbanes-oxley.com.
	Gramm-Leach-Bliley: http://www.ftc.gov/privacy/privacyinitiatives/glbact.html.
	HIPAA: http://www.hipaa.org.

INDEX

SYMBOLS

$Target variables (IP addresses), 121

A

AAA servers, NAC Framework, 213

Action option (query interface), 96

actions
- alerting actions list, 125
- rules, attaching to, 125

addressable implementation specification (HIPPA Security Rule), 30

admin groups, troubleshooting e-mail notifications, 203

Administrative Safeguards (HIPPA Security Rule), 30-31

Advanced Regex queries, 287

alerting actions list (rules), 125

alerts, 13

All Events and NetFlow-Top Destination Ports graph (Dashboard), 23

All False Positives section (Dashboard), 22

All-Top Destinations chart (Network Status page), 24

All-Top Event Types chart (Network Status page), 24

All-Top Reporting Devices chart (Network Status page), 24

All-Top Rules Fired chart (Network Status page), 24

All-Top Sources chart (Network Status page), 24

antivirus software, Maintain a Vulnerability Management Program category (PCI Data Security Standard), 49

ANY variables (IP addresses), 121

appliances, inherent security, 78-79

approver role (CS-Manager), 184

archives
- archive server
  - *configuring, 165-166*
  - *planning/selecting, 164-165*
- CS-MARS, configuring, 166
- direct access of archived events, 173

directory structures, 283

querying
- *Advanced Regex queries, 287*
- *command-line queries, 284-285*
- *common query text files, 288*
- *customizing queries, 286-287*
- *ES directories, 284*
- *marchive.py utility source code, 289-292*
- *user rights, 283*
- *web applications, 285*
- *zgrep command, 284-285*

restoring
- *from, 168-169*
- *to reporting appliances, 170-172*

retrieving raw events, 173-174

subdirectory structures, 284

Attack Diagram (Dashboard), 22

B - C

batch query reporting method, 93

batch reports, 108-114, 117-119

beeping noises (MARS hardware), troubleshooting, 194

botnets, 38

Build and Maintain a Secure Network category (PCI Data Security Standard), 45-46

built-in reports
- default reports list, 92
- report groups list, 89-91

case notes, incident investigation, 151

case studies, CS-MARS deployments, 71-72

Check Point logs, troubleshooting, 200

Cisco CSC Module, 226

CISP (Cardholder Information Security Program), PCI Data Security Standard, 42

civil penalties, 23-24, 29

compliance validation requirements (PCI Data Security Standard), 56

configuring
- archive server, 165-166
- CS-Manager, 184-187

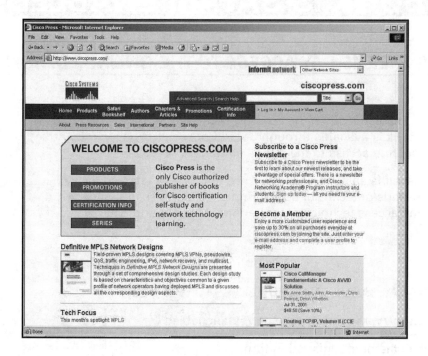
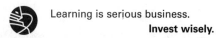

Safari

BOOKS ONLINE

ENABLED

THIS BOOK IS SAFARI ENABLED

INCLUDES FREE 45-DAY ACCESS TO THE ONLINE EDITION

The Safari® Enabled icon on the cover of your favorite technology book means the book is available through Safari Bookshelf. When you buy this book, you get free access to the online edition for 45 days.

Safari Bookshelf is an electronic reference library that lets you easily search thousands of technical books, find code samples, download chapters, and access technical information whenever and wherever you need it.

TO GAIN 45-DAY SAFARI ENABLED ACCESS TO THIS BOOK:

- Go to **http://www.ciscopress.com/safarienabled**

- Complete the brief registration form

- Enter the coupon code found in the front of this book before the "Contents at a Glance" page

If you have difficulty registering on Safari Bookshelf or accessing the online edition, please e-mail customer-service@safaribooksonline.com.